Modern
Canadian
Architecture

Leon Whiteson

Modern Canadian Architecture

Hurtig Publishers Ltd.
Edmonton

Hurtig Publishers Ltd.
10560-105 Street
Edmonton, Alberta

Canadian Cataloguing in Publication Data

Whiteson, Leon, 1930-
    Modern Canadian architecture

Includes index.
ISBN 0-88830-248-7

1. Architecture, Modern — 20th century —
Canada.   I. Title.
NA745.W494   720'.971   C83-091278-9

Printed and bound in Canada

Photo Credits

Bob Acciaro, 226
Applied Photography Ltd., 143, 173, 175, 182, 183, 188, 189, 191, 193, 195, 205
Bank of Nova Scotia Archives, 10
Marten Bot, 89
Dick Busher, 52, 55 (left)
Fraser Day, 198
William Dekur, 41
Jim Dow, 85
Michael Drummond, 216, 217
C. Moore Ede, 131
Ellefson Photography Ltd., 13 (upper)
Esto Photographics Inc., 36
E. Feistel, 227
John Fulker, 28, 30, 44, 45, 46 (upper), 48, 50 (upper), 77, 78, 79 (lower), 81, 102, 103
Yukio Futagawa, 154
Sandy Gage, 12 (upper left)
F. B. Griblin, 55 (right)
David Harford, 125, 127
In-Pro, 96
Roger Jowett, 18 (upper), 139, 142, 150, 151, 214, 255, 256, 257
Henry Kalen, 99, 100, 101, 104, 105, 106, 107, 109 (lower), 110, 111, 113, 114, 115, 117
Balthazar Korab, 156, 159, 160, 162, 163, 165
J. A. Kraulis, 17, 24, 25 (lower), 27, 32, 37 (upper), 67, 70, 73, 74, 76 (upper), 91 (upper), 98, 124, 128, 131 (upper), 169, 171 (upper), 184, 185, 238, 239
Lenscape Inc., 168
Alan Maples, 234, 235
North Light Photographic, 264, 265
Panda Associates, 11, 12 (upper right), 132, 133, 135 (lower), 192
Cedric Pearson, 236, 237
Robert Perron, 140, 141
Victor Prus, 13 (lower), 223, 224, 230, 233, 259, 260, 261
Bent Raj, 152, 153
John Roaf, 53
Ian Samson, 79 (upper), 155, 167
Simon Scott, 66
Julius Shulman, 231
Fiona Spalding-Smith, 19, 134, 196, 199 (lower), 208, 209, 210, 211
George Stockton, 174
Wayne Thom Associates, 37 (lower), 38
Webb, Zerafa, Menkes, Housden, 187

Every attempt has been made to identify and credit sources for the photographs. Hurtig Publishers Ltd. would appreciate receiving any information on the uncredited photographs for subsequent editions of *Modern Canadian Architecture*.

Contents

Foreword

Raymond Moriyama

1982 will remain a year of historical significance for all Canadians — the year our Constitution, however imperfect, was patriated. In keeping with our character, this coming together of past and future was achieved by evolution rather than by revolution.

On June 1, 1982, I and many other architects converged on Winnipeg to attend the Royal Architectural Institute of Canada's Convention and to participate in the first Governor General's Awards program for architecture. Of course, there were expressions of concern for immediate problems faced by the profession and the country — the state of our depressed economy, the widespread unemployment, and the need for more open democratic practice in selecting architects for public projects. However, for those of us gathered in Gustavo da Roza's Winnipeg Art Gallery to witness the collective expression of the fifty finalists and the twenty award winners, it was a day for optimism and reflection of a different sort. The display was a confirmation of what many of us have been declaring for years: architecture in Canada has matured, diversified, and achieved a place second to none in the world.

The firms and individuals who established new standards of excellence over the past two decades — Gordon Atkins, Jack Diamond, Arthur Erickson, Barton Myers, Ron Thom, Thompson Berwick Pratt, and a dozen others — demonstrated that originality and elegance continue to find new expression. This is reason enough for optimism and celebration, of course, but the Winnipeg exhibition had an added dimension in the significant contribution now being made by a new generation of architects. A charming library in Markham, Ontario, by Phillip Carter, IKOY Architects' high-tech design for their offices in Winnipeg, the renovation and preservation of historic structures and sections of Ottawa by the staff of the National Capital Commission, and the restoration of the Grand Theatre in London, Ontario, by Lett/Smith are examples that come immediately to mind. The diversity of invention ranged in size from the smallest shelter — four metres by four metres — designed by our own office, to the Toronto Eaton Centre, designed by Bregman and Hamann and Zeidler Roberts.

These are only a few examples of the architectural flowering that has been taking place in all parts of Canada. At the same time, our architecture has been developing rapidly as a competitive and increasingly important Canadian export to the United States and many other countries.

The Winnipeg lessons are confirmed and elaborated by the sixty architectural projects discussed in this book. This is why I did not hesitate to accept Leon Whiteson's invitation to set down my own thoughts about the place and potential of Canadian architecture in the interdependent, multicultural world of the immediate future. Whiteson's book represents yet another convergence. Four architects — Ray Affleck, Peter Hemingway, John Parkin, and Ron Thom — provide an introduction and focus to four regions of our country.

Included here are completed projects by many architects I continue to admire: Ray Affleck, John Andrews, Douglas Cardinal, Macy Dubois, Etienne Gaboury, Roger Kemble, Rocco Maragna, Rhone and Iredale, Peter Rose, Moshe Safdie, Short Tilbe Henschel Peters, James Strasman, and Clifford Wiens, to name a few. As demonstrated by their work, and the achievements of others included in this book, architecture is more than the provision of shelter. It is a response, even to the point of subservience, to the land, climate, and nature; it is an understanding of time, geological and human, that insight of a moment we all experience, which shifts the mind and changes the course of life; it is appropriateness of thoughts and action to serve social needs in the context of place as well as time; it is acceptance of the transitory nature of architecture in the evolutionary continuity of life. These, and the vital connection with past and future, are the elements that keep architecture alive and integrated with the culture it expresses. I was not consciously aware of this, though I may have been influenced by intuitions, when I made up my mind to become an architect. That was largely the result of an accident in Vancouver shortly before my fifth birthday. I think I remember it so well because of pain.

Fifty per cent of my body had been scalded and I had to think the pain away while confined to bed for eight months. I fantasized about many things but mostly about buildings and streets. I tried to think as I imagined an architect might think when designing a house, a fire station, a candy store. Later, when my body had healed enough to let me enjoy again the freedom of the outdoors, the old Interurban became my magic carpet. As it clanked and lumbered from Vancouver Station to New Westminster it carried me through a kingdom of patterns and surprises: row after row of offices, stores, movie houses, schools, parks, houses, gardens, open spaces between gasoline stations, hills, valleys, trees, distant mountains, and more offices and stores. Who made these arrangements that seemed so magical to me, I wondered. Did the architects come first or the planners? Why is perception, the experience of these arrangements, so different in drizzle, in sunlight, at night?

As a child, I learned three other lessons that have remained with me ever since. During the Second World War every Japanese Canadian had direct personal experience with contradiction. On the one hand, Canada had gone to war in defence of democracy, human rights, and freedom. On the other, we Canadians of Japanese heritage were interned in ghost towns. Some were even sent to prisoner-of-war camps. The three lessons I learned were these: first, that democracy is indeed very fragile; every individual is responsible for its preservation and must be vigilant for the rights of others as well as for his or her own. Second, that nature, in its transience, is permanent and is the only reliable and stable source of solace in times of social and political turmoil.

And third, that any institution, public or private, big or small, can (by insensitivity, not malice) do violence to the need of an individual to grow, especially spiritually, thereby creating an incalculable loss to the community, the country, and the world.

These lessons formed some of the reasons for my belief that architectural goals and social goals should converge, to give dignity to every individual.

The experiences of my childhood are fundamental, I suppose, to my own design and work and my perceptions of architecture as an interplay of diverse, harmoniously connected elements, some old, some new. They also explain in part why I welcome the new opportunities and freedoms represented by the waning of the so-called International Style and the emergence of what is now being called Post-Modernism. Of course, the work of most architects cannot and should not be classified so simply.

Post-Modernism began as a reaction, an expression of a widely felt nostalgia for the tactile and infinitely varied world of the past. People had become uneasy, unsure of the impersonal, standardized urban environment springing up around them without any sign of the technological Utopia it envisioned. As a result, Post-Modernism quickly became the dominant trend in writing, dance, and the Arts as well as in architecture. Its promise is the freedom to range through all of history for the connections and continuity that must be considered in creating the expressions appropriate to our time. Its danger lies in the tendency to narrow and distort these freedoms into yet another "style" or mannerism. However, properly considered, Post-Modernism can prove to be precisely the condition necessary for each architect to grow personally and to contribute more directly to diversity in a world that becomes smaller and more interdependent by the year.

We are living in a new world: a global economy. The trend is toward the rapid development of an international society tied together by information as well as by industry and trade. Canada, with its official policies of bilingualism and multiculturalism, is in the forefront of this trend. It is also in the forefront of an accompanying trend toward political decentralization.

The link between these trends and the diverse architectural projects dealt with in this book is the need to function in the world of tomorrow with a clear understanding of both integration and variety. On a planet where everything is rapidly converging, healthy diversity can only be maintained by responding specifically and appropriately to local conditions, to local people, to their moods and premonitions. Those unsung architects who work closely with people in small communities to improve the local environment should be lauded and celebrated. Sometimes the most important contribution of such architects is to look for alternatives to, or even to terminate, projects that offer no long-term social and environmental benefits.

Canadian architects have rapidly become effective competitors in many countries. With computers and telecopiers as tools of transportation, translation, and communications, operating globally is no longer a hardship, no longer heroic. Within our own boundaries, however, we remain curiously bound by old attitudes of parochialism and protectionism. So long as professional or government regulations inhibit architects from one region in their efforts to practice without restriction anywhere in Canada, only a few firms will be able to establish practices sensitive enough and strong enough to compete in the international arena. For this reason and others, new attitudes must be adopted by provincial and federal governments and by provincial architectural associations to facilitate the mobility of architectural skills. We have the experience and the political and social framework to be able to think in global terms while acting in response to conditions in individual locations.

This book should be evidence of that potential. This country speaks 130 languages, only two of them officially. The land conditions, climate, and people are more varied than those found in most nations of the world. The training available to architects in Canada represents the experience of the whole world in microcosm.

Designers, planners, and architects now no longer need to be called in from other countries to solve all our problems. Quite the reverse, they come now from all over the world to study our architecture, our cities, our processes, and our success in preserving the freedom and dignity of the individual within a multicultural community. They recognize that the Canadian experience takes the world one step beyond the melting-pot democracy of the United States.

I admire but do not envy the task Leon Whiteson has undertaken in writing this book. However, it is a book that needed to be written and the author is uniquely qualified, as both architect and writer, to present these examples of Canadian architecture. All of us — the public as well as architects — stand to benefit.

Glossary

AIR MODULE SUPPLY UNITS: air-conditioning machinery designed to service a section of a complex layout to allow for varying environmental needs.

ALUMINUM PROFILE SHEET: metal cladding with a pronounced three-dimensional configuration.

APRON THRUST STAGE: stage that projects into a theatre's auditorium, with a rounded front edge.

ASHLAR: masonry of cut stone used to face rubble or brick.

BEARING WALLS: walls that carry the structure as well as enclosing space.

BELVEDERE: a summerhouse or turreted lookout.

BERMS: low earth banks, freestanding or against walls.

BITUMEN: a fluid form of asphalt, laid and finished hot.

BLASTWALL: concrete or metal screen for transformers or other high-risk apparatus subject to explosion or fire.

BOX GIRDERS: massive structural trusses that form a hollow square or "box" in section.

BULLNOSED: prominently rounded edges to blocks or bricks.

BUSH-HAMMERED: a technique of rough-finishing concrete by chipping away the surface cement to reveal the stone aggregate in the mix.

CAISSONS: a type of deep column foundation in unstable soil.

CANTILEVER: beam, slab, or bracket projecting beyond a column or wall.

CATENARY: the curve formed by flexible rods hanging freely between two fixed points.

CENTRES: spacing between columns or mullions measured to the centre of the members.

CHAMFER: bevelled edges to a groove or channel.

CHECKER PLATES: metal sheet punched out in pattern of holes resembling the squares of a chessboard.

CHORDS: the top or bottom main structural strut in a truss.

CLEARSTORY: a high-level window in a wall, usually in the form of a continuous horizontal strip.

COFFERS: sunken panels in a ceiling, divided by ribs.

CONTINUOUS HINGED SLIP JOINTS: a type of connecting hinge that allows surfaces to slide past one another.

CONTINUOUS RETURN-AIR PLENUM: recirculated volume of air kept in continuous movement.

CURTAIN WALL: external building skin, usually of glass and metal, not bearing any load.

DROP PANELS: removable sections of metal or plastic slotted in place.

ELEVATION: the façade of a building; an architect's two-dimensional drawing of a façade.

FIN TUBE CONVECTORS: cylindrical metal heating units with a series of circular fins along the length.

FLASHING: strips of metal or other material used to seal roof junctions around projections or parapets.

FLUORO-CARBON FINISH: a high-strength, weather-resistant surface to metal sheeting.

FLUSH: surfaces in a smooth plane with no projections.

FLY ASH CONCRETE: a technique of adding industrial furnace ash to the cement in reinforced concrete to increase bonding strength and speed up the hardening process.

FLYLOFT TOWER: theatre tower over the stage to contain secenery to be raised or lowered.

FUME HOODS: hoods over work or laboratory areas to extract noxious gases.

GEODESIC DOMES: structure developed by American architect-engineer Buckminster Fuller in which light-weight spheres with surfaces divided along lines following Great Circle routes enclose a maximum of space in a minimum of structure.

GRADE: average ground level on a building site.

GREENHOUSE STACK ACTION: the tendency of rising heat to get trapped at the top of a volume and prevent effective air circulation

GRID (DIAGRID): a regular network of divisions in one or two planes or directions.

HOLLOW-SECTION DOUBLE TRUSS: doubled structural span constructed of square-section hollow metal members.

HYPERBOLIC PARABOLOID: extremely thin, light roof structure curved in three dimensions as in an eggshell to achieve a high strength-to-weight ratio; technically, the exploitation of a geometric formula concerning the sections of a parabolic cone curve.

IN-SITU: on site; in place.

MODULE: standardized unit of space used to systematize building components and layouts.

MULLION: vertical window division or support.

PARTY-WALL: wall dividing self-contained units.

POINT FOOTINGS, LOADINGS: loads concentrated on a point rather than distributed over a wider area, in foundations, columns or supports.

POST TENSIONED: technique of tightening steel reinforcing rods in cast concrete to maximize pressure after the structural elements are in place.

PRECAST: building elements, usually concrete, prefabricated or manufactured separately from the main structural process.

PRESSURE-TREATED: factory method of forcing preservatives into timber under high pressure to increase the material's weathering and fire-resistant properties.

RACEWAYS: channels or pathways for services, such as cables or piping.

"RAIN SCREEN": weather-protection principle developed by the National Research Council for dealing with wide ranges in temperature and climate; combines a permeable outer skin backed by a waterproof membrane with controlled drainage and ventilation.

RING BEAM: stabilizing perimeter beam used to tie a structure together.

R AND U VALUES: tabulated, standardized system for grading the insulating properties of materials.

SCREED: smooth cement surface laid on rough concrete to take a floor finish, or left bare.

SECTION: drawn projection of a vertical slice through a building to show its interior design and construction.

SHEAR WALL CORES: "shear" is the slipping or sliding stress called into play when a structure is subject to twisting or bending strain; this kind of stress is acute in a tall, freestanding structure and must be countered by massive core walls or column grids.

SHUTTERING: the formwork, usually of timber or metal, into which liquid concrete is poured and moulded into shape.

SOFFIT: underside of ceiling, arch, or lintel.

SPACE-FRAME: roof or floor structures created by linking a large number of struts to produce a three-dimensional light-weight lattice.

SPANDRELS: wall panels.

STACKBOND: bricks or blocks laid with the joints lined up vertically.

STRESSED SKIN: external membrane of plywood or metal used as an integral element in the structure.

TIE RODS: steel bars used to connect and stiffen beams, trusses, or walls by holding them in tension.

TRIODETIC: triangulated structural web of spars or rods.

TRUSS: a structural beam made up of open, triangulated struts.

WYTHES: separate leaves of material forming a complex structural wall or laminated beam.

Modern Canadian Architecture
A General Introduction

Leon Whiteson

The intent of this book's title seems obvious; yet, within these three apparently patent words — Modern Canadian Architecture — all sorts of resonances occur.

What is *Modern*? What is *Canadian*? What is particular to the architecture that links these labels?

In one sense the title's intent is easily explained: in this book I have used it to include projects designed in Canada by Canadians since the Second World War. It is when one advances from this simple description that the questions multiply.

Modernism — that very twentieth-century notion — is a way of conceiving the natural and human world as raw material to be energized by what Marx, in a vivid phrase, called "the lightning flash of the Idea." The idea of Modernism has been used to energize social reform and revolution, to technologize the collective unconscious, to provide a style for the Machine Age. In architecture, Modernism began as a kind of poetics of technology wed to a yearning for a Utopia of social justice.

Le Corbusier, in *Vers une architecture* in 1923, set, with a poet's precision, the emotional tone of Modernism: "You employ stone, wood and concrete, and with these materials you build houses and palaces: that is construction. Ingenuity is at work. But suddenly you touch my heart, you do me good. I am happy and I say: 'This is beautiful.' That is architecture."

In the same bible of Modernism, Le Corbusier continues: "If we eliminate from our hearts and minds all dead concepts...we shall arrive at the House Machine, the mass production dwelling, healthy (and morally so too) and beautiful in the same way the working tools and instruments which accompany our lives are beautiful...."

Happy, healthy, moral, beautiful, free of dead concepts — these are the key terms of Modernism's dialectic. The political dialectics of social reform, developed in the nineteenth century, are crossed with a visionary faith in the perfectability of man through the esthetics of the machine.

This yearning for a Brave New World, rational and technical and so healthy, happy, and moral, and beautiful, was given urgency by the mass slaughter and social chaos of two world wars. It was sharpened by the ferocious irony of the contradiction between mankind's marvellous technical ingenuity and murderous confusions of soul.

Modernism, in its original innocence, in the simplicity of its hope for human transformation by design, was moving. But it was this very innocence that bent it to become at once the high style of corporate capitalism and the gesture of the nature-mystic and social reformer.

And then there's Canada, peripheral and colonial; vague about its own soul, defined too often by negatives of not this, not that....

Historically and emotionally, Canada is a filling spread thin between two slabs: to the south, America's dense fact; to the north, a thick wilderness compacted by Arctic ice. Canadians commonly experience the southern slab of this cultural sandwich more than they do the northern. But the wasteland is always there, a timbered, rocky, frozen breath at our backs.

This compression between densities glues the nation's parts even as it pressures our fragile cross-continental linkages. Our many solitudes — English, French, Atlantic, Prairie, Pacific — strung out from east to west, are united as much by a resistance to being crushed between America and the Arctic as by any more complex ties.

Canada and the United States, for all their early similarities of settlement, drew different strands from the unravelling undershirt of eighteenth-century Europe, their common dam. Rousseau's lament, "Man is born free, and everywhere he is in chains," leads to the Pursuit of Happiness and the emotional force for republicans.

Canadians, both Catholic and Protestant, were less seduced by the delusions of freedom; they tended to the Hobbesian intuition that men are born brutish, to be civilized by convention and law. And Canadians were so thin on the ground, had so much space around them, that law and loyalty were vital links.

In the wilderness of 3,850,000 square miles, populated even now by fewer than twenty-five million inhabitants, the politics of continuity served better than those of confrontation. If this were not a basic fact underlying frequent petulance, Canada would long ago have fragmented.

This social provenance gives Canadian architecture of all epochs its particular quality. Architecture is a most social art requiring a consensus of agreement to generate the funds needed to build. Our architecture is as distinctly Canadian as our cultural landscape, and as elusive to define.

For all its practicalities, architecture is moved by abstract concepts, by ideas of how to be human as well as the direct experience of living. Ideas have consequences, as Dostoevsky once remarked, and concepts of Modernism and Canadian-ness have fused and fought with one another in our contemporary design.

Modernism is by inspiration the International Style, as it was once known. It is universalist in tone, one-world by hope, expressive of a common humanity free of those narrow nationalisms and regional quirks that have caused so much grief in the past and still do in the present. Its populism is intellectual, not grassroots; its humanism is abstract, not sentimental; its metaphysic is technological, not traditional. *Purity* is a key note; a sense of new beginnings, of "starting from zero," of eliminating "from our hearts and minds all dead concepts," and even the inherited, confused, and deadly past itself. Nietzsche's cry, "History kills!" echoes though the corridors of Modernism. Modernism, in its morality of purity of surface and intent, its yearning for a clarity of form-following-function, inherited a lust as old as Luther.

Figure 1.   Bank of Nova Scotia, Halifax.

Modernism in architecture has been, above all, a source of vehemently clear and universal answers to very complex questions about the nature of things, social and cultural. This is the main thrust of its energies. Yet Canada's continuity, its vital sense of history and place, is stronger, in most regions, than the force of any idea.

This rooted inertia has saved Canada from many of the worst crudities of the International Style at its most arrogant and urgent. On the other hand, not knowing exactly who you are, lacking ready answers to questions of identity, is most un-Modernist. It is also a subtle means of survival, this resistance to the cogency of concepts. In our century, ideas — political, cultural, social, spiritual, and esthetic — have been often lethal to body and mind.

Modernism came late to Canada, in architecture as in other areas of sensibility such as writing and painting. Before the Second World War it was very thin on the ground. We did not receive influential emigrés from the Bauhaus like Mies van der Rohe, Gropius, Neutra, Breuer, Moholy-Nagy, Albers, et al., who settled in the United States in the 1930s and 1940s. These refugees from Nazism preferred the real centres of North American power — New York, Chicago, Los Angeles — as bases from which to convert the continent to Modernism. Nor did we generate home-grown originals like Frank Lloyd Wright to marry Modernism to a native genius.

Yet, ironically, the *idea* of Canada was potent in the modern European mind. As early as 1913 Gropius wrote in the Werkbund Yearbook: "The silos of Canada and South America, the coal carriers on the great railways...offer to the observer an architectural composition of such precision that their meaning is made forcibly and unambiguously plain. The natural perfection of these buildings [lies] in the clear and independent vision the designers had of these great, impressive forms."

These "great impressive forms," though to some extent developed by Canadians, were unappreciated locally for their symbolic force. Conceptualized as modern images by the busy European mind, the forms were re-imported as foreign inventions. This weakness in conceptualization, in the gift of organizing thought into coherent systems, is very Canadian.

However, the cross-cultural influences were there from early on. Canada unconsciously contributed to modern architecture's original inspiration as a unity of art and technology; a pure instance, in Prairie grain silos, of form-follows-function.

In the 1930s a few Canadian pre-modern designers were touched by the new notions promulgated in Europe. John M. Lyle, associate architect of Toronto's Beaux-Arts Union Station, travelled to Europe, "particularly anxious to study the Modern Movement in architecture which is now sweeping over the world...."

The phrase, "particularly anxious," is revealing. Architects in North America were beginning to be agitated by the ferment of ideas across the water. Like his contemporary in Montreal, Ernest Cormier — also trained in the Beaux-Arts tradition — Lyle was moved by Modernism to seek "that personal and distinctly Canadian note" conceived as a marriage of received ideas

Figure 2.   Halifax; window.

and the country's natural forms and local building materials.

A fresh Modernist vigour sharpens Lyle's designs for the Bank of Nova Scotia buildings in Calgary and Halifax in the early 1930s. (Figures 1 and 2) The banks' clean Art Deco lines are stripped neoclassicism enlivened by Canadian motifs carved in low relief. These designs, along with other rare instances such as McCarter and Nairne's Marine Building in Vancouver and Cormier's own house on Pine Avenue in Montreal, were a new note in our architecture.

"What road will [Canadian architecture] travel?" Lyle asked, in an address to the Royal Architectural Institute of Canada in 1932. "Towards a Modernism based on international forms and ornament or on Canadian forms and ornament — or is it to remain a dead thing chained to the moss-grown chariot of Rome or to the mystic spirit of the middle ages?"

Lyle's concept of Modernism was, a trifle naively, "simplicity of wall surface ...a use of incised relief ornament...a daring use of sunshine colours...." His notions of "Canadian forms and ornament" were, to some extent, the typical sentimentalization of nature of urban man — beavers, bears, and turkeys — jostling carved panels of industry and fishing. Cormier, Québecois, and more subtle, could be less fervently indigenous in his metaphors, more sumptuously eclectic in his rich borrowings of motifs for design and decoration.

Montreal, then Canada's most populous and urbane metropolis, appreciated Modernism. The profound conservatism of Québecois culture was leavened by a Gallic instinct for the elegance of ideas, by a sophisticated grasp of Modernism as the coming style. In the late 1930s Marcel Parizeau designed a suburban Montreal house in the International Style. (The term *International Style* was coined in 1932 by Henry-Russell Hitchcock and Philip Johnson for their exhibition at New York's Museum of Modern Art.) In the 1950s Charles Trudeau, a student of Walter Gropius, designed a pavilion house in the Laurentians that was pure Bauhaus.

In the development of modern architecture in Canada, Quebec is, as it is in so many instances, a special case.

The split between Anglophones and Francophones that deepened during the Quiet Revolution of the 1960s drove a number of Québecois designers to seek a "relevant architecture," a national style not wholly captive to imported *idées reçues*. Architects such as Roger D'Astous, a student of Frank Lloyd Wright, and Paul Marie Coté drew, in the decade, upon sources of cultural resonance, and upon a wider Latin style, such as Niemeyer's in Brazil, for a counterblast to mainstream Modernism and its Germanic-Protestant puritanism.

The energy of this style of Québecois Expressionism sprang from its "visceral metaphors exposing the bias of the dominant Anglo-Canadian taste," as one local critic expressed it. Coté's Saguenay churches, with their swirling concrete curves and romantically sculptural silhouettes, derive from the structural poetry of Catalonia's Antonio Gaudi and America's Bruce Goff, crossed with a stoic local idiom. Such structures, isolated in the wide landscape of northern Quebec, set up hopeful echoes of the lone *voyageurs*, the trappers and traders who opened up the harsh Canadian interior in journeys of wild enterprise.

Québecois Expressionism was ploughed under by the manifest destiny of internationalism confirmed by Montreal's Expo '67. In this World's Fair

Figure 3. Ortho Pharmaceutical offices and factory.

it was the anglophone architects of the city, allied with their colleagues in Toronto and Vancouver, whose cultural confidence conquered. French Modernists of the technocratic mainstream like Guy Gérin-Lajoie, Louis Papineau, and Michel LeBlanc who designed the Quebec Pavilion at Expo '67, joined in this celebration of Modernism.

Yet the desire to creat "relevant architecture" — regional styles reflecting the diversity, variety, and local heritage of the nation — persisted, and still persists in various provinces. More than merely maintaining a wilful awkwardness, such attempts helped give Canadian modern architecture its distinctive tone.

Ontario is, by geography and by sentiment, close to the traditional centres of American industrial and political power. As such it is the heart of mainstream Modernism in architecture, particularly since the relative commercial decline of Montreal following the rise of Quebec chauvinism in the 1970s. As Canada's main concentration of capital, services, and manufacturing, Ontario has a deeply vested interest in modernity. All of this applies in particular to the city of Toronto.

Toronto's note of purist Modernism was struck in the mid-1950s in such projects as John B. Parkin's Ortho Pharmaceutical offices and factory (Figure 3) — a design that is still a classic of the International Style. Parkin's later Toronto International Airport Terminal One building, though innovative in its time, is less enduring.

The Finnish architect, Viljo Revell, won the international design competition for Toronto's New City Hall, completed in 1965. New City Hall's twin curved towers cupping the flat dome of the council chamber gave Metro, in Ron Thom's words: "A strong symbol that can accommodate all the love and abuse that can be heaped upon it." The design expressed, in the requirements of its program, "government, continuity of democratic traditions and service to the community...." This continuity and contrast of traditions is pointed by New City Hall's proximity to the red sandstone, Victorian Romanesque Old City Hall designed by E. J. Lennox sixty-six years earlier. (Figure 4)

New City Hall gave Toronto the cultural confidence to go along with its rapid post-war growth, its transformation from provincial "Hogtown" to major metropolis accommodating immigrants from many foreign cultures. This new confidence was dramatized in the late

Figure 4. (top left) Toronto city halls.

Figure 5. (top right) Mount Royal Post Office.

Figure 6. (bottom) Mortifee house.

1960s and early 1970s by the upthrusting of Metro's skyline, led by four bank skyscrapers and the rampant symbol of the Canadian National Tower — the world's tallest freestanding erection. Mies van der Rohe, in his design for the Toronto Dominion Centre, gave the city its epaulettes as the nation's commodore of Modernism.

Montreal had reached its peak of Modernist potency earlier than Toronto. Place Ville Marie and Place des Arts, designed in 1963 by a consortium of local architects in association with America's I. M. Pei, and Place Victoria, designed in 1965 by Luigi Moretti, were major forerunners of Expo '67. Even earlier, in 1955, Ray Affleck had designed the small Mount Royal post office (Figure 5), which matches Parkin's Ortho Pharmaceutical building as a perfect piece of purist Modernism. (Figure 3)

Yet it was the so-called Vancouver School, remote from these eastern centres of power, that first caught the country's eye as a distinctively Canadian modern style....

In the 1950s a combination of opportunity, climate, and talent produced on the West Coast the fortunate circumstance for the emergence of a body of regional architecture of a consistently original character.

The influences were multiple: in style Japanese, perhaps through the filter of Frank Lloyd Wright's imagination in such masterworks as Tokyo's Imperial Hotel, and that of Wright's Japan-based disciple Antonin Raymond. This new awareness of British Columbia's position on the Pacific Rim spurred young designers like Arthur Erickson, Ron Thom, Douglas Shadbolt, Bud Wood, Barry Downs, Fred Hollingsworth, Paul Merrick, Bruno Freschi, and Ned Pratt to develop a local idiom based on the western framing system of timber post-and-beam native to their magnificently forested mountain region.

One of the purest examples of this cultural cross-reference is Ron Thom's Mortifee House (Figure 6) designed in the late 1950s when Thom was still with the office of Thompson Berwick Pratt and Partners. This formal Japanese pavilion, westernized in a typically Wrightian manner, is, along with the Thea Koerner House designed by the same practice, a counterpoint to the dreamy romanticism of many "organic" local dwellings on misty, steep, sea-stunned sites.

Private homes were the Vancouver School architects' main field of fantasy.

It was in the design of single-family residences for amenable and enlightened clients that talents such as Erickson's first flowered. On this small canvas could be sketched demi-paradises of natural communion where divisions between inside and outside, the everyday and the eternal could be blurred. Yet, as Bruno Freschi wrote: "The detached single-family dwelling is not a mainstream architectural problem. It is rather a vehicle for the development of a personal statement — an invaluable step in the evolution of a personal form vocabulary." Also, as Fred Hollingsworth pointed out soberly: "Less than one per cent of housing, multiple and single, is handled by architects."

Nurtured by a soft climate and spectacular topography, inspired by Frank Lloyd Wright and American West-Coast designers like California's Richard Neutra and Oregon's Pietro Belluschi, given a formal rigour by the admired disciplines of Japan, the Vancouver School tempered its talents. British Columbia's many gifted designers were experienced when, powered by a surge in economic and population growth, Canada built a truly modern, mainly urban, scene in the busy 1960s and 1970s.

Until the early 1960s the number of modern architects in Canada was small. One school of architecture — McGill's, under Professor John Bland — was very influential.

Bland directed the McGill School of Architecture for three decades from 1941. Under his benign eye many of the young talents who were to form the future met and mingled. Montrealers like Affleck and Desbarats attended studios with westerners like Erickson. Younger students such as Safdie followed; European immigrants like Prus taught there.

At more or less the same period the University of Toronto was graduating designers such as Moriyama and Markson. John C. Parkin was then the partner in charge of design at John B. Parkin Associates. When, in 1961, Ron Thom moved from Vancouver to Toronto to carry out the winning

scheme for Massey College, the three main centres of Canadian Modernism were cross-referenced.

This local horizon was widened by the immigration in the 1960s of architects from the United States, Europe, and the Commonwealth. Talents such as Zeidler, from Germany; Annau, from Hungary; Andrews, from Australia; Diamond, from South Africa; Myers, DuBois, and Long from America enriched our architecture's range.

The 1960s saw the triumph of Modernism in Canada, as it did in most other developed countries. The decade was the high point of the hope that, "if we eliminate from our hearts and minds all dead concepts," we shall arrive — to paraphrase Le Corbusier — at an architecture that is beautiful, happy, healthy, rational, and, above all, moral.

However, a sardonic reality decreed that the major patrons of this brave new morality in design were businessmen and bureaucrats. Though inherently conservative, both of these powerful social forces came to see an imagery of progress and profit in the cost-efficiency, technical logic, and futuristic aspirations of Modernism. It was an architecture that — again to wryly conjure up Le Corbusier — made them happy.

"'This is beautiful.' That is architecture...." Truly, their hearts were touched in those brave, booming days.

Major university projects manifested government's embrace of Modernism, particularly those at Trent, Simon Fraser, Scarborough, Lethbridge, and Laval. (Figure 7) In the 1960s education was expanding at all levels, becoming open to all, available to every student

Figure 7.   (above) University of Laval.

Figure 8.   (below) Metro Bonaventure.

who merited a place. The Brave New World of meritocrats that was dawning in that golden time required many trained minds. Along with Toronto's New City Hall and Montreal's splendid new subway system (Figure 8) linked to an extensive underground downtown pedestrian network, the new universities proclaimed the union of modern design and modern government.

1967, the year of Canada's centennial since the British North America Act created its Dominion, was the peak of Modernist confidence. All across the country, government at the federal, provincial, and municipal levels commissioned works of celebration, completed at the time or in the next few years.

In Charlottetown, Prince Edward Island, it was the Fathers of Confederation Memorial Building; in Quebec City, le Grand Théâtre; in Toronto, the Ontario Science Centre (Figure 13) and Ontario Place; in Ottawa, the National Arts Centre; in Calgary, the Centennial Planetarium (Figure 14) and so forth. Local governments welcomed official buildings executed in a radically Modernist manner, such as Kopsa's boldly Brutalist raw concrete city hall for Brantford, Ontario.

Montreal's World's Fair, Expo '67, was modern Canada's coming of age, its bold claim to brilliance. Expo's emperor was Mayor Jean Drapeau. He was the Napoleonic overlord who marshalled millions of dollars, who bullied, cozened, coaxed, and cajoled the large resources needed to display Canadian — and Québecois — modernity. Drapeau was splendidly successful in these campaigns, and almost seemed to have conquered hearts and minds forever; yet, in the moment of its triumphant claim to be modern, Montreal was actually in decline. And in its rush to modernize, the city had junked huge chunks of its architectural heritage.

Montreal is a most particular *urbis*. "An English city with French Canadian inhabitants, floating — an island in the river — on the edge of French Quebec," is how one local writer has it. Historically, it is a city of parsimonious, formal, nineteenth-century grey stone edifices for bankers and other money men, surrounded by the *quartiers populaires* of the working class. The urban architecture of these *quartier* rowhouses, with their stacked front porches and multiple open staircases, is as distinctive as that of the French Quarter of New Orleans.

In the 1960s Montreal opened its civic arms wide to welcome development. Restrictions, zoning control, preservation by-laws were cut to the bone to attract outside capital, much of it foreign. Huge superblocks such as Place Ville Marie, Place Victoria, Westmount Square, Place Bonaventure, and the later Complex Desjardins took

Figure 9. Ontario Pavilion, Expo '67.

over the centre of the city to become Montreal's new urban squares as their corridors and subterranean pedestrian linking tunnels became new metropolitan "streets."

This was the local context of Expo '67 — that "engineer's nightmare of exotic designers, kooky film producers, dubious intellectuals and arty spooks all spouting their private variant of McLuhanese," as *The Canadian Architect* tartly summarized the event in retrospect.

The Fair was built on islands in the St. Lawrence River with Montreal's newly-modern skyline across the water. It was designed as a "plug-in" city of nodes linked by transportation loops of monorails. Silver express trains brought in the more than fifty million visitors who saw Expo that summer of '67.

Theme pavilions, a Buckminster Fuller geodesic dome, tensed spaceforms of steel, canvas, plastic, and glass (Figure 9) created prismatic futurist shapes charged with confidence in the coming Utopia of Technological Man, that curiously bionic creature beloved of architects, industrialists, and politicians alike.

"A new world of architectural design was opening up," a prominent journalist enthused. "Some of us imagined we might even be in at the beginning of a revolution." Another equally famous pop-pundit declared: "The modernization of Canada will be dated from this Fair."

Almost a decade after Expo '67, Montreal made one more try for that *folie de grandeur* that inflated Mayor Drapeau's style — the 1976 Olympics.

This international festival of sports, whose costs rocketed from just over $100 million to around $2 billion, left as relics an unfinished concrete stadium and velodrome designed by France's Roger Taillibert in an overblown grandiose manner matching the Napoleonic afflatus of Drapeau, and a pyramidal Olympic Village, designed by Montreal's D'Astous and Durand, that was accused of plagiarism and corruption. As relics of failed grandeur, these almost impossible structures have a certain pathos. As monuments of civic insensitivity, they are magnificent.

In contrast, Montreal's Melvin Charney designed a most modest festival of architecture as urban art titled "Corridart." Along five and a half miles of Sherbrooke Street, Charney mounted witty displays of scaffolding, fake façades, photos, and giant red plastic fists whose rude fingers pointed out the glories or miseries of Montreal's vernacular and its destruction by development. These contemporaneous acts — the Olympic structures and Corridart (demolished by Drapeau in a fit of pique) — dramatized opposite visions of the modern city; a site of ruinous grandiosity or of quiet humanity.

"Every time I travel across the country I am moved anew by the Canadian landscape," said John C. Parkin in a 1976 speech. "This is no place for the lover of languid airs and soft, yielding flesh. It is ...a country of cold winters and long nights. Half the continental land mass is occupied by thick, bony plates of Precambrian rock. The rest is a dwarfing sweep of Prairie, or a convulsion of fresh, jagged mountain peaks. No one can live with such a geography without being shaped by it."

Yet, in the same eloquent address, Parkin added: "Our habitat is most Canadian where the best available solutions have been borrowed and adapted to the unique Canadian circumstances." The Canadian psyche, Parkin continues, "deplores conspicuous consumption or extravagant show. It is not widely original, radical or experimental. It is modest, and it is apt."

This impression of our modesty is confirmed by a distinguished English visitor — Lance Wright, editor of *The Architectural Review.* "The Canadian architect seems able to respond more naturally than architects elsewhere to the public demand for an architecture people can live with," Wright wrote in an issue of his magazine (May 1980) devoted to Canada. "[He] seeks to make their century acceptable to them by an imaginative fusion of archetypal images.... In Canada, technical advance and historical memory go hand in hand." Out of this inspiration, Wright concludes, "is arising an interpretation of architecture which is unaffected, unique — and of world-wide interest."

It has to be said here, quite emphatically, that modern architecture is the one major field of cultural endeavour in which Canada is considered world class. It is perhaps the only art in which we not only have a few outstanding stars but, more importantly, achieve and maintain an internationally recognized level of excellence, a body of substantial work.

Yet, as Parkin points out, and the Briton gently implies, we are famous more for our humanism than our brilliance. No innovators, we are best at domesticating borrowings from more fervently original cultures. The archetypal images we so imaginatively fuse are usually dreamed up elsewhere.

This is a general truth applicable in most regions of Canada, with one possible exception — the Prairies.

"Flat horizons prompt an architecture of powerful silhouettes," writes one Albertan architect. "The textural edge of the terrain against the Prairie sky is something that requires poetic sensibilities."

"Such sensibilities don't appear to be central concerns with most clients, or their architects," a Saskatchewan designer bitterly retorts.

These comments reveal the tensions of designing for the vast flatlands that occupy the centre of Canada. They suggest the deep conservatism, even indifference, of the populace; and the contrary imperative to conjure up strong, symbolic shapes to stand up in such a hard context of man and nature.

"The Prairie climate is unforgiving," says Gustavo da Roza, a Winnipeg architect. "Every little mistake in design shows up." On the other hand, an architectural historian comments: "Edmonton owns the poorest examples of commercial architecture in Western Canada.... In the space of a few years an alliance of the more mediocre and least responsible architects with the most avaricious, Philistine developers has succeeded in reducing what could have been a lively, forward-looking metropolis to a desert of unrelated glass boxes."

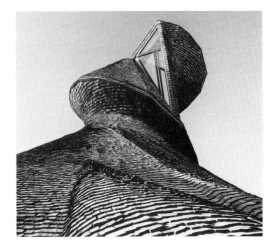

Figure 10. (above) Heating and Cooling Plant, Regina, Saskatchewan.

Figure 11. (below) Precious Blood Church, St. Boniface, Manitoba.

"There isn't a Prairie architecture as such," Clifford Wiens of Regina flatly declares. "Technological advances have been so rapid and the population continues to be so mobile that we are rapidly becoming insensitive to regionalism in a climatic sense, or in terms of scale." Yet it is Wiens himself who has created some of those "powerful silhouettes" that distinguish modern Prairie architecture. (Figure 10) Silhouettes, it may be remarked, derived from the silos Gropius so admired for "the natural perfection...[and] clear and independent vision their designers had of these great, impressive forms...."

15

Once again we have a Canadian fact re-imported as a concept. This trade is typical of the Prairies, as it is of all Canada. The grain elevator, the log cabin, the railway hotel, the ethnic church, the formal official buildings, the banks, firehalls, and forts, and the 1930s gas stations and storefront vernaculars beloved of Prairie Post-Modernists like Calgary's Dan Jenkins, are all borrowed forms "adapted to the unique Canadian circumstances." Even the Prairie farmstead took the European courtyard farm tradition and sprawled it open to the winds.

Yet native designers like Wiens, Gaboury, and Cardinal have developed a stubborn Prairie poetry of place. Of the trio, Gaboury is perhaps the most purely imaginative, bringing a Gallic flamboyance to the steeple twist of his church in St. Boniface, Manitoba. (Figure 11) Wiens is more Mennonite fundamentalist, while Cardinal is a wayward poet of place often too impatient with the stodginess of his bureaucratic clients and the cavalier rigidity of the materials of construction. Cardinal is, as critic Peter Hemingway has suggested, drawing upon Nietzsche, the Dionysius to Wiens's Apollo, while Gaboury fuses both polarities of temperament.

Alberta's cities, particularly Edmonton and Calgary, are "going through a period of rapid growth, both in physical size and economic importance," Hemingway has written. "Coincident with this boom the cities face a series of related issues ranging from the annexation of surrounding municipalities to the construction of new civic centres....[They are] having to cope with an awakening social conscience personified by the activities of a number of neighbourhood pressure groups...." The extravagant crudities of "boomtown urban design," as the catchphrase has it, have begun to provoke a backlash among citizens concerned with the environment of Prairie cities.

Outside architects, based most often in Toronto or Vancouver, have contributed much that is good as well as a great deal that's awful. Diamond and Myers's Citadel Theatre, and Moriyama's Meewasin Valley 100-year

Figure 12.   Scarborough Civic Centre.

Conceptual Master Plan for Saskatoon are brilliant examples of the best of these extraneous contributions.

"The South Saskatchewan River, with all its subtle and sometimes violent voices, speaks a unique and special language in this Prairie environment," the Meewasin Study concludes. "It would be wise to learn that language, and listen to it, before acting."

Wise indeed.

Despite the caveats, doubts, and pessimism of many Prairie designers, despite Hemingway's assertion that "the 1950-1980 cycle of building did not develop a focused image of the region because examples of good Prairie architecture were relatively few and far between...," Prairie architects, at their rare best, have given Canadian architecture new and particularly native forms at once thoroughly modern and deeply indigenous.

Original images are rare. Architects, like the rest of us, derive visual ideas from a ragbag of received images out of movies, magazines, newspapers, travel, television, books, history, and obscure social and personal memory.

We live in an eclectic and imagistically incestuous time. Styles feed off one another, exploited by professional image hustlers such as advertisers, fashion designers, and film makers. Modernism itself has already become a mannerism, generating its own instant nostalgias. Art Deco, the Bauhaus, and the sentimentality of technology known as High Tech are parodied daily.

The entire catalogue of architectural history, to the pyramids and beyond, is a treasure trove of tricks, of evocative cultural signs to delight a semiologist. Even the neon pop-modernism of Las Vegas casinos and California hamburger heavens is offered as symbology. Cultural cannibalism, the image devouring itself in its greed for meaning — any meaning — is the rage.

Canadian designers are, as always, less sophisticated than the most advanced Americans or Europeans. They are less hip, less street-smart, less sharp. The nice irony is that this simplicity gives their work a kind of innocence. Not so acutely aware of the agitation of the times, they are often cheerfully creative.

A fine instance of this cheerful innocence is Scarborough Civic Centre in Ontario, designed by Raymond Moriyama. Typically, the centre's style has many derivations, echoes from Japanese tradition, Finland's Aalto and the Saarinens, latter-day Art Deco sleekness in its detailing. Yet there is something uniquely Canadian in this building's response to its social scale, to its need to be a symbol for a dormitory suburb of Toronto, to its clarity and seriousness not at odds with a certain innocent sensuousness. (Figure 12) The centre is that all too rare event — a truly modern symbol that is yet humane.

There are many ways of expressing our humanity in concrete materials, in "built form," as the jargon has it. A humane architecture can be grand, like the cathedrals of Chartres or Salisbury. It can be humble, like villages on the islands of Greece, or the pueblos of the Navajo, or African mud huts. But it is always an expression of belonging to a culture that nourishes, that confirms your identity, heightens your humanness.

Such coups of cultural enhancement are infrequent in modern architecture, as in modern life. It can be claimed that Canada has rather more than the common currency.

Our powerful, troubled neighbour to the south readily accepts this claim. "Relax," an article in the *American Institute of Architects Journal* opens mock-facetiously. "Forget those fears that the city of the future will inevitably be like Houston, for there is a quite delightful alternative: It could be like Toronto."

The genesis of this "quite delightful alternative" is rooted in the Canadian social, political, and personal temperament. It is rooted in the quality of our civic government. Toronto, for example, in 1953 was the first city in North America to create a Metropolitan Council to respond to the new fact of the regional city needing an expanded tax base to finance a modern infrastructure mix of mass transit, freeways, and services. It is rooted in the character of our major real estate developers who — despite vociferous and often deserved ciriticism — have taken long-term equity positions in their properties, have recognized the legitimacy of advocacy planning (a notion imported from Britain) and, most of all, have quickly understood that keeping cities liveable is in their future interest. Canadian developers have, relative to their American counterparts, accepted the involvement of government in the economy with some good grace, avoiding an often brutal confrontation between bureaucrats and entrepeneurs.

The post-war policies of the Canada Mortgage and Housing Corporation, a federal body, and the developers' alliances with major national banks, insurance, and trust companies on the other hand have helped companies like Cadillac Fairview, Trizec, and Olympia and York to become extraordinarily profitable — to the extent that they have begun to penetrate the American urban scene, carrying their architects with them.

Jane Jacobs, whose influential work, *Death and Life of Great American Cities*, helped spark the counter-revolution against rampant urban Modernism, chooses to live in Toronto. Her writings and her presence have stimulated architects like Zeidler, designer of the Eaton Centre.

Yet it must be admitted that Canadians are as instinctively anti-urban as Americans. Our city plans are, for the most part, the same rigid rectangular street grids burned like the brand of Civilization into the body of the wilderness — a revelation of the early

Figure 13.   (above) Ontario Science Centre.

Figure 14.   (below) Calgary Planetarium.

settlers' terror of the scale and savagery of the New World.

Canadians, too, fled to the suburbs in large numbers in the post-war decades, creating that profligate sprawl that is such a waste of territory and resources. The main virtue of Vancouver for many people has been that residents can get out of town, to the sea, the slopes, and forests in under half an hour. Yet it is Vancouver that is now attempting to lure its citizens downtown to play and live as well as work, in excellent urban designs such as Granville Island, False Creek, and Robson Square.

Canadian civic politics are, for the most part, less polarized than politics in the United States or Europe. Party allegiances are less compelling than local loyalties. Also — except in boomtowns like Edmonton and Calgary — a traditional restraint reins in the rush to redevelop, even at the cost of lost investment. A famous instance is Toronto's two-year moratorium in the mid-1970s on buildings higher than forty-five feet in the downtown core. The people of Metro and their Reform Council felt overwhelmed by the high tide of unrestrained development, the upthrust of countless corporate towers punching the placid skyline, and cried *halt!*

Bold actions such as this, and the preservation of lively urban villages, help keep downtown cores alive, save cities from that nocturnal *danse macabre* where the metropolitan heart is abandoned to criminals and cops after office workers flee at five.

Toronto's Eaton Centre is a prime example of keeping the city core alive by urbanizing a suburban form. The centre is a megastructure fusing several city blocks, and its long, glass-roofed galleria draws formal provenance from European malls married to the commercial format of a typical suburban shopping plaza. Scale, movement, enclosure are exuberantly expressed in a late Art Deco–High Tech manner made serious by Zeidler's Germanic instinct for the hierarchy of proportions. The centre is less successful in its attempts to relate the street façades to the tumultuous Yonge Street strip alongside. But the generic tensions of downtown versus suburbs remain, intensified by the very success in keeping Toronto's core vital.

With the post-war flood of immigrants slowed to a trickle, Metro's core population has declined as the prospering seek the suburban dream. However, a post-surburban generation of young professionals and middle-class singles and couples has recently rediscovered the excitement of urban life. Their return to live downtown has at the same time revived aging housing stock and deprived the less privileged of much of their historic reserves of cheaper accommodation. Also, luxury condominium developments attractive to middle-aged couples whose children have left home have displaced older

ALEXANDRA PARK
SITE DEVELOPMENT PLAN
ARCHITECTS
KLEIN & SEARS
WEBB, ZERAFA & MENKES   JEROME MARKSON
SITE PLANNERS & LANDSCAPE ARCHITECTS
SASAKI, STRONG & ASSOCIATES

Figures 15, 16.   Alexandra Park, Toronto.

housing downtown. The core has become, some commentators claim, "a ghetto for the rich."

This reveals one of the structural weaknesses in municipal housing policy: the failure to provide enough subsidized urban accommodation for those many people who simply can't afford inflated market prices. Along with this, architects and planners have failed to invent a humane urban idiom for the few such projects that have been built.

Alexandra Park, in downtown Toronto, (Figures 15, 16) and Flemingdon Park in the city's northeast, are typical 1960s examples of mass urban housing developed with the best of social and architectural intentions.

As architect Irving Grossman, designer of Flemingdon Park, expressed it, the overriding concern was with "the idea of the identity of the cell."

Alexandra Park was defended by one of its planners as: "A living environment of reasonable density and high child count, inserted into the fabric of a central city situation — certainly not a ghetto." Today, however, this apparently enlightened scheme is the closest approach to a black ghetto Metro possesses.

The Ontario Housing Corporation, which is responsible for most public housing in Metro, was the client here. "Where such projects mostly fall down," Grossman says, with hindsight, "is in the lack of outdoor privacy — living room window facing living room window, with hundreds of kids running between."

A later attempt to provide downtown public housing in Toronto, begun in 1976 and still, at the time of writing, in progress, is the St. Lawrence Neighbourhood. Again, the intentions were impeccable — the revitalization of a declined core district by a model urban housing project mixing subsidized and co-operative units at a density of 320 people per acre. (Figure 17)

Once more, the results are very mixed. Socially, the two classes, middle and working, have different aspirations. Architecturally, the deadening lack of diversity in the buildings, the use of the same raw red brick throughout, the confusion in the street pattern, the overall failure of imagination in the invention of a contemporary urban vernacular generates an ambience one critic has described as, "dreamlike verging on sadness."

Yet Toronto provides excellent precedents for urban housing in its older downtown districts, its lively urban villages with their neat, porched rowhouses and leafy avenues. Perhaps when planners and architects prepare to design for the "underprivileged," they become much too careful, too self-consciously concerned; they become, as one commentator put it: "Middle-class Baptists on a crusade."

"Architecture is a matter of selection rather than innovation," comments Raymond Moriyama. "Besides, Canadians don't like cleverness. The religion of superstars you tend to find in the States is not our style. We design and build more scrupulously than Americans tend to do. We have to, with our climate, and our more cautious

Figure 17. St. Lawrence Neighbourhood.

national character. Our buildings are usually well put together, and we call the contractor into our offices early on, to consult during the design process. Engineers, too, are integrated. The contribution of structural consultants, such as the firm of M. S. Yolles and Partners, is crucial to the success or failure of a design."

Architects control only a fraction of all building construction. On the other hand, in large projects, private or public, the architect often becomes the mediator as well as the designer.

The architect may be the one person involved in the design and building process who can deal even-handedly with all parties, from client to contractor. He or she may need to help formulate a client's program. The architect may well be the only participant who has an overall vision of the impact of the finished product, who asks the truly radical questions — questions like, "Is this project really necessary?"

After all the functional, financial, and social imperatives have been satisfied in a design, it is the architect who makes an essentially philosophical choice about the nature of shaped space. The fact that he or she has no training in the dialectics of philosophy and may not even realise that the ultimate decisions on the shape and look of a building are not functional but metaphysical — a concrete expression of a way of viewing the social reality — seldom deters the designer.

"Architecture is a fusion of functional logic and cultural memory," says Eberhard Zeidler, designer of the Eaton

Centre and Ontario Place. "It operates by a kind of informed intuition, an emotional instinct derived from an understanding of structure and social necessity. It is, at best, an art derived from technology, yet free to express feeling. Of course," Zeidler adds, "the architect is the last amateur in an industry of professionals."

Indeed, the architect is "the last amateur" in an industry that ultimately resists basic mechanisation. Despite tower cranes, hoists, plastics, prefabrication, high-tensile steels, quicksetting concretes, and computer calculations; despite the boundless technical innovations and copious new products that overwhelm the building industry, the construction process remains essentially pre-industrial in its on-site assembly of largely nonstandard components. Social diversity, the variety of sites, the disorganization of the market, all prevent any significant standardization of structures.

Also, there are certain common building types that resist any real "fusion of functional logic and cultural memory," certain building types architects have simply failed to master. The suburban shopping plaza is one such. Speculative suburban housing subdivisions are another, as are gas stations. Perhaps these common elements of the built environment are simply too intractable, too bluntly populist, to submit to any significant symbolic transformation.

"A fusion of functional logic and cultural memory...." This formulation takes on an extra resonance in the light of the current tensions between mainstream Modernism and what is loosely known as the heritage movement.

Compared to Europe, Canada came late to the appreciation of its architectural history; compared to America, it may well be in advance. Professor Eric Arthur of the University of Toronto published his excellent book, *Toronto: No Mean City,* in 1964. "Posterity will rightly judge that we were unworthy," Arthur wrote in the book's epilogue, decrying the desecration of one of the city's finest avenues. "We once had an architecture where man was the measure in the greater, as in the humbler thoroughfares."

The rediscovery of the past, and of vital civic elements like the street, so disdained by earlier Modernists (Le Corbusier banished it from his visionary Radiant City) is a recent phenomenon linked to Post-Modernism and its ironic nostalgias. Thoroughfares that were, in the early post-war years, mainly movement corridors for cars, are beginning to revert to real highways and byways for all sorts of traffic, including pedestrians. The North American has rediscovered his feet after a long passion for wheels; this more leisurely pace of passing by, whether jogging or strolling, encourages preservation of the urban scene. Instances of this new sensibility, this need to reconnect with the continuities of the past ruptured by Modernism's urge to "start from zero," are multiplying from coast to coast.

In Halifax, Nova Scotia, the Waterfront Historic District has had its old stone warehouses, banks, and shops restored to a seaside splendour, with the addition of a new indoor, skylit promenade. In Toronto, ninety-two acres of disused docks and quays are being developed as "Harbourfront," with a mixture of new architecture and renovated industrial structures. Vancouver has the thirty-eight-acre Granville Island project. Even Montreal, once the developers' playground, has begun to ponder the social and cash values of its architectural heritage.

Single acts of restoration, renovation, and reconstruction, private and public, are becoming common in many Canadian towns, cities, and villages. One of the most subtle fusions of past and present, of "functional logic and cultural memory," is to be found in Etienne Gaboury's design for St. Boniface Cathedral, Winnipeg. A 1968 fire destroyed the soft fabric of the old church, sparing the limestone structure and sections of the curved sanctuary wall. The architect set a new basilica into the rear of the ruin, using the preserved front façade as a symbolic gateway to a courtyard as a gesture of continuity between the historic and the modern, the old Roman Catholic liturgy and the new. This delicate conjunction of ruin and renovation induces a

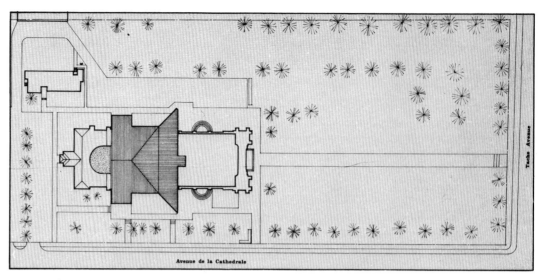

Figure 18. St. Boniface Cathedral, site plan.

sense of cultural pathos, of the overlays of human hope constantly upset and renewed, rare in current design. (Figure 18)

Pathos; irony; staginess: these are fresh and witty grace notes expanding the puritan matrix of Modernism. An example is Rose, Righter, and Lanken's 1977 ski lodge, Pavilion Soixante-Dix, at Mont St-Sauveur, Quebec. This sly structure crosses the Laurentian barn vernacular with histrionic hints of mock-Palladian villas and rustic Grand Hotels out of a Hollywood backlot as it faces the slopes with a cheery wink, welcoming the visitor to Playland. This is architecture as literate fun. literate fun.

Modernism, once a morality, a vision of contemporary Utopia, an ethical hope for the future in the holy union of art and technology, has become a manner. It has become, on the one hand, sleek, sexy, and urbane; on the other, ironic, conserving, civic, and culturally sophisticated. Like any ideology, Modernism in its triumph spawned many heresies. Wiser and older, Modernism, once messianic, is now essentially mannerist.

Nowadays its enthusiasms are as often shallow as hectic. The hot issue of energy conservation is a case in point. When the urgency of energy conservation first flourished in the mid-1970s, after oil embargoes and price hikes, many studies were commissioned, many guidelines published. The 1978 *Energy Conservation Measures for*

Buildings is an example. New building forms sprang into fashion, foremost among them the so-called "atrium," a misnomer for a climate-controlled, glass-roofed indoor courtyard often, unlike its putative Roman ancestor, many stories high. (Figure 19) This form makes a lot of sense in Canada's long winters; it's odd it was so little used in the past. A rare historic example was the Toronto Arcade, constructed in 1888, demolished in 1955, which provided four floors of shops along an internal street with a peaked glass roof 130 feet long. But Canadians, perversely, have seemed to prefer to suffer their winters rather than avoid them. Few cities, for instance, have such obvious amenities for protection from snowfalls as arcaded sidewalks.

The atrium form, on a practical level, has obvious advantages and obvious drawbacks. The lower, more compact building profile reduces the energy-inefficient, heat-stack effects of highrise structures. Conversely, the excessive heating and lighting levels in most offices and other public buildings are exaggerated in a low mass. Also, atria tend to replace public amenity areas with private, or semi-private interior space.

Energy conservation and the forms it seems to validate have often proved to be more a manner than a must. The actual savings in fuel costs are probably minimal in the present state of the art. "The young architect has little knowledge of complex building technology," an expert has tartly remarked.

It is perhaps only in really harsh conditions, illustrated by the Leaf Rapids Community Centre location, that the logic of conservation is unarguable. The winter-city concept of placing all amenities, government and commercial, under one roof to create an indoor civic space transcending the common shopping mall, makes excellent sense in these northern latitudes.

There are many excellent modern buildings in Canada — a fact worth repeating, for it seems stubbornly unacknowledged at home. In its modern architecture, Canada boasts its only truly major first-class art. "Out of this climate is arising an interpretation of architecture which is unaffected, unique — and of world-wide interest. . . ."

This general level of excellence complicates the choice of particular projects for an overall and definitive survey of the field. Many fine projects have had to be left out, or else this book would have become unwieldy. I made the decision to limit the selection to sixty projects and so give each one more space.

The criteria of choice I have used here are as objective as I can make them. In a broad sense, they are based on balance: I have tried to provide as wide a regional spread and to include as full a range of current building types as possible, balanced to some degree in proportion to their occurrence. For instance, fifteen of the sixty projects are residential, and these include multiple, commercial, and private housing. British Columbia has five of these because housing is distinctive to the West-Coast style.

The search for balance has meant that some provinces that have a plethora of good modern architecture — Ontario, for example — have had to be

Figure 19.   Atria North, Toronto

restricted to some degree so as not to overweigh the survey. Other areas — the Atlantic Provinces — are very much less fertile as sources of Modernism.

These were my broad parameters of choice. Within these, I have chosen examples of building types I consider representative, and that I feel will stand the test of time. These projects, to my mind, have a certain enduring quality of design that transcends fashion and formulation. This last judgment must of necessity be subjective.

To balance this detachment, and this subjectivity, I have asked five architects prominent in their regions and in their time to provide a personal view of what it has meant to be a modern designer in Canada. These comments, by Ron Thom for British Columbia, Peter Hemingway for the Prairies, John C. Parkin for Ontario, and Ray Affleck for Quebec, with Raymond Moriyama commenting overall, are very personal. These are all men who helped invent the tone of Canadian Modernism.

What matters most in our modern architecture, it seems to me, is not any particular trend or tendency, or any "religion of superstars," but a body of building of a consistently high and humane quality, lit up by flashes of magnificence. What matters is not what is narrowly Canadian in character — whatever that is — but what the architecture's impact is on the scene of our daily lives.

Modernism in architecture has transformed our built landscape, for good or ill. Many burning hopes have turned to ashes, much hot passion has gone cold and sour. The bastard offspring of Le Corbusier's utopian vision of towers in a park are the crude Cubist highrises that ring our cities. Dreamed-of Garden Cities have become suburban wastelands. The downtowns of many a modern metropolis are museums of glass, metal, and masonry making geometries out of a Cubist's nightmare.

"By their designs shall you know them." This is the heart of the matter, when all rhetoric, debate, and controversy have faded into remote cacophony. Architecture is a direct revelation of who we really are, how we enhance or diminish ourselves as human beings. If there is a moral basis to architectural excellence, it must lie in this judgement.

"Suddenly you touch my heart, you do me good. I am happy and I say: 'This is beautiful.' That is architecture." This lifting of the spirit, this sense of being made happy, this feeling of being enlarged by the common good is what a truly humane architecture is all about for the people who need to feel at home in their built environment.

It is no small matter, therefore, in our confused, stressful, impermanent, and often violently disturbed late twentieth century to be applauded for our talent, "to respond more readily and more naturally than architects elsewhere to the public demand for an architecture people can live with."

Modern Architecture on the West Coast

Ron Thom

"The first personalities to dominate art in British Columbia came chiefly from the British or European academies. They brought with them the tradition of art as a gentlemanly preoccupation, a skill, a mystery vouchsafed to the initiate, a worshipful and intense preoccupation with the direct imitation of nature in her romantic moods…and ran their little outpost of Empire with confident flourish." This introduction to an article by Douglas Shadbolt in a 1946 issue of *Canadian Art* magazine sets the tone of the context in which modern art and architecture developed on the West Coast. It gives a whiff of that curious mix of colonial condescension, pastoral dreaminess, and cultural isolation that characterized the province up to the middle of the twentieth century.

Early settlers came directly to Vancouver, arriving by sea. In the field of domestic architecture, colonial, Cape Cod, and Tudor reigned for generations prior to the Great War. Areas of Vancouver such as Shaughnessy, developed in the 1920s and 1930s, were very much in the manner of nineteenth-century Britain.

A new generation of post-Second World War architects discovered a new fact: the West Coast was part of the Pacific Rim, that vast region bordering the globe's largest ocean. And the culture that, to western eyes, dominated the Rim was Japan's.

The idea of the Japanese that illuminated the minds of young designers after 1945 — most of whom had never visited Nippon — was received through Frank Lloyd Wright's fascination with that ancient culture. This idea of building in the very special West-Coast landscape gave post-war architects a release from the stale European nostalgias.

Our use of wood was learned from the Japanese. Timbers such as hemlock, pine, and cedar had remained in excellent condition in Japanese structures for over a thousand years, yet in Canada wood had never achieved full respectability as a permanent building material.

The importance of roof forms in the Pacific Rim tradition was of great significance in our designs. The beauty of these roofs was a product of their various forms, developed over centuries, such as the *kirizuma* (gable), *shichū* (central ridge pole), *irimoya* (a hybrid of the previous two types), and *hōgyō* (a sloping roof without a ridge pole). The particular character of the various covering materials — thatch, shingles, sheet bronze, tiles — was given by the specific environments in which the structures were located. Slope proportions, overhangs, surface curves, and eaves lines were all calculated to add grace and stability.

The main impact of this Japanese influence was on West-Coast domestic architecture. Domestic architecture, it has been said, betrays us to history more than any other form of art. There are few more poignant events in the realm of art than the juxtaposition of the human dwelling and its setting.

Another Pacific Rim influence acted upon British Columbia designers after the war: California and Oregon. A group of American West-Coast architects attracted young Canadians who were travelling up and down the coast as they began their post-war careers, looking at the work of Bernard Maybeck, the Greene brothers, Richard Neutra, Pietro Belluschi, and John Yeon. Neutra visited Vancouver regularly in the 1940s and 1950s to lecture and talk to the younger generation. Developers, too, were influenced and helped provide the opportunity for architects to spread new design ideas up and down the B.C. coast.

The most profound single influence was Frank Lloyd Wright. On the surface, this may seem surprising; Wright was a man of the American Middle West, his culture was of a very different background. Yet the manner in which Wright's "organic" architecture married a methodology of structural framing and the use of natural, non-industrial materials together with a formal discipline learned from the Orient was intensely appealing. Wright's planning created a flow of interior and exterior spaces with fused planes, unlike the hard-edged urban mode of Le Corbusier and the Bauhaus, repellent to our softer West-Coast sensibilities.

By 1945 architecture in British Columbia was coming alive after the Great Depression slump. Practices that had built little since 1929 were suddenly deluged by commissions of every sort to fill the vacuum created by the years of stagnation. The few progressive firms such as Thompson Berwick Pratt, Peter Thornton, C. B. K. Van Norman, Bill Birmingham, and Percy Underwood designed many fine homes and commercial and industrial projects. These established practices were given new energy by a vigorous younger generation recently graduated from Manitoba, Toronto, and McGill, and by others who had come up through the B.C. apprenticeship process. In addition, there was an important cross-over of influences between those who had had their training in eastern and American schools and others (like myself) whose education and experience was purely West Coast.

Teaching at the Vancouver School of Art in the 1930s and 1940s was B. C. Binning, an artist who had a real impact on local architectural development. Binning designed and built his own house and gave a course in design at the Art School which turned many young artists in the direction of architecture. With Fred Amess, another teacher at the school, Binning founded the "Art in Living" group, which was concerned with educating the public to community planning and urban issues.

The Vancouver environment was changing rapidly under the impact of the post-war building boom — seldom for the best. Among the many ugly office and commercial downtown developments, certain projects shone out as exceptions. One of these was the British Columbia Electric head office building, designed by Thompson Berwick Pratt and completed in 1957. The B.C. Electric building was an early example of design in the service of corporate expression conceived in a mood of technological and esthetic pioneering; it was an attempt to find an urban idiom for the West Coast that was regional as well as Modern. It was an early curtain-wall tower with a delicately articulated grid of metal that took account of the city's cloudy skies and moody climate.

Vancouver has a strong character of its own, given by the drama of its location, the character of its landscape, its curious sense of floating on the edge of the known world, confronting vast oceanic space. Its mistiness is psychical as well as physical; distinct outlines, hard abstractions, clear thought are not its style. It is unlike any other Canadian city.

Unfortunately, over the last decade, developers and their architects have come in from outside with little appreciation of Vancouver's special sensibility. So many of their new buildings could be anywhere; many sections of the downtown core cannot now be distinguished from that Urban Anywhere that has ruined the particularity of so many cities.

And the city is cramped by its geography, shut in between mountains and the sea. The ocean front is a hard edge, and the slopes can be colonized only so far. Fraser Valley farmland is already threatened by development in search of expansion. Vancouver's pride and glory, its spectacular setting, is also a severe limitation.

Vancouver is, in effect, a city-state; its metropolitan area includes more than two-thirds of British Columbia's population. Yet, paradoxically, the city's people have always had a sense of being masters of endless space, of living in a nature that takes care of all problems with its luxuriant, soft generosities.

But this sense that "nature will take care of things" must now come to terms with hard urban facts. The city is not just a place to earn your daily bread, pay your dues so you can fish and swim or ski — the real life. Vancouverites must now develop a sense of urban pattern, accept a density among streets they've traditionally fled. They have to begin to take account of their neighbours, to build collectively rather than with wild individualism. This is the price they must pay to preserve "nature in her romantic moods."

Simon Fraser University

Central Mall and terrace under glazed roof.

Master Plan Architects: Erickson Massey
Associate Architects:
   Academic Quadrangle: Zoltan Kiss and Associates
   Library: Robert Harrison and Associates
   Theatre and Gymnasium: Duncan McNab, Harry Lee,
      and David Logan
   Science Block: Rhone and Iredale
Location: Burnaby, British Columbia
Completion date: 1965 — Phase One
Construction cost: $25 million — Phase One

"An Acropolis for our time," is how Arthur Erickson describes his design for Simon Fraser University, chosen by competition in 1963. "It's an urban complex overlooking the marvellous prospects of the landscape and the city [Vancouver] that produced it."

The university was established to meet the rapid increase in student population in the 1960s. It was planned for twenty-five hundred students in the first phase, rising to eighteen thousand.

Simon Fraser was built to complement two other universities in the province and, like its contemporary, Scarborough College in Toronto, it was founded on the principle of the interrelationship of academic faculties rather than their traditional separation into colleges. Based on a system of large lecture halls and small tutorial groups, the aim was to foster student mingling. Interdisciplinary work between its three faculties — arts, science, and education — is encouraged in an open campus.

To give shape to this concept, and to match the drama of the university's ridge-top setting on twelve hundred forested acres of Burnaby Mountain, overlooking an inlet and the city to the west, Erickson conceived a "simple skeleton of walkways," a series of formal terraces focused on a central mall.

The approach road winding up the mountain passes under the building. As most of the students commute, this is their main introduction to the complex. Above the parking level of the transportation centre, a dome with precast concrete ribs and cylindrical glass lights makes an occasion of entry. Running along the ridge, the transportation centre and the central mall link the student complex to the west with the academic quadrangle and science complex to the east. A library and a theatre also open off the mall.

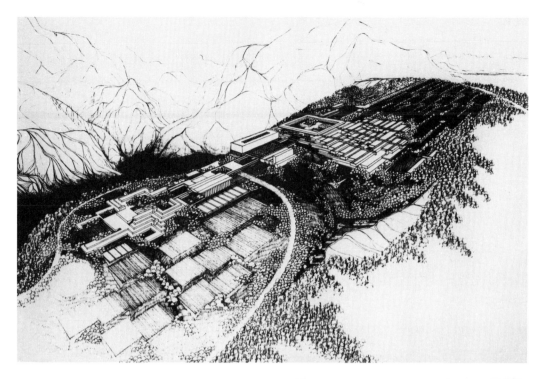

The heart of the university, in plan and concept, is the central mall. This three-storey open "Acropolis" is covered by a glazed over-sailing roof 297 feet by 133 feet, constructed of a spatial web of laminated fir beams tensioned by steel tie rods. Though many glass panes have cracked under heavy snow, calling for extensive replacement, and though gusty winds can make it bleak, this vast and luminous umbrella remains the university's most dramatic symbol of unity.

Concrete — "the marble of our time," in the architect's words — is the main building material. The planes are horizontal in a muscular response to the ridge-top site and its surrounding peaks. Vertical concrete sun-breakers counterpoint the massive horizontals. The concrete finishes are varied between smooth, sandblasted, and rough-pebbled to articulate the structural mass.

The inward-looking 440-foot-square academic quadrangle stands two floors high on columns around a stepped grassy mound reminiscent of a Mayan temple. The science complex includes five large lecture halls and laboratories. The labs are positioned along spinal corridors; 50-foot post-tensioned beams allow flexible partitioning.

Above: sketch of campus on Burnaby Mountain.
Below: main entry dome.

The 250,000-book library on the north side of the mall has four levels, two above the mall, two below. Its ceiling is constructed of four-foot-square recessed concrete waffles with soffit lighting. The finish is exposed sandblasted concrete. The 520-seat theatre has a curved, steep auditorium built of reinforced concrete with steel roof trusses. The gymnasium and pool to the west of the mall are enclosed with translucent insulating wall panels of reinforced plastic.

The campus has expanded steadily along its horizontal east-west ridge axis since its inception. If its mountain-top location has been criticised as "pantheistic," if its aspiration to the status of Acropolis jars with the reality of prosaically blue-jeaned students lounging on its terraces, it remains a superbly optimistic gesture, in a "mar-vellous prospect," toward a faith in a future few now, sadly, seem to share.

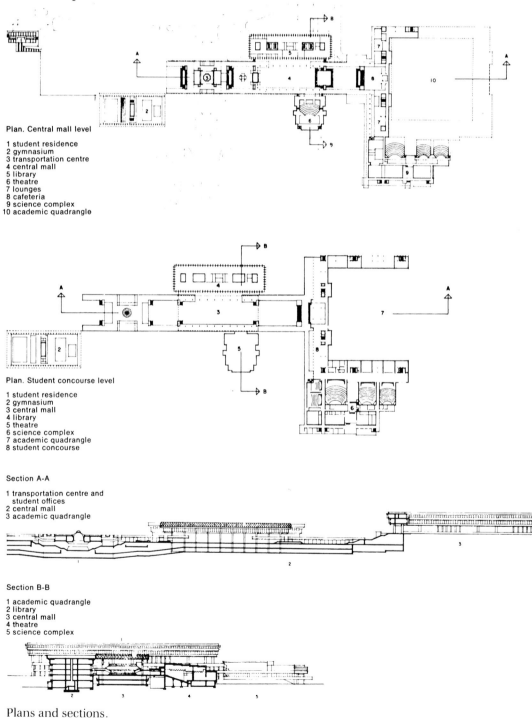

Plan. Central mall level

1 student residence
2 gymnasium
3 transportation centre
4 central mall
5 library
6 theatre
7 lounges
8 cafeteria
9 science complex
10 academic quadrangle

Plan. Student concourse level

1 student residence
2 gymnasium
3 central mall
4 library
5 theatre
6 science complex
7 academic quadrangle
8 student concourse

Section A-A

1 transportation centre and
  student offices
2 central mall
3 academic quadrangle

Section B-B

1 academic quadrangle
2 library
3 central mall
4 theatre
5 science complex

Plans and sections.

Central Mall, *above*, with view towards academic quadrangle, shown *below*.

Smith House

Horizontal planes in the landscape.

Architects: Erickson Massey
Location: West Vancouver, British Columbia
Completion date: 1966
Gross floor area: 1500 square feet, excluding accessories
Construction cost: $40,000
Clients: Gordon and Marion Smith
Project Team: Arthur Erickson, Mo Van Nostrand, Gary Hanson

A visionary simplicity lies at the heart of Arthur Erickson's architecture, an almost puritan urge to realise profoundly lucid images for a confused and complex world. "I want to build with all details suppressed," Erickson is quoted as saying. "I want to compress everything into a few words...to make what I build look as if it had just happened."

Blown up to a very large scale, in Alberta's Lethbridge University, for example, this simplicity can become simplistic. The suppression of detail in a structure 900 feet long induces visual boredom. Simplicity at this scale kills all resonance, leaving the observer oppressed by one simple-minded idea endlessly restated.

But in a small scale, Erickson's simplicity can be superb. His lucidity of vision is perhaps most purely realised in the many West-Coast houses he has designed in the past twenty-five years. The Filberg, Eppich, Catton, Hilborn, Graham, Smith, and Wright houses in and around Vancouver are all uniquely simple in concept and detail. In each case one clear idea is carried through with rigour and sensitive conviction.

The Smith house is an excellent example. In the mountainous and forested shoreline of Erickson's origins, the architect's urge for dramatic lucidity is matched by a lush landscape. Nature is a drama here, provoking a designer's disciplined yet deeply theatrical response.

View through living room to courtyard.

29

The dining-living space.

The Smith residence, commissioned by a couple who are both artists, is marvellously simple in design. Set in a declivity on a rocky hillside forested with firs and cedars sloping to the sea, it is conceived as a "square spiral": a pavilion climbing upward around a timber-paved courtyard.

The building materials are equally simplified in massing and detail. Clear expanses of almost mullionless glass walls are articulated by running timber horizontals at floor and roof level. The unevenness of the site is levelled by a bush-hammered concrete base and a wide flight of courtyard steps. The red cedar beams and siding, and the oak flooring are pressure-treated to a patina of gold and olive green.

Entry is through the carport into the courtyard with its ornamental pool. A double-height studio opens off the hallway; its walls are covered in white-washed burlap between rough-sawn structural timbers. From this level the house steps up to the living-dining areas and further to the master, and only, bedroom. The vertical rise is only five feet overall, but the slope of the site allows the living room to bridge between rocky outcroppings in a flying platform.

The view from the living room and its adjoining decks is at the same time magnificently open toward the Strait of Georgia and sheltered by the thrusting rocks and trees among which the house hides. The forest reflects the house's raw timber; the glass mirrors the woods. Landscape and habitation are intimate yet distinct, like a wild mother and her civilised child.

Erickson has designed grander residences, some, like the Eppich house, quite opulent. But in the Smith house he has best achieved an economy of image and idea, a simplicity of sentiment almost Japanese in its classical clarity. It's a building that, indeed, "looks as if it had just happened."

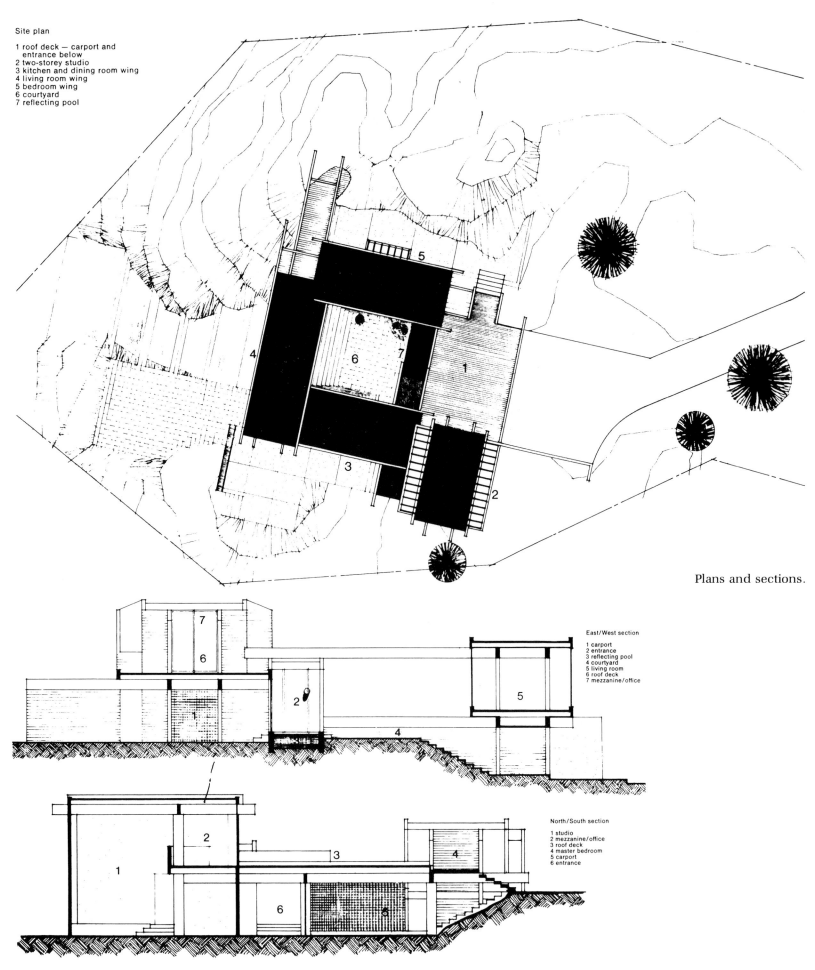

Site plan

1 roof deck — carport and
  entrance below
2 two-storey studio
3 kitchen and dining room wing
4 living room wing
5 bedroom wing
6 courtyard
7 reflecting pool

Plans and sections.

East/West section

1 carport
2 entrance
3 reflecting pool
4 courtyard
5 living room
6 roof deck
7 mezzanine/office

North/South section

1 studio
2 mezzanine/office
3 roof deck
4 master bedroom
5 carport
6 entrance

Museum of Anthropology

Architect: Arthur Erickson
Location: West Vancouver, British Coumbia
Completion date: 1976
Gross floor area: 66,000 square feet
Construction cost: $3,100,000
Client: University of British Columbia
Structural Engineers: Bogue Babicki & Associates Ltd.
Contractors: Grimwood Construction Ltd.

Above: main elevation;
Below: entry;
Opposite: Massive Carving Gallery.

Anthropology — the science of man — carries a freight of cultural condescension. It is weighted with the notion of "primitive." Sociology — the science of the society — is the term we apply to the study of our own "civilised" cultures.

The act of paying cultural homage to peoples we have more or less destroyed in the march of manifet destiny carries many overtones of irony. Even so magnificent a monument as this museum of Northwest-Coast Indian culture at the University of British Columbia leads one to wonder how a Haida might feel on visiting such a mausoleum to his people's vanished glories, raised by the very folk who accomplished their decline.

"On this coast there was a noble and great response to this land that has never been equalled since," Arthur Erickson declares. His museum is a metaphor of this splendid humility. Its main structural element mimics a traditional Kwakiutl longhouse frame of posts and crossbeam. Here, however, this simple structure is transformed into a cadence of sandblasted precast concrete posts up to fifty feet high supporting post-tensioned channel crossbeams up to a hundred eighty feet long. A narrow native frame, in cedar carved with sea lions, stands in the museum's Massive Carving Gallery as an ironic model for the sophistication of modern concrete technology.

On display are the vital, celebratory totems of the Haida, the Kwakiutl, and the Nootka. The museum's structure translates their icons of mimic awe into a grand architectural poetry whose manner is essentially theatrical. A "noble and great response to this land," provokes an act of theatre.

The museum is set on an eleven-acre site at the edge of cliffs on the campus. Its siting, between forest and sea, under the snowcaps of the Tantalus Mountains overlooking the Pacific, is yet another derivation from local Indian custom. The west side's artificial lake, reflecting the setting sun and the concrete "longhouse" posts and beams, adds yet another dimension of metaphor.

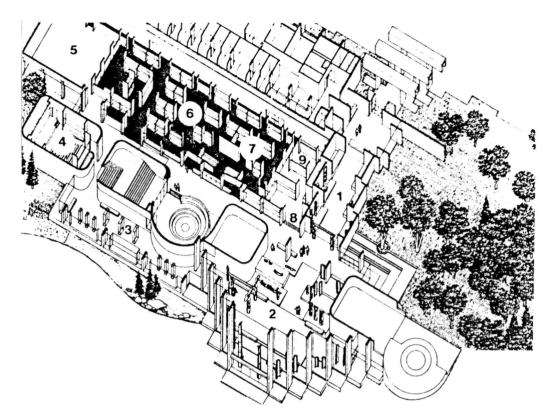

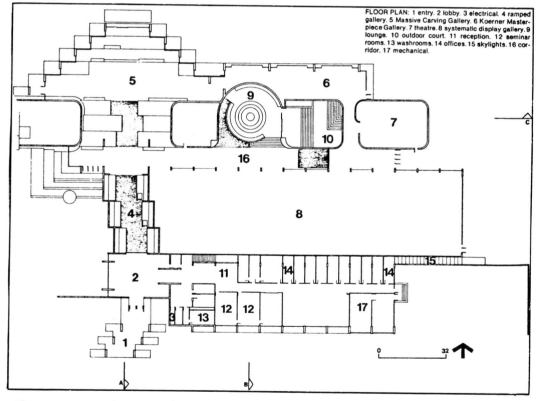

Above: axonometric view; *Below:* plan.

The post-and-beam motif marks the entrance. The concrete in these elements is pebbled and finished a warm weathered grey. From the entry the main asymmetric axis ramps gently down to the Great Hall, the Massive Carving Gallery where totems up to forty-five feet high are on display against a backdrop of suspended tempered glass. The ceiling steps up as the spans lift and narrow, urging the eye to the soft, misty West-Coast sky.

All nine concrete post-and-beam units have the same dimensions whatever distance they span. Curved and bronzed acrylic skylights link them, filling the halls with a golden glow. Although the museum is a research and teaching facility, all its artifacts are open to public view. Each space is scaled to its displays, from the most delicate jewellery to the tallest totem.

Concrete gun emplacements on the site, left over from civilisation's last great conflict, form the neck of the Great Hall. Another bunker is made into a circular lounge focused on a modern Haida carving, toplit by a fourteen-foot-diameter ribless acrylic dome.

The site is landscaped as an ethno-botanical outdoor museum complete with local flora, log houses, and totems. The homage is total: "civilised" man salutes the "primitive" whose culture he has overwhelmed.

Modern structural technique achieves spans that the original natives of this shore would have found miraculous. The contrast of scale between the Kwakiutl longhouse on display and the concrete elements it inspires is startling. Yet a native house, carved with beasts and demons, speaks to an ancient mystery in a language we have lost. For the Haida, the sciences of man and of society were one with their worship of life. Theirs was truly a "great and noble response" we can only acknowledge in an act of dramatic humility in this splendid museum of anthropology.

The Museum in its context, visual and historic: "A noble and great response to this land . . ."

Robson Square

View of Robson Square from the north; Law Courts at top.

Architect: Arthur Erickson
Location: Vancouver, British Columbia
Completion date: 1979
Gross floor area: 1,156,000 square feet, excluding landscaping
Construction cost: $100 million
Client: British Columbia Buildings Corporation
Structural Engineers: Bogue Babicki & Associates Ltd.
Landscape Consultants: Cornelia Oberlander, Raoul Robillard
Construction Management: Concordia Management Co. Ltd.
Project Team: Arthur Erickson, Junichi Hashimoto, James Wright, Rand Jefferson,
    Barry Johns, Eva Matsuzaki, Rainer Fassler, Ron Beaton, Nick Milkovich, Roger Morris

"A city matures when its citizens flock to the centre not for work but for pleasure," Erickson has said, describing the essential impetus for his design of the Robson Square development in downtown Vancouver. Pleasure — a visual delight in pools, plants, and architecture — is the genius of this landscaped urban park.

Three entire blocks on a north-south axis in the city's core are integrated into a low-rise complex adjoining Georgia Street, a major roadway running east-west. The top block contains the city's old neoclassical courthouse, renovated into a municipal art gallery. A Food Fair is situated under its main plaza. The centre block, linked by ramps and stairs over a street open only to pedestrians and buses, houses new provincial government offices buried under landscaping. The bottom block is occupied by a nine-storey Law Courts building.

The complex, funded by the provincial government, is served by an underground truck tunnel system which links with the Pacific Centre commercial district to the east. This submerged services feed, together with below-grade parking for 450 cars, frees the pedestrian level of heavy traffic.

Robson Square steps up from north to south in a subtle interplay of platforms; from the domed Palladian colonnades of the old courthouse to the great glass roof of the new one, whose flat top matches the height of the old cupola. Pools, waterfalls, trees, and plant-troughs interact with paving, sunken plazas, canopies, mounds, steps, and ramps to create a unique "metropolitan forest" of concrete, water, and greenery.

The provincial government offices in the centre block are set mostly below grade. The office levels, which step up to three storeys above ground at the southern end, are hidden by glass-bottomed pools, glazing screened by waterfalls, and lush planting. The office areas are open with wide corridors serving as internal streets. A media centre and a public atrium with an "underwater" view of the pool above are included in this section.

Law Courts: *above*, from Robson Square; *below*, from Nelson Street.

The Law Courts

Glazed, sloping space frame over main public areas.

The Law Courts building connects with the square by a bridge over Smithe Street. It is capped by a sloping steel space-frame that forms a glazed green-house canopy seven storeys high and 150 feet wide, supported on a series of two-storey concrete "knees." Thirty-five civil and criminal courtrooms, double-height and arranged in an interlocking stack, run the length of the building. Access for the public is on the west side, for court officials on the east. Each courtroom, either window-less or toplit, is finished in blond wood with warm red carpeting. The Law Courts' air is cooled by greenhouse stack action with lower level diffusers and top exhaust vents.

The vast, glazed public concourse of the courts plays to the notion of "open" justice. The Law marches in its majesty up grand staircases which lead to terraces between undetailed raw con-crete horizontals and elbowed verticals. In this huge space, despite the humane aspirations of the architect, structure, like legal process, predominates.

Erickson's desire to "build with all details suppressed" serves him poorly in this urban context. The inherent operatic urge of his architecture works best in a wide and dramatic natural setting, such as that of Simon Fraser University's Burnaby Mountain ridge-top. In a city, distancing is difficult, and detailing is crucial in buildings constantly seen up close.

In the landscaping of Robson Square's "metropolitan forest," however, Erickson achieves a splendid urban vista. The long views north and south over the open terraces are superb, providing Vancouver with its own miniature Central Park, an urban focus to match the magnificence of the city's surrounding peaks.

It is to the mountains that Robson Square speaks as well as to the streets. In its articulation of shady, almost rural paths, its soft sounds of rushing water amid traffic, its cascading steps, grand pools, and intimate plazas, the square is both restful and exhilarating. The bravura gestures of the architecture, like the clumsy conjunctions of the glass canopy and its concrete limbs, work less happily.

Erickson is a master of the daring gesture on a virgin site. His sense of drama is highly developed and requires a matching context, which cities seldom provide. Nature is his fondest mistress. In Robson Square his urge to "green" the streets succeeds brilliantly in the landscaping, poorly in the structures. The back end of the Law Courts, on the corner of Howe and Nelson streets, is awkward. The submerged offices under the plaza are oppressive for the people who work in them.

Pleasure, as Erickson conceives it, is seldom urban. The crush and jostle of buildings, people, and traffic hardly appeals to his nature-mystic soul. Urban drama is more complex, confused, and shoulder-rubbing than he seems to like. When he designs in an urban context he must crate his own theatre — most successfully in Ottawa's Bank of Canada, least so in Toronto's new concert hall.

Robson Square's success happens despite its architecture. It is an all-weather "people place" meant for pleas-ure, deriving from an old tradition of urban parks. Most of its structure, wisely, disappears under water and greenery. As a pleasure garden it is, in-deed, a symbol of Vancouver's maturity.

Plans and sections.

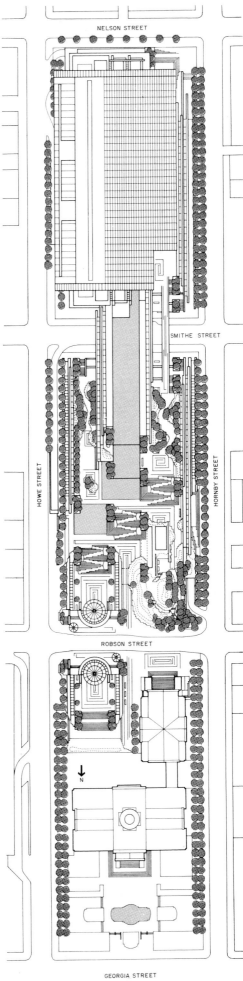

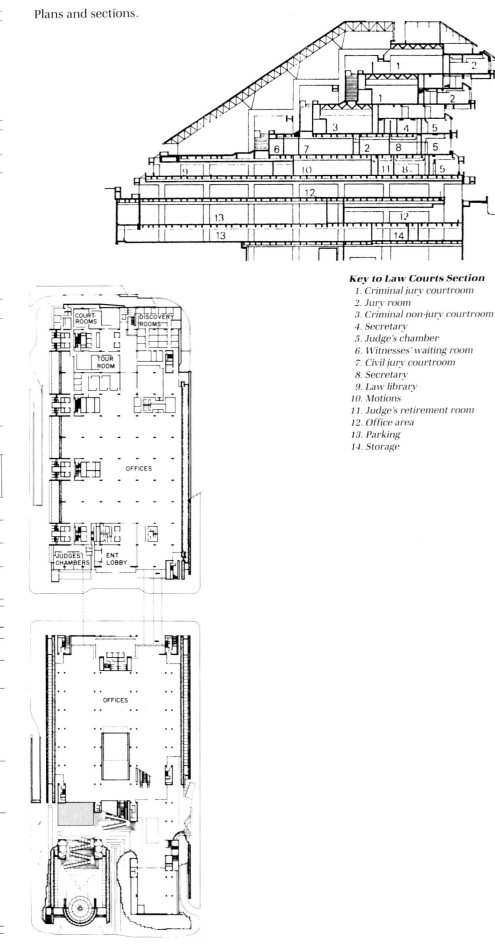

Key to Law Courts Section
1. Criminal jury courtroom
2. Jury room
3. Criminal non-jury courtroom
4. Secretary
5. Judge's chamber
6. Witnesses' waiting room
7. Civil jury courtroom
8. Secretary
9. Law library
10. Motions
11. Judge's retirement room
12. Office area
13. Parking
14. Storage

Central Control Building, Peace River Dam

Central control building.

Architect: Rhone and Iredale
Partner-in-charge: Randle Iredale
Location: Portage Mountain, British Columbia
Completion date: 1968
Construction cost: $18.5 million
Client: British Columbia Hydro and Power Authority
Structural Engineers:
    International Power and Engineering Consultants
Contractors: Foundation-Comstock Consortium

The division between the mutual disciplines of architecture and engineering has too often become lamentably rigid, especially in the English-speaking world. A kind of amiable contempt frequently characterizes the two views held of one another by these two professions: the designer's disdain for the "nuts-and-bolts" man; the structural specialist's derision of the "artist."

Too seldom do architects and engineers work together in harmony, fusing their different talents to create a form that is both structurally honest and forcefully expressed. The $400-million Portage Mountain Project, in northeastern British Columbia, is a rare and excellent exception.

The 600-foot-high Peace River Dam, eighty miles west of Fort St. John, holds a 640-square-mile reservoir. Above the crest of the dam is a gallery of ten massive concrete intake towers. Below the vast curving wall are the generator breaker buildings, transformer pockets and blastwalls, a 300-KV relay station and switchyard, and the central control building.

All these elements were designed by a team headed by the structural consultants, attached to the British Columbia Hydro and Power Authority. The architects, concerned with the visual impact of the overall design, collaborated intimately with the engineers responsible for structural stability. In this remarkably unforced fashion, unity of form and function was achieved throughout the project.

This seamless fusion of disciplines is best illustrated in the design of the central control building, located below the dam beside the 900-foot long powerhouse structure. The control building houses transformer maintenance and repair functions in the lower levels, hydro-electric monitoring in the upper. It also acts as an information centre and mimic display facility for the hundred and fifty thousand tourists who visit the site annually.

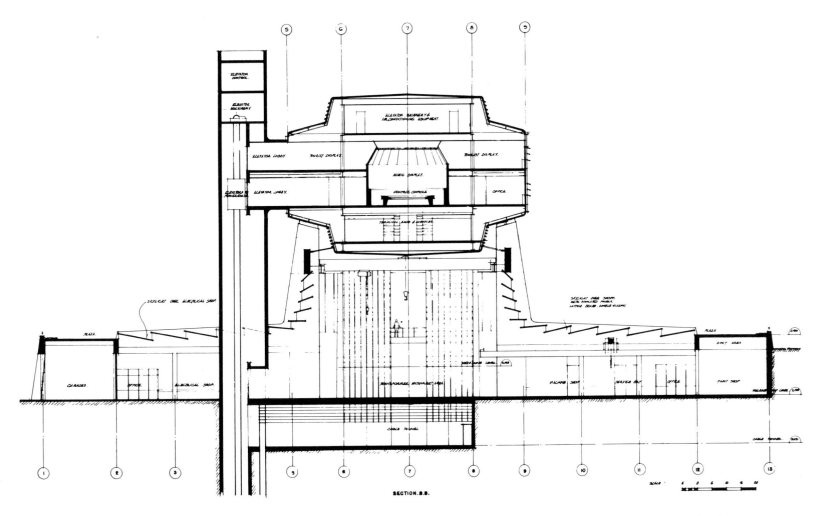

SECTION. B.B.

Section: maintenance and repair on lower levels; hydro-electric monitoring and information centre on upper levels.

Transformer maintenance entry.

The massive power of electrical transformers on this scale provides the metaphor for the control building's configuration. Constructed of reinforced concrete on spread footings set on bedrock and fill, its four pairs of sloped corner bastions support a four-storey metal-faced cap. The squat cap's cladding, of pop-riveted aluminum profile sheet backed on the "rain screen" principle with an interior aluminum liner and rigid insulation, is meant to mimic a generator's potent presence.

The 120-foot tall concrete tower on the west, housing two elevators that descend 620 feet below ground to the lowest level of the powerhouse, imitates the idiom of the penstock intakes above the dam. The four-thousand-pound capacity elevators operate at speeds of up to five hundred feet per minute.

Their shafts are lined with rough-sawn cedar boarding. The tower also houses antennas and a microwave dish linking the dam directly with Vancouver five hundred miles to the southwest over the Rockies.

The context and the climate of the Portage Mountain Project is muscular and severe. Temperatures range from minus 50°F to plus 90°F. The control building is designed for a snow-load of sixty pounds and a thirty-pound wind-load.

In this fierce yet magnificent setting, the architects and engineers, working in tandem, have contrived a design that matches nature's grand scale. The notion that form should follow function is here realized in the architecture of engineering as more than merely a metaphor.

Plan at tourist access level; elevator tower at left.

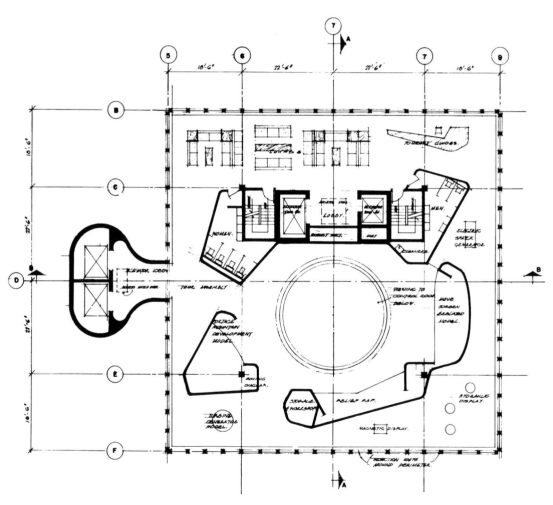

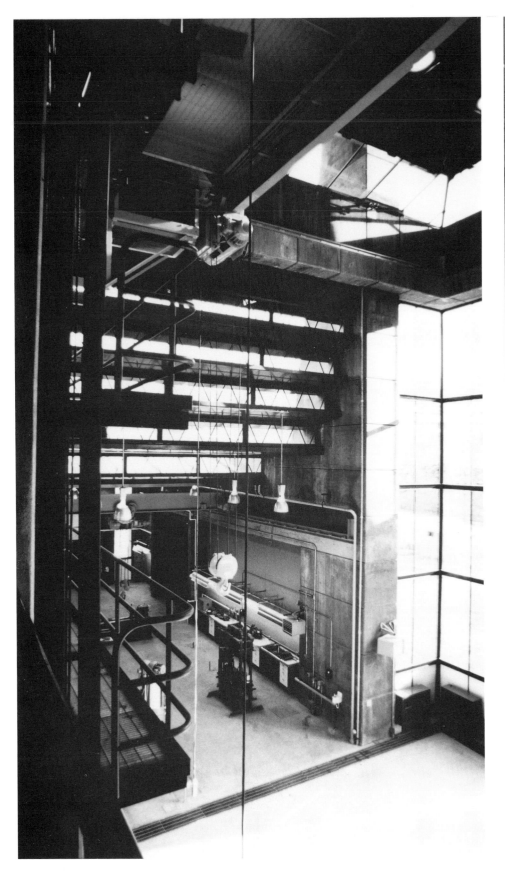

Close-ups: a muscular idiom for a tough job.

Fairview Place and Steamboat House

Fairview Place court in foreground;
Steamboat House beyond.

Architects: Rhone and Iredale; Randle Iredale
Location: Vancouver, British Columbia
Completion dates: Fairview 1 and 2; 1974, 1976;
      Steamboat House; 1980
Gross commercial floor area: 15,000 square feet
Construction cost: Fairview Place; $2 million
Client: Kara Resources Ltd.
Landscape Architects: Don Vaughn Associates

Steamboat House is a Vancouver mansion built in 1891 on Fairview Slopes in the local timber-frame vernacular known as "carpenter Gothic." This style featured fretworked porches with turned pilasters and carved eaves brackets. Dormers decorated shingled roofs; white trim framed double-hung sashes in horizontal clapboarding.

Between the wars Fairview Slopes, overlooking False Creek from the south, became unfashionable. By the early 1970s Steamboat House had declined to the status of rooming house, surrounded by cheap industrial and commercial buildings. In 1976 the house was designated a heritage building as part of the national revival of interest in historic preservation.

In 1973 architects Rhone and Iredale began the redevelopment of the properties adjacent to Steamboat House. Their clients introduced the concept of mixed housing and office development in the Fairview Slopes area which, with the False Creek development to the north, was part of the city's plan for urban renewal.

The two sections of Fairview Place frame Steamboat House, itself renovated for rental as professional office space. A paved and landscaped courtyard opens off West Eighth Avenue, giving access to all three elements of the renovation and redevelopment. The site drops about thirteen feet to a lane at the rear, allowing lower-level parking.

Each section of Fairview Place includes eleven townhouses built over an equivalent area of semi-sunken commercial space. The fourteen-foot-frontage town houses are on three floors opening off a raised pedestrian street overlooking the courtyard. The houses comprise two-bedroom units of 1000 square feet, and smaller one-bedroom units. All units have skylit lofts for storage or studio space.

The narrow interiors are made spacious by double-height living rooms with mezzanines and tall glazing linked with skylights. The finishes — light pine-boarded ceilings and balustrades and white-painted walls — add airiness. The views over the courtyard and towards the city skyline and mountains beyond are both intimate and urbane.

Fairview Place: integration of residential and commercial spaces.

The lower commercial level, reached from the sunken court, integrates casually with the residences. Stairs from the courtyard lead down to the common garage level.

Steamboat House is the crown of the complex. The beige stucco of the new architecture framing it echoes the tone of the historic structure's clapboarding. Bronzed mullions match the paintwork on the house's eaves. The glazing is mirrored by the new aluminum storefronts that replace the original siding and French windows on the renovated veranda.

Townhouse living room with mezzanine bedroom.

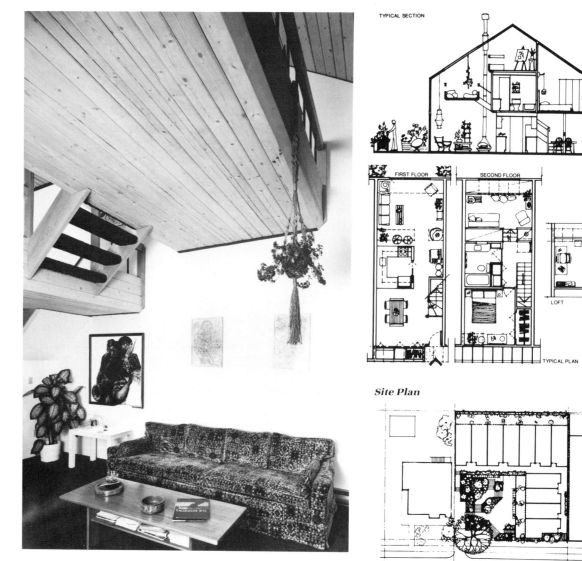

Steamboat House veranda: a detail in "Carpenter Gothic."

Fire stairs added to the rear of the house have been expanded into wide landing decks. New foundations created the opportunity for skylit rentable basement space. New dormers open to a view over the city. The interior, organized around a central staircase, opens into a series of suites on four floors. A section of the wraparound glassed-in sunporch is a lawyer's library. Offices retain the old fireplaces. Windows matching the original style were relocated where required. The interior of Steamboat House is cool and white and gracious in its sensitive modernization.

The Fairview-Steamboat development presents a subtle integration of renovation and new building, of inherited and contemporary manners. The differing scales, grand and intimate, residential and commercial, set one another off in a charming interplay of old and new. The new architecture makes no fake gestures of humility or nostalgia towards its historic neighbour, yet has the excellent manners to act as a fit setting for a revived grand old house.

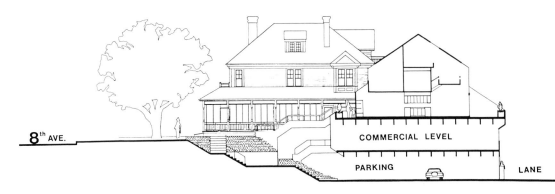

Section through Fairview Place: townhouses over commercial level and parking.

Lester Pearson College of the Pacific

View down over Pedder Bay.

Architects: R. J. Thom; Downs Archambault
Location: Vancouver Island, British Columbia
Completion date: 1975
Gross floor area: 61,300 square feet
Construction cost: $3,150,000
Client: United World Colleges
Structural Engineers: M. S. Yolles and Partners Ltd.
Contractors: Farmer Construction Co. Ltd.
Project Team: R. J. Thom, Barry Downs, John Mathews, R. McIntyre

Education's internationalism, its civilising capacity to dissolve barriers of nation, race, religion, and class, is a deeply held principle of the liberal mind. The belief that people who have studied together will never quite regard one another as alien was a noble faith dear to the heart of Lester Bowles Pearson, Canada's first full Ambassador to Washington, President of the United Nations General Assembly, Liberal Prime Minister and recipient of the Nobel Peace Prize.

The college named after him, on Vancouver Island twenty-five miles west of Victoria, embodies this faith. Erected by United World Colleges, an international organization dedicated to bringing young people of all races together to study, the cluster of buildings on a wooded hillside overlooking Pedder Bay is Pearson's memorial. "On a worldwide scale," Pearson once said, "this system could become...one of our best bets to reduce the risk of a third world war."

The seventy-acre south-facing site has nearly three thousand feet of rocky shoreline on the bay. It rises steeply to an elevation of two hundred fifty feet, with views to the water down forested vales and knolls. Firs, cedars, hemlocks, white pines, and spruces a hundred feet tall overhang garry oaks and arbutus, cottonwoods and willows. A dense underbrush is rich in wildfowers, watered by a twenty-five-inch annual rainfall.

In this lush West-Coast rain forest the planners have zoned the college by the docks. An approach road from the north comes down the slope, to a wooded level overlooking the channel. The fourteen buildings, including five student residences, a dining hall, a seafront common room, and academic and administration buildings, are arranged in an informal village. The student residences occupy the high ground just below the access road. Each residence accommodates forty in four-bed rooms on two storeys. The upper-floor bedrooms are double height with mezzanines. Washrooms are communal, and each residence provides a common room for recreation and seminars, and suites for the supervising masters.

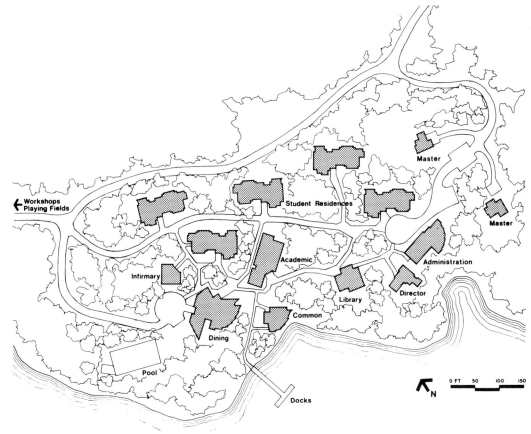

Sketch plan of College layout.

The campus in the woods.

Residence dining room.

Like other United World Colleges, Pearson College is more a prep school than a university. Its fifteen- to eighteen-year-old students stay for a two-year course with a syllabus based on language and community service study. The school dormitory layout of the residences reflects this fact. Yet the college aspires to be more of a community than an institution, balancing control with a feeling of friendly mingling.

The dining hall down by the docks is the community's focus. Its large main room is a quarter segment of a circle, facing south and west to a wide view over the bay. Its exposed cedar roof beams fan out and down to floor-to-ceiling glazing from a central brick and stucco fireplace core thirty feet high at its peak.

Red cedar on timber framing is the main building material throughout. The steep roofs are covered in cedar shakes, the walls and ceilings are rough-sawn boards. The wide overhangs and projecting terraces protect the large glass areas and frame the rich rain forest from within, welcoming its luxuriance without surrendering to its overwhelming lushness.

Students at the college come from many nations on the Pacific Rim, and from Europe, Africa, and the Middle East. The college was, in Pearson's widow's words, "The project closest to his heart." It is, in inspiration and architecture, a global village dedicated to the civilising faith of international education, "One of our best bets to reduce the risk of a third world war."

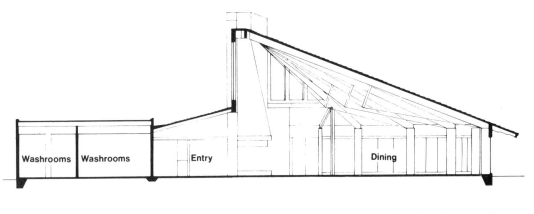

Main dining hall: exterior view and section showing open-timbered ceiling.

Housing by Hassell-Griblin

Szijarto house: view down over dining level.

Designers: Robert Hassell and Barry Griblin
Location: Vancouver, British Columbia
Completion dates: 1965-1975
Construction costs: $25,000-$45,000 (including land)
Client/Contractors: Comprehensive Architectural Services Ltd.,
    Stratawest Projects Ltd.

The conventional process of design and construction, rigidly separates client, designer, and contractor; this is a frustration to many architects. On projects large and small, from multi-million dollar complexes to individual houses, designers have constantly sought ways to emphasize co-operation rather than antagonism between the sectors of the construction industry.

A number of graduate architects, feeling hampered by the restrictions of professional registration, operate without licences from their particular provincial Institute or Association. This allows them to freely combine the functions of designer, client, and contractor; to provide, in Robert Hassell's words, "a more comprehensive approach than architects are prepared to offer...avoiding the padded costs of competitive building."

Hassell developed his desgin philosophy early on, in his very first house, built in 1965 for his own family while he was still a student. This basic cube, contracted by Hassell himself, cost under $10,000. The housing that followed during the next decade, built in partnership with Barry Griblin, remained in the economic range of $15-$20 per square foot, both for cus-tom-designed and speculative units.

Most developed from that first basic cube. The simple three-storey resawn cedar box, perched on point footings on the typically steep terrain of the lower mainland, minimizes its roof area. A typical section has family bedrooms on the lowest level, main living floor in the middle, master bedroom and study on top, connected by a central stair. Decks extend the space out into the site; windows, usually vertical to echo the surrounding tree forms, are integral to the geometry; generous skylights bring light to the interior in the region's misty climate.

The Szijarto house, constructed in 1975, is a prime example of the partner-ship's work. Here the basic cube has been enhanced by the shrewd design of open split levels, projecting decks, and large skylights into a perky little pavilion of fifteen hundred square feet

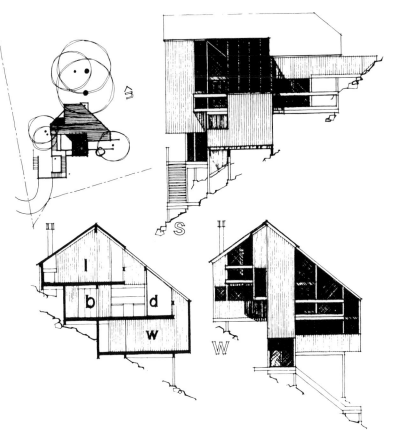

Szijarto house: plan, sections, side elevation.

Chesterfield Court townhouses.

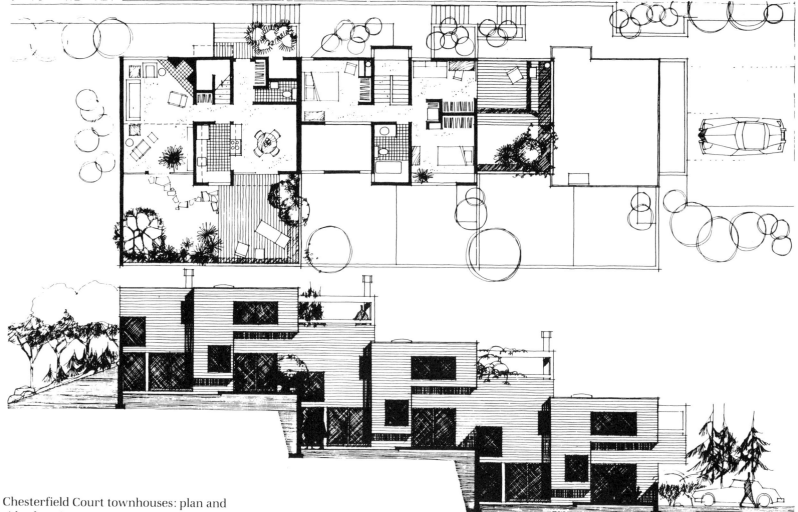

Chesterfield Court townhouses: plan and side elevation.

built for $40,000 on a sloped lot in the village of Lions Bay. Point footings on a foundation core wedged into the hillside leave the terrain intact. Simple timber millwork details define the structural geometry; rough cedar, pressure-treated externally, left unfinished as resawn inside, encourages the integration of intimate interior shelter and grand natural vistas.

The Hassell-Griblin principles of simple basic design, sensitive siting, and economical construction have been applied successfully to subdivisions and multiple housing.

The 1973 Chesterfield Court town-house project includes three two-storey three-bedroom units clad in stained cedar siding on a small corner lot with a building width of only twenty feet after setbacks. The houses, designed around courtyards, drop down the slope one full floor per unit.

This provides privacy and clear views, and trellised deck space. For their modest floor areas of 1230 square feet, the houses are remarkably spacious and free of any sense of confinement caused by the narrow site.

"We have systemized proportions and developed typical details, which remain constant," Hassell says. "Our buildings are responsive to the character and climate of the region...wrapped in as simple a shell as possible. We cope with consumer needs, municipal planning policies, land and building costs, and even sales promotion. We feel it is essential for architects to provide a truly comprehensive service. At the same time," the architect adds, "we have a strong emotional involvement with the West Coast — its landforms, vegetation, rain, and quality of light."

Szijarto house: simple basic design and sensitive siting.

Culhane House

Architect: Roger Kemble
Location: North Vancouver, British Columbia
Completion date: 1974
Gross floor area: 2250 square feet
Construction cost: $74,000
Client: Vera Culhane
Contractor: Daniel Boone

Plywood in primary colours contrasting nature's opulence: "An air of gaiety should prevail . . ."

In the 1960s and 1970s Roger Kemble led
the development of the use of plywood
for West-Coast houses. In twenty years
the architect has built over a hundred
custom-designed residences in Vancouver's lower mainland area, many of
them constructed of half-inch medium
density overlaid fir plywood on a traditional western frame skeleton. The
plywood has a double function — as an
economical sheathing membrane and
as a structural stressed skin.

Kemble's use of plywood, often
painted primary reds, blues and yellows, runs against the grain of the West
Coast's idiom of natural fir and cedar
finishes that blend with the hilly
rain forests of the region. Houses such
as those for the Gray and MacLellan
families startled the neighbours with
their bright and cheery "packing case"
appearance on rocky, wooded slopes.

Kemble's houses have no overhangs
— another departure from tradition.
Their geometry, determined by the
simplicities of the framing system, is
pure and crisp, choosing sharp contrast
with nature rather than blending. "The
simultaneous contrast of colour, texture,
form, and space are simple facts of
architectural design," Kemble declares.
"An air of gaiety should prevail."

The Culhane house is one of
Kemble's most radical designs. It sits on
a rock bluff at the top of a steep and
narrow fifty-foot lot that drops sharply
to the shoreline five hundred feet below.
The approach road descends through
dense undergrowth and tall conifers to
a cul-de-sac, giving views of deep inlets
and snowy mountain peaks at every
turn.

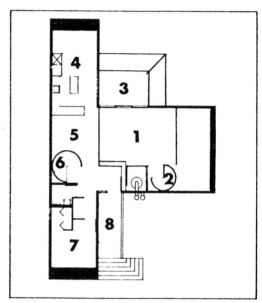

FLOOR PLAN: 1 conversation area. 2 spiral staircase down. 3 deck. 4 breakfast nook. 5 dining. 6 spiral staircase up. 7 bedroom. 8 entry bridge.

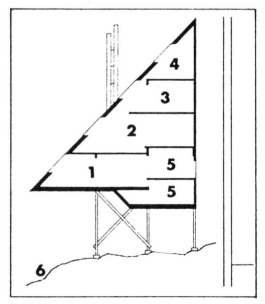

SECTION: 1 music room. 2 main living level. 3 main bedroom. 4 study. 5 bedroom. 6 existing rock grade.

In this dramatic region of misty green the Culhane house's sharp, triangular red-orange shape is a shock. The shock is intentional, as a relief from the overwhelming coniferous forest. The painted plywood walls and Neoprene-hyperlon roof surfaces are sleekly geometric in the context of rounded rocks and lush undergrowth.

The house perches on nine small concrete footing pads and a twelve-foot bracing wall upon an exposed rocky platform. Glue-laminated fir framing supports six levels on posts, from the lower bedrooms through the main living space and deck to the master bedroom and attic study. Timber beams cantilever twenty feet on both sides of the main structure in projecting triangles stiffened by the plywood stressed skin.

The house is thus a conjunction of plywood prisms mimicking the steep slopes. Internally the spaces and levels flow together, unified by the roof angles. Four tiers of slot windows orchestrate the seaward views. The warm interior finishes of red and yellow rough-sawn cedar boarding, following the triangulated hypotenuse, add cosiness and gaiety in the cascade of surrounding greenery.

A considerable amount of living space is economically enclosed. The owner of an earlier Kemble house claimed: "We have built a first-class residence with a top specification for about twenty per cent less than the going rate. Above all, our place is fun to live in."

Kemble complains that the Culhane house "has been allowed to deteriorate badly." This designer's lament is, sadly, all too common.

"Our place is fun to live in." The triangular sections, emphasized by diagonal cedar boarding and sloping slot windows, gives visual verve to a simple and economical space.

Granville Island Redevelopment

Co-ordinating Planners: Norman Hotson Architects
Planning Project Team: Norman Hotson, Joost Bakker, Greg Ball
Location: Vancouver, British Columbia
Inception date: 1977
Site area: 38 acres
Streetworks cost: $4.5 million
Client: Canada Mortgage and Housing Corporation
Development Consultants: Urbanic Consultants Ltd.
Structural Consultants: Buckland and Taylor Ltd.
Landscape Consultants: Don Vaughn Associates

The dredged sandbar known as Granville Island in Vancouver's False Creek inlet had become, after the last war, an industrial semi ghost town. Overshadowed by the hundred-foot-high Granville Bridge that marches over it, the island, though close to downtown, was in decay. A few factories and workshops remained, in battered corrugated iron buildings, Generally, it was an eyesore.

In the early 1970s the federal government stepped in and bought up the island for redevelopment, adding its contribution to the overall urban renewal of False Creek, whose south shore is now new housing. The Canada Mortgage and Housing Corporation (CMHC) appointed Norman Hotson to co-ordinate the plan for the revival of the ovoid peninsula (an island in name only) attached to the creek's waterfront, under the supervision of the Granville Island Trust.

Hotson's brief was to create a development program and design the island's public space, including streets, parks, and parking; to suggest recycling of existing structures for public use; to establish guidelines for the built form of the renewal. The key slogan was "the revival of a lost urbanity...encouraging randomness, curiosity, delight, and surprise." The architects envisioned the redevelopment as "a return to the original roots of settlement, to a time before zoning segregated and sterilized our urban environment....To create an urban village inspired by the particular history of place."

The strategy for achieving this imaginative action took the form of "controlled intervention." Public areas retain the industrial street patterns, parking lots are recycled as a flea market or an outdoor amphitheatre, the railroad tracks remain as part of the urban texture. Several existing industries — manufacturers of chains, paper convertors, drill bits, nails, and cement — have been mixed in with the new recreational, educational, cultural, and small-scale craft and market components. In short, the old Granville Island industrial ghost town has been revived by being transformed into a modern urban village where visitors mingle for fun and shopping. It is, in effect, a kind of Tivoli Gardens spilled in among working factories, a federal face-lift giving new life to a relic of Vancouver's tough and tatty past.

To set the tone for this transformation, which is ongoing, Hotson introduced several unifying design elements. The crumbling edges of the old bulkheads containing the island's dredged silt were reinforced by a new granite ashlar seawall, that runs around the perimeter, giving way to piers, docks, and boardwalks. Parkland, planted with shade trees, rolls down to the water's edge at the green slopes of the island's east-end outdoor amphitheatre.

Paving is another unifier. Inter-locking concrete paving stones laid on sand form unseparated roadways and sidewalks. Cars and people mingle freely, slowing traffic, ending an old antagonism. A unified street-hardware vocabulary of thick timber posts tied together with three-inch-diameter running steel tubing loops along the buildings at heights varying from three to eighteen feet. This brightly painted piping alternately forms railings, electric light conduits, canopy and awning carriers, and zone boundary markers.

The buildings are permeable to pedestrians. The Public Market complex, for example, which Hotson recycled out of five old industrial structures into a 46,500-square-feet open sale space, uses internally the same street vernacular of tube and post. A studio and office building by William McCreery, constructed out of cor-rugated iron, curves the edge of its bright red façade to demonstrate its playfulness. The wide doorways of the old factories, now refurbished, are articulated with concrete thresholds. Bright colours are everywhere, in the tubing, painted corrugated iron, boardwalks, piers, floats, and docks.

Plan and street views showing use of paving and running steel tubing to integrate diverse urban elements to "encourage curiosity, delight and surprise."

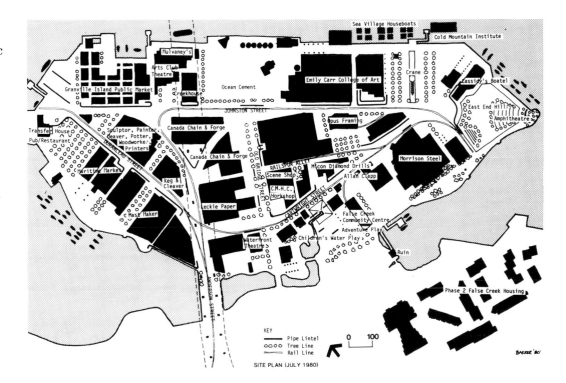

Granville Island in its setting; Vancouver's downtown skyline as backdrop.

The island houses the Emily Carr College of Art, a maritime market, a Sea Village for houseboats, a community centre for Phase 2 of the False Creek housing development, pubs, restaurants, an arts club, and two theatres. It is intended to be, when fully leased, self-supporting from its revenues. The federal government's original investment of about $30 million laid the groundwork.

The small peninsula can be appreciated from three angles of view: from the water, from the streets, and from the bridge above. The scale of the steel bridge, under which some buildings are tucked, dominates Granville Island. It establishes an urban dimension in tension with the villagey character of the cheerful bustle below — a kind of witty visual metaphor for the "greening" of Vancouver's core.

In Granville Island an industrial ghost town has become a jolly Disneyland. Its many visitors can peep in at chains being forged in clanking factories, buy fruit, watch working potters, dawdle over handmade jewellery, stroll along the seawall, refresh themselves with seafood and hamburgers, beer and wine, while their children frolic over this wide and varied playground. "Randomness, curiosity, delight, and surprise" are present at every turn. Cranes, winches, trucks, and streetcars are mixed in with trees, cars, trellises, awnings, and crowds in a cityscape of corrugated iron and open storefronts, boats and bridges. The island is an instant popular urban theatre of High-Tech Post-Modernism, at once relaxed, nostalgic, and great fun.

Views of Granville Bridge, *above*, Public Market, *below*.

False Creek Housing

Urban renewal — the reclamation of derelict city districts — is a crucial contemporary concern. As the tidal sprawl of suburban development begins to recede, curbed by local resistance to the endless consumption of valuable agricultural acreage and by a post-suburban generation's fresh appreciation of the pleasures of the city, attention is increasingly turned to the revival of the urban core as a place to live and enjoy, not just to visit for work or excitement.

Vancouver, though a relatively young city, is confined by its geography. Mountains hem it in, water divides it into peninsulas. Its scope for endless suburban sprawl is limited. For reasons of topography, among others, it came early to the notion of urban renewal.

False Creek is a small inlet to the south of downtown Vancouver. Its north shore was rail yards, its south shore a rundown industrial slum. Impetus for the redevelopment of the area grew through the 1960s. In the early 1970s the city held a competition for an overall development strategy for the south shore of False Creek.

The development area is bounded on the north by the inlet, on the south by Sixth Avenue, a major road artery, and a rail corridor, and on the west by Granville Island, itself a newly rehabilitated urban centre. The shoreline looks across the creek to the downtown skyline silhouetted against mountains.

The major social planning guidelines for False Creek set out a medium-density, mixed-income development, half subsidized housing, half free-market units, leased from the city for a sixty-year period. The development is divided into three phases with a projected population of about four thousand. The social mix includes families with young children, childless couples, the single, and the elderly.

Each phase is divided into a number of smaller enclaves — urban "villages," along the continuous landscaped rough

Architects:
  Phase 1 Plan: Thompson Berwick Pratt & Partners
  Phase 2 Plan: Downs Archambault, Davidson Johnston
Location: Vancouver, British Columbia
Completion dates:
  Phase 1 – 1976
  Phase 2 – continuing
Site area: 400 acres, with an average density of 35 to 70 units per acre
Overall co-ordination: False Creek Development Group
Contractor: Frank Stanzl

False Creek Housing Co-op: aerial view, *opposite*; elevations and sections, *above*.

granite ashlar seawall. The development is intended to bridge the rail and road corridor and link with the concurrent housing on Fairview Slopes to the south.

Construction of Phase 1, the eastern section, began in 1973. It is divided into two neighbourhoods, Spruce and Heather, on either side of a twenty-three-acre public park. It includes a school, a community centre, a commercial complex, an outdoor theatre, and two marinas.

The Heather Neighbourhood, in the extreme east, has five enclaves with a possible total population of twelve hundred. The higher densities of Phase 1 are concentrated here, around the civic focus of Leg-in-Boot Square. Two-thirds of the units are of concrete construction, up to twelve storeys high. A ferry landing and a marina occupy the small bayfront.

The Spruce Neighbourhood, to the west beyond Charleson Park, has three housing enclaves and a live-aboard marina, with a population of a thousand. The elementary school with its gymnasium and playing fields adjoins the park. The buildings are low-rise timber frame structures, many finished with pebble-dash stucco and sloped asphalt shingle or metal roofing.

The Alder Bay Neighbourhood, in Phase 2, is divided by a system of narrow pedestrian streets running north-south. It occupies a curve of the shore abutting Granville Island. The high, steel, box girders of Granville Bridge are a backdrop. The development is a mix of stacked maisonettes and eight-storey concrete units arranged in a semi-urban streetscape with closed vistas of the island and the distant city skyline.

Phase 2 will house fifteen hundred people. Its westernmost section contains office, commercial, and recreational components. Phase 3, the smallest section, west of Granville Bridge, is yet to be developed.

Access by car to all the neighbourhoods is restricted. Parking is limited to preserve the pedestrian character of

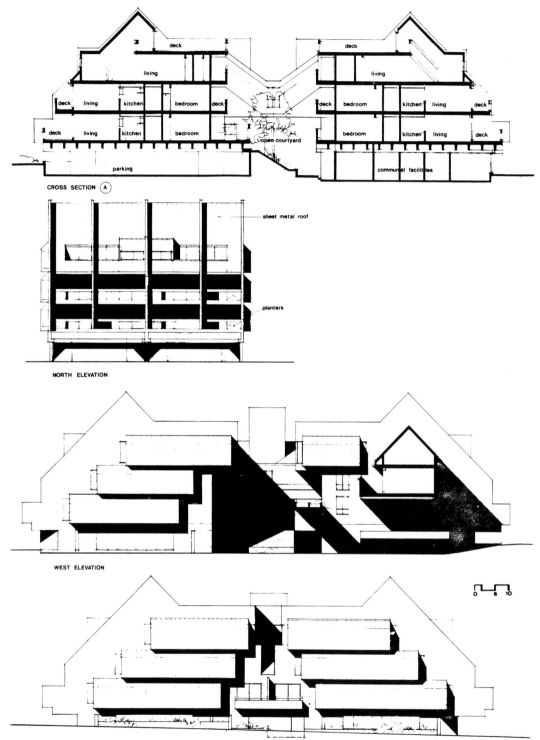

CROSS SECTION Ⓐ

NORTH ELEVATION

WEST ELEVATION

EAST ELEVATION

the precincts. A transit system links False Creek with downtown.

More than twenty architectural firms are and have been involved in the design of False Creek, under the overall co-ordination of the planners of each phase and the city's False Creek Development Group. The variety and quality of their work is diverse yet integrated within False Creek's dominant vernacular, which is a slightly curious overlay of mock-Mediterranean village, suburban subdivision, and waterfront urban.

The False Creek Housing Co-op, by Henriquez and Partners, is planned around an irregular central courtyard. Living rooms face outward toward the surrounding park, or inward into the court. Steep red metal roofs, recessed balconies, and a sculptural use of external stairways, curved and straight, give this enclave distinction in the tight modelling of its 170 units.

The smaller Waterfront enclave, by Romses Kwan and Associates, uses a similar courtyard layout. In this fifty-unit, low-to-middle-income grouping the massing is more varied than in most other enclaves. The roofline is broken up for visual variety, the exterior finish is natural stained cedar — a relief from the prevailing stucco.

The Alder Bay Co-op, by Downs Archambault, Davidson Johnston, has ninety-six units in two enclaves laid out along paved pedestrian streets. The houses are stacked two-storey maisonettes with bay windows in a stucco façade modulated by staircases. In this neighbourhood a rare urban streetscape is achieved, with closed vistas, contrasting with the suburban inspiration of most of the other housing groups.

This indecision between urban and suburban inspiration is one of the main tensions of False Creek. Although the development is close to downtown, in sight of the commercial core, much of its housing has the character of a typical suburban subdivision. As in most suburbs, the street is not the unifying factor so much as merely a means of access.

The classic sense of isolation suburban development generates is heightened by False Creek's geography.

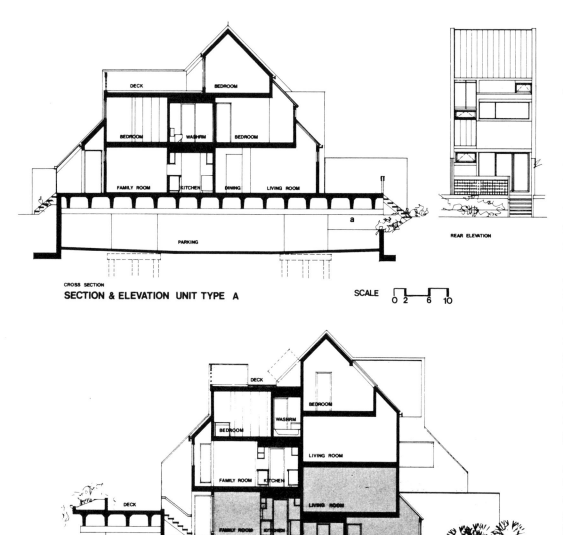

SECTION & ELEVATION UNIT TYPE A

REAR ELEVATION

CROSS SECTION

SCALE 0 2   6   10

SECTION UNIT TYPE B

SCALE 0 2   6   10

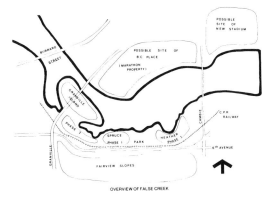

OVERVIEW OF FALSE CREEK

Opposite: Waterfront Enclave rowhouses; *This page:* maisonettes and apartments. A variety of residential types mixing market and assisted housing.

Hemmed in by the water and the transport corridor, by the bridge and slopes behind, False Creek, for all its proximity to Vancouver's West End, gives its residents a feeling of being cut off from the rest of the city. This isolation is increased by the deliberate restriction of car access and parking space. The enclave layout further cuts up the community, sacrificing a truly urban dimension for intimacy and semi-privacy.

The enlightened social and age mix, so beloved of utopian city planners, also sets up tensions. The single and the elderly are bothered by noisy kids playing in the courtyards. Inadequate soundproofing in the housing units, many of which are built to minimal National Building Code standards, also limits privacy.

Mixing market and assisted housing has its problems. Resentments develop in both directions, between those paying commercial lease rates and the subsidized; in the comparison of different amenities and room sizes in the two classes of unit. People have a natural tendency to arrange themselves in hierarchies of privilege, which planners prefer to ignore.

False Creek might have been more boldly conceived as a thoroughly urban development rather than a series of suburban "villages." However, despite all these reservations, it is a source of pride and pleasure for its residents and the city that had the foresight to promote this imaginative example of radical urban renewal.

The last word must lie with one of the people who lives in False Creek. "It's much easier to meet people here," he says. "Residents sit and chat along the seawall. You see joggers, bikes, and kids on skates. This is a people place."

Prairie Architecture
An Introduction
Peter Hemingway

I suppose it is a truism that it is impossible to judge an epoch in history from the viewpoint of that particular age. In order to properly assess modern architecture on the Prairies, we would have to be transported forward in time, say to the year 2050; then, perhaps, we could look back and interpret developments during the years 1950 to 1980 with some accuracy. However, as this is written there are strong indications that our present building cycle is coming to a close and so is ripe for review. If, indeed, the post-war building boom is ending, then we can count three major construction cycles on the Prairies since the original pioneer settlements were founded.

The earliest period predates the First World War, peaking in the Edwardian years between 1900 and 1912 when the arrival and consolidation of the railways stimulated major investments in real estate and building. Land speculation was rife; fortunes were made and lost before it all came to an end in the trenches at Verdun or Ypres.

The optimism of those years was unequalled even by the euphoria in Alberta during the 1970s. It is not unusual to discover from the records of small Prairie towns that their planners saw them attaining the size of major cites such as Calgary or Winnipeg, the latter a city particularly rich in architecture of the Edwardian and earlier eras.

Throughout the Prairie provinces, one comes across examples of this early architecture. There are mansions built by merchants and entrepreneurs; churches of many faiths, often the only buildings of any significance in the villages and hamlets of the West; magnificent masonry warehouses that housed the trade goods that sustained the region's settlement. And then there

are the great romantic structures — the provincial legislative buildings and the railway hotels, still as imposing as they were seventy-five years ago. My own favourite is the Banff Springs Hotel, not because it is a finer piece of architecture than, say, the Manitoba Legislature, but because it is so unexpected and improbable in its setting. The audacity of the architects in inserting a Baroque Baronial castle amid the peaks of the Bow Valley is remarkable and still not fully appreciated. In its own way the Banff Springs Hotel rivals the folly of Ludwig at Neuschwanstein.

The second building cycle followed the Great War, but was neither as robust as the preceding cycle nor as frenzied as the most recent. In truth, it never had the chance to burst into full flower before the Depression of the 1930s forced a virtual suspension of construction. A few designs from that period pay lip service to the Art Deco movement, particularly some of the department stores and movie palaces. But the Depression was so pre-eminent on the Prairies that the new International Movement had little chance to emerge. As a consequence, the years between the wars there are of limited interest to an architectural historian.

Perhaps the most potent period of Prairie architecture is the one that began about 1950 and has continued to the present. A rapid increase in economic activity and construction accompanied the post-war waves of immigration. It seemed the world wanted to emigrate to Canada; the cities — Winnipeg, Regina, Edmonton, Calgary, Saskatoon — were once again seized by a fervour for development.

This economic explosion was felt in different ways in different provinces. Manitoba was the least affected, mainly because it does not possess the natural resources of Alberta or Saskatchewan. However, Manitoba had cultural resources the younger regions lacked. For instance, at the University of Manitoba, a well-established faculty of architecture encouraged a high standard of design. Until the early 1970s, when the University of Calgary began to grant degrees in Environmental Design, this was the only accredited school of architecture on the Prairies.

Saskatchewan's historical suspicion of outside entrepreneurs deterred the arrival of heavy investment capital. Regina was the birthplace of the Prairie populist movement, rooted in Fabian socialism, which until fairly recently was a tough homespun weave of conservative religiosity and bread-and-butter Marxism.

Alberta has been called the "Texas of the Canadian Prairies." Following the discovery of the Leduc oil field in 1947, the free-enterprise zeal of the province's Social Credit politicians encouraged all manner of investors to profit from the bonanza. International oil companies and real-estate conglomerates invaded Alberta with capital and people. The skylines of Edmonton and Calgary are one result. But in the rush to build, little attention was paid to form, to detailing, or to the impact on the urban infrastructure. It may take many years to digest this hurried development.

This sudden demand on their professional skills all but overwhelmed local architects. With the ink hardly dry on their diplomas, they were often called upon to design huge commercial complexes. Frequently construction commenced before financing was fully in place or the working drawings completed. It is no surprise that so much post-war Prairie architecture is — to put it politely — undistinguished. The circumstances of frantic boom and architectural inexperience seldom achieve design distinction.

Yet, as the examples in this book show, some architects still managed to produce designs that captured both the optimism of technology and its interaction with Prairie tradition — no mean task, given the headlong rush to profit of the three decades since the war.

The Prairies present a harsh and unforgiving environment. No matter how beautiful the Alberta Rockies or Saskatchewan sunsets or Manitoba lakes, the threat of early frosts and hard winters is ever-present in all three provinces. Cross this climate with a cost-conscious developer concerned only with speed of construction and economy of means and you have a very difficult context for design.

If I had to select one architect who has nonetheless achieved a synthesis of twentieth-century technology, Prairie fundamentalism, and cost-economy it would have to be Clifford Wiens of Regina. In some ways Wiens had more obstacles to overcome than his colleagues in Manitoba or Alberta. Saskatchewan is a most infertile soil for architectural innovation, lacking the wealth of Alberta and the cultural sophistication of Manitoba, yet Wiens has been able to produce designs that transcend economic limitations while remaining deeply committed to their social and physical context.

Wiens, in my opinion, has built from his primal Mennonite gut. The Central Heating and Cooling Plant in Regina is a vertical building that punctuates the flat Prairie landscape in the same way as did the pioneer churches and the grain elevators. His own office is a similar act of poetic defiance in a mediocre sreetscape.

Etienne Gaboury of Winnipeg is another designer who has been able to achieve a similar synthesis. I sense in him the same unregenerate Prairie "geist" as energizes Wiens, tempered by a French-Canadian experience. Gaboury is a dreamer striving to retain the enthusiasm and dedication of his pioneer Catholic antecedents. His work is rich in paradox, fruitful for the future; it is most unfortunate that economic downturns have limited his output.

Douglas Cardinal in Alberta began with a refusal to accept the conventional wisdom of the International Style in favour of developing a personal idiom that owes a great deal to Gaudi and the later Le Corbusier. Yet, oddly, Cardinal had as clients conservative government agencies with limited funds; these seem unlikely patrons for his personally poetic statements. The building skills that such personal architecture requires are increasingly hard to find. For all these reasons few of Cardinal's buildings are entirely satisfactory; St. Mary's Church in Red Deer remains his finest and most complete work in which interior and exterior fuse in a dynamic balance. The church is a potent and evocative architectural sculpture, only slightly diminished by its suburban surroundings.

Gustavo da Roza in Winnipeg is a teacher at the University of Winnipeg and a practising architect. An immigrant, he has shown an understanding of his adopted environment few native-born Prairie designers have achieved. Da Roza feels deeply about the technology of building in a cold climate, yet manages to invest his architecture with an enthusiasm that transcends his concern with vapour barriers. The Winnipeg Art Gallery is as much a sculpture as Cardinal's church, but fits more aptly into its urban context.

The Diamond and Myers buildings, such as the Citadel Theatre and the Housing Union Building, are outsiders to the Prairie esthetic. These designs are adventurous in the High Tech style of Toronto rather than Alberta. Yet it must be said that the Citadel is surely one of the most successful theatres in Canada, much appreciated by both audiences and performers. If the HUB building is less popular it is because it tries to bend too radically our stiff Prairie psyche.

The Centennial Hall at the University of Winnipeg is handsome and accomplished, but it lacks the magnificent willfulness of Wiens or Gaboury. But then it is a structure in another idiom and for another time, like the little architects' offices by the IKOY Partnership. These buildings have a Prairie sense if not a Prairie image.

Leslie Stechesen's Leaf Rapids Community Centre suggests a possible future direction for Prairie architecture to function as something other than pure building design; this multi-use complex is more concerned with human behaviour than with style or symbolism. The centre concedes the unforgiving nature of our environment, both climatically and socially. Pioneer societies do not appreciate attempts to change their world.

We are now at the end of one more Prairie building cycle. Economic and social pressures are forcing us to re-think many of our assumptions. Put simply, we have for too long tended to design people for buildings, rather than communities for people; in the next decades architects will have to learn a great deal more about the relationship between life sciences and architecture. This possible fusion of psychology, socio-biology, economics, and design offers new challenges. The greatest is to conjure up major form-givers like Wiens and Gaboury to give back to us profound and original images of the Prairies at the end of the twentieth century.

The Prairie region, in its geographic immensity, climatic hostility, and social rigidity requires its architects to be potent givers of form. This, in my opinion, is why the most powerfully original buildings in the post-war era have come from here. I would go further and say that perhaps the only truly Canadian — as against adopted — architectural images have been created on the Prairies, out of this harsh necessity for strong forms in a landscape wide as Heaven or Hell.

Saint Mary's Church

Above: the sculptural shell; *Opposite:* the altar and its light-cannon.

Architect: Douglas J. Cardinal
Location: Red Deer, Alberta
Completion date: 1968
Gross floor area: 13,000 square feet
Construction cost: $345,000
Client: St. Mary's Parish
Structural Consultants: Ricketts and Evers, Calgary, Ltd.
Contractors: N.Y. Construction Co. Ltd.

"We design from the inside out...and wrap a sculptural shell around...a natural curvilinear form out of our own unique Prairie environment," says Douglas Cardinal.

St. Mary's Church, serving six hundred parishioners in a residential section of this pretty Prairie town, springs from the omphalos of its altar — a six-ton block of rough-sawn white limestone lit by a light-cannon like a navel in the convex belly of the church's concrete catenary roof.

All liturgical and structural concepts wrap around the altar. The congregation gathers round it in curving oaken pews on a gently sloping floor, the choir and confessionals flank it, a skylit tabernacle is its counterpoint, an open-pipe organ its backdrop. A circling shell of brick encloses this intimate hierarchy of worship, a canopy of ceiling covers it like a tent.

Cardinal, great-grandson of a Stony Indian woman and a European settler, grew up locally. "My roots are firm in this land," he says. With Father Merx, the parish priest, Cardinal created a church that "grew from the main altar

in the manner of a seashell around its soft creature."

But Red Deer is a long way from the sea. Perhaps an idiom more apt for the rippling, earthy, variegated-brick enclosure of St. Mary's, that rises and falls around its altar as it sails in the flat Prairie "sea," is that of the pattern of shadow of wheat waving in the wind. The sculptural expressionism of its architecture is the offspring as much of purely formal "organic" precedents, such as Erich Mendelsohn's 1921 Einstein Tower in Potsdam, as of the designer's own root imagery.

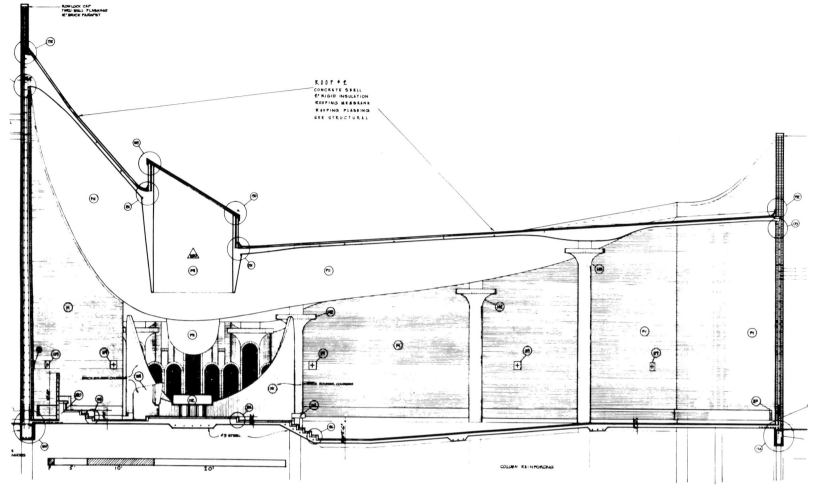

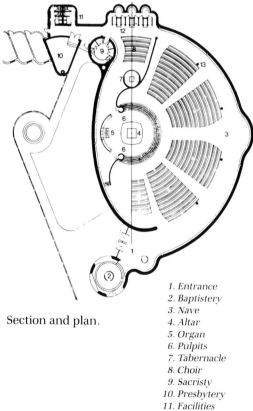

Section and plan.

1. Entrance
2. Baptistery
3. Nave
4. Altar
5. Organ
6. Pulpits
7. Tabernacle
8. Choir
9. Sacristy
10. Presbytery
11. Facilities
12. Confessionals
13. Pilasters

Tapering double-brick wythes form bearing walls filled with reinforced concrete. The walls and a series of concrete pilasters support a reinforced ring-beam from which the canted canopy is suspended. The 120-foot-wide catenary is formed of radial pre-tensioned cables in a computer-calculated spider-web pattern sprayed with cement. The roof is finished externally with two-inch rigid insulation and a Neoprene membrane. The ceiling soffit is coated with up to two inches of limpet asbestos fibre with fire-resistant, acoustical, and thermal properties.

"The people of God gather around the altar for a communal banquet," Cardinal writes. "This new liturgical concept is mirrored in the fluid form." Entry to this "banquet" is past an open circular baptistery under a curving bell tower. The font is in full view under sunken arches. The skylit confessionals, which penitents approach from behind, are judgement seats facing the altar.

Cardinal's designs, as in his Grande Prairie Regional College, or in the model for his own house in Edmonton, favour the curvilinear. Yet attempts to seize upon this characteristic as some sort of "Indian" architecture are both misguided and condescending. Cardinal's sculptural poetics are sophisticated, drawing as much from a modern European idiom as from his own innate imagery. The inventive design is matched by a technical sophistication necessary for its implementation, and by a high quality of execution, as St. Mary's illustrates. Cardinal's work is, in fact, highly ambitious and sometimes expensive. The original budget for St. Mary's was exceeded by fifty per cent. No funds were left over for landscaping or a projected rectory.

When Cardinal declares that "I place man at the centre, and ask myself how I may create a feeling of well-being in the surrounding space," he is expressing an aspiration common to all architecture.

View of entry flanked by baptistery.

Close-up of curving, textured brick in strong shadow.

Muttart Conservatory

Glass pyramids at roof level.

Architect: Peter Hemingway
Designer-in-charge: Paul Chung
Location: Edmonton, Alberta
Gross floor area: 26,000 square feet
Construction cost: $1 million
Client: City of Edmonton
Structural Consultants: B. W. Brooker Engineering Ltd.
Mechanical Consultants: Panner Engineering Ltd.
Contractor: Alta West Construction Ltd.

Snow lies long on the ground around Edmonton, Alberta's capital city. Sub-zero temperatures last from November to March, and often beyond. Fifty degrees below zero has been registered on both Fahrenheit and Celsius scales. Rivers are iced over and the Prairie landscape is pure white for months on end. In this context, the eye yearns for a change of scene. The Muttart Conservatory, on the banks of the North Saskatchewan River close to downtown Edmonton, provides such a welcome relief.

Four glass pyramids cap concrete chambers buried under grassy earth berms. A central reception area, also half-buried, links the pyramids, which vary in size from the sixty-foot-high, seventy-eight-foot-square Tropical house to the thirty-nine-foot-square Arid enclosure. In between are two intermediate pyramids, one for the plants, trees, and flowers of the world's temperate zones, another for changing shows of flora.

The conservatory is approached through ramped forecourts. Each pyramid has its own exit cut into the berm. The sunken reception plaza, toplit by its own miniature pyramidal skylight, is an island of carpet and benches surrounded by the quarry-tile paving that runs through the building.

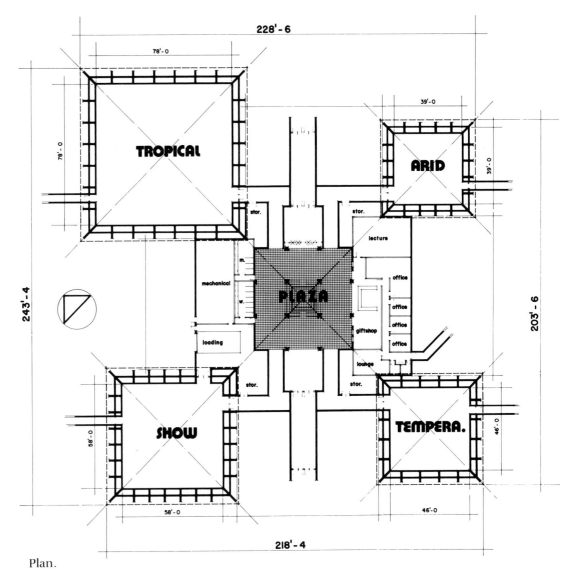

Plan.

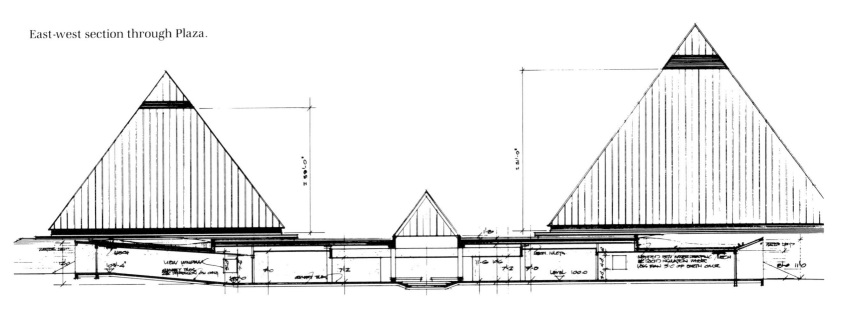

East-west section through Plaza.

Above: pyramids in the landscape; *Below:*
the Plaza.

Pyramid interior: aluminum greenhouse framing anchored to concrete curbs.

The buried conservatory walls are ten-inch reinforced concrete finished with hot-mopped bitumen and rigid insulation, and banked with earth to retain the heat. Interior precast panels, beams, and columns have a rough sandblasted finish. Drain tiles buried in the berms carry away seepage.

The superstructure of the pyramids is an industrial, prefabricated steel and aluminum greenhouse framing anchored to concrete curbs. Aluminum grills at top and bottom of the pyramids allow air circulation. Mechanical systems provide temperature, humidity, and ventilation control specialized to each environment.

The flat roof around the central plaza and over its surrounding offices, lobbies, gift shop, and washrooms is surfaced in asphalt, as are the troughs bordering each pyramid. This allows the roof to be flooded in summer, turning it into a reflecting pool which mirrors the magnificent blue Prairie sky with its cloud formations.

The miniature botanical garden in the river valley stands out sharply against the city's skyline. This quartet of transparent technological tepees, huddling at the foot of a low slope, reflects the summer sky and sparkles playfully in the winter sun, promising relief from the uniform snow and cold.

Citadel Theatre

Main corner with glazed arcade overhang.

Architects: Diamond, Myers, and Wilkin
Location: Edmonton, Alberta
Completion date: 1976
Gross floor area: 90,000 square feet
Construction cost: $6 million
Client: Citadel Theatre Company
Structural Engineers: M. B. Engineering Ltd.
Acoustics Consultant: Valcoustics Ltd.
Theatre Consultant: Andis Celms
Contractor: Carlson Management Services Ltd.
Project Team: Barton Myers, Rick Wilkin, David Murray, Don Clinton

Edmonton's Citadel Theatre has been described as "a gleaming, rust-lacquered jewel box." Like a jewel box, it is a neat enclosure containing a number of compartments that gives great pleasure among a clutter of commonplace objects — the highrise confusion of this vigorous city's rapidly expanding downtown.

The site, on the edge of a major development area adjacent to the North Saskatchewan River, was restricted by an existing multi-level underground garage and a thirty-foot-wide pedestrian right-of-way running north-south. On this tight lot the popular regional theatre company required three theatres seating 700, 300, and 200 people respectively.

The architects organized these complexities into a lucid composition. The pedestrian right-of-way became a street level internal mall with access to the lobbies of all three theatres. A restaurant, shop, and meeting rooms also open off the mall, which is linked by an elevator to the sub-grade parking. The stairway mezzanines and vaulted ceiling of the underside of the main auditorium make the mall a lively space while linking the internal street to the surrounding city.

The front end of the building is enclosed in a light-weight steel and glass envelope that wraps around the stairs and lobby serving the main theatre. This aluminum-sash curtain-wall and skylight glitters in the sun and twinkles with light at night. It makes the "jewel box" gleam and opens its activity to the street. A glazed arcade overhang protects the sidewalks from the weather — a feature that could be usefully extended through the urban core in Alberta's severe climate.

The "back of the house" — the flyloft tower, the rehearsal rooms, and the ramped delivery entrance for scenery — is encased in a contrasting solid structure of reinforced concrete columns and slabs faced with a terra cotta-red brick traditional to Edmonton's older architecture. The enamelled steel spandrels and aluminum sashes of the front-end glazing are finished in a rust tone to match the brickwork.

Main lobby; an interplay of crowds and levels in a high-tech "jewel box" with a strong sense of theatre.

Section.

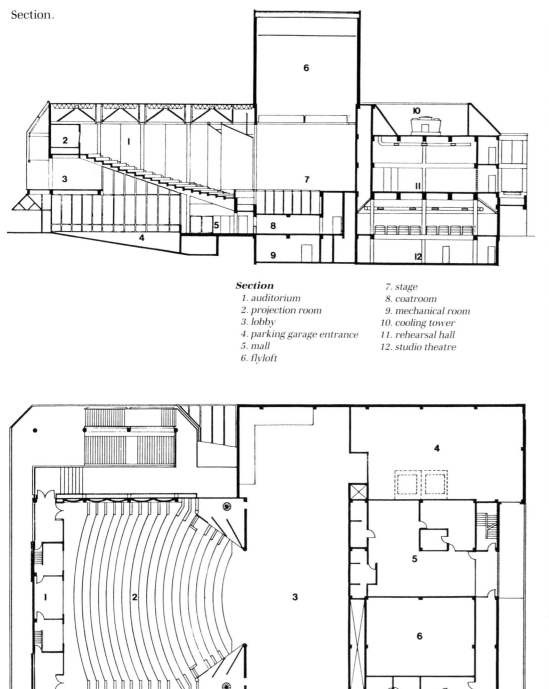

Section
1. auditorium
2. projection room
3. lobby
4. parking garage entrance
5. mall
6. flyloft
7. stage
8. coatroom
9. mechanical room
10. cooling tower
11. rehearsal hall
12. studio theatre

The 700-seat proscenium theatre has its stage eighteen feet above street level. Its seating is arranged in a single rake up from the stage in wide curves with no centre or cross aisles, and no seat further than sixty-five feet from the proscenium. Hollow section double trusses span the auditorium, tied by a deep concrete ring beam. Checker plates across the bottom chords make catwalks. The stage apron can be lowered to form an orchestra pit. The theatre is panelled and ceilinged in fire-treated flush redwood lined with sound-absorbent packing.

The two smaller theatres — one with movable seating and stage thrusts for experimental productions; the other for cinema, poetry readings, lectures, and recitals — are located on the opposite side of the mall. One is panelled, the other painted. Unglazed red clay tile floors the mall, matching the exposed brickwork inside and out. Brass railings, tempered glass balustrades, bubble lights, painted exposed ductwork, ribbed maroon carpeting and matching upholstery, and heavy red plush quilted velvet curtains used to insulate the curtain-walling complete the rich interior design.

Heating is provided by a gas-fired forced-air system fed through fin tube convectors. An enclosed rooftop cooling tower houses the airconditioning plant. Lighting in the theatres is flexible and accessible. Steel stairs and walkways are suspended from large hollow steel beams which also house ducting.

The Citadel "jewel box" sits on the edge of the city's core as if encouraging the confused urban fabric to rise to the level of its own urbane sophistication. It is a model for a town that hopes to be truly modern rather than merely expansive.

level 130
1. projection, sound, light rooms
2. auditorium
3. flyloft
4. upper part of workshop
5. costume and design workshop
6. rehearsal hall, upper part
7. offices
8. elevator
9. library and boardroom

Plan at main auditorium level.

The Theatre in its setting: urbane
sophistication in Boom Town.

Housing Union Building

Architects: Diamond, Myers, and Wilkin
Location: Edmonton, Alberta
Completion date: 1972
Gross floor area: 350,000 square feet
Construction cost: $5,600,000
Client: University of Alberta Students' Union
Structural Engineers: Read Jones Christoffersen Ltd.
Contractor: Poole Construction Ltd.

Over the past fifteen years Barton Myers has developed a design philosophy of "urban consolidation": the acceptance of the existing architectural fabric as the city's living history, to be enhanced by new structures rather than willfully destroyed, as so often happens. This radical conservatism is allied to an advanced style, influenced by Louis Kahn and Charles Eames, in the clear definition of service elements and the use of standard industrial components boldly displayed.

Myers's philosophy of "consolidation" is applied in many projects, particularly the urban infill of the Dundas-Sherbourne housing in Toronto and Myers's own house in the same city. Its clearest expression is seen in the University of Alberta's Housing Union Building in Edmonton.

The university's Long Range Development Plan, drawn up by the architects in the late 1960s, called for the connection of existing buildings on the dispersed campus by a network of new

Opposite: the Galleria; *Below:* HUB in the campus.

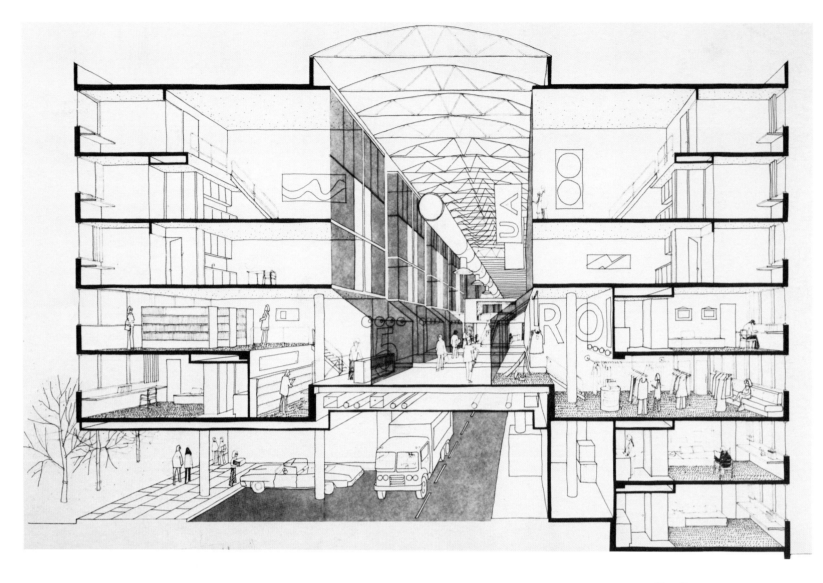

structures and by linear movement systems for pedestrians, cars, and buses to provide the maximum of shelter from Alberta's harsh climate. It planned a doubling of site coverage to accommodate an expected increase in student enrollment.

The HUB, commissioned by the University of Alberta Students' Union and paid for out of its own funds, provides on-campus housing for a thousand students in one-, two-, and four-person apartments built along both sides of an existing street. Above the street the seven-storey 957-foot-long building is unified by an enclosed glazed gallery five storeys high that creates a pedestrian precinct with its own sidewalk cafes, shops, lounges, and a daycare centre.

The economics of the project were investigated by the architects working with a quantity surveyor, A. J.

Vermeulen. A rock-bottom budget of $15.50 per square foot was set, using a structural system comparable to commercial apartment construction. Flat plates and concrete columns form the framework, clad in four-inch precast concrete panels. The gallery roof is a light steel frame spanning twenty-eight feet and glazed with clear acrylic bubble domes. Ductwork that keeps the gallery under a positive pressure to limit fire spread is boldly exposed and painted in primary colours.

All apartments are reached by a series of private stairs off the gallery, which is linked to the street below and parking. Several overhead bridges connect both sides of the building. The apartments have their bedrooms on the quieter outer face of the structure; the glass-walled living-dining rooms overlook the concourse. Each student has his or her own bedroom and the living spaces are double height in the large units. The ceilings are sprayed with sound-deadening material and partitions between apartments are acoustically absorbent.

The HUB gallery, a cheerful urban space of pleasantly human scale, derives from an old European tradition of protected indoor streets. The medieval university town of Bologna, for instance, is connected by twenty miles of covered passages. This tradition expresses an historical urban humanism in contrast to the highrise Utopias of much contemporary city planning.

"A good architect always appreciates the past," Myers says. "But that doesn't imply imitation. Design can be radical and conservative together: radical in manner, conservative in its sensitivity to the inherited fabric. Cities weren't born yesterday. History is continuous, and we are a link in a long chain of urban evolution. The past made us and we make the future."

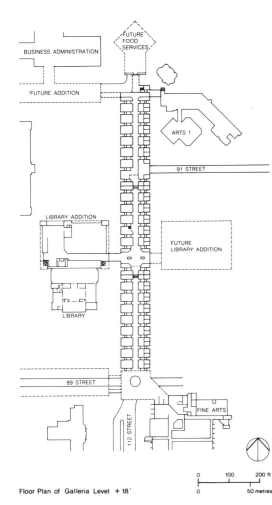

Floor Plan of Galleria Level + 18'

0   100   200 ft
0   50 metres

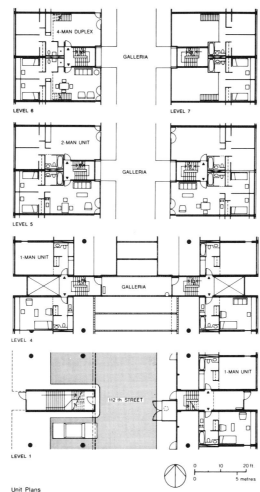

Unit Plans

0   10   20 ft
0   5 metres

Plans, exterior, and, *opposite*, sections and interior of a two-storey apartment unit.

Court and Remand Centre and "Plus 15" System

Architects: J. W. Long & Associates
Location: Calgary, Alberta
Completion date: (main structure) 1974
Gross floor area: 142,000 square feet
Construction cost: $7 million
Client: Department of Public Works, Province of Alberta
Structural Consultants: T. Lamb McManus & Associates
Contractors: Cana Construction Ltd.
Design Team: Jack Long, Don Snow, Jake Mayell, Bob Miller

Above: offices; *Opposite:* central atrium.

Calgary's Court and Remand Centre brings under one roof eight provincial Judges' Courts with attendant services, and a holding facility for people in custody awaiting trial. The building, located at the east end of the city's core urban renewal area, is connected to the central police station, the main city library and to City Hall.

The centre is planned on eight levels. The main entry level — connected by bridges to the city's "Plus 15" pedestrian walkway system — and the floor above house the criminal and traffic courtrooms. Below, at street level, is the jail; above are the remand cells and dormitories. A central three-storey atrium with mezzanines and a grand staircase is the centre's main public circulation space.

The two functions, judicial and incarcerational, are differentiated by their external skins. The court levels are clad in oversized brickwork in a variegated reddish brown; the upper floors of the remand facility — an extra fourth level was added in 1978 — are enclosed in dark-coloured metal siding. The structural system of *in-situ* reinforced concrete columns and waffle-plate slabs is exposed internally, setting off the masonry walls and matching tile floors.

The centre forms the southeastern entry point into Calgary's "Plus 15" pedestrian system. It is designed to integrate the elevated walkways into its internal space perhaps more completely than any other structure in the city's core. The central atrium, connected at its mezzanine court level by the yellow-tinted, curved, acrylic-covered bridges over the street, forms an ample, expansive resting place for people passing through.

"Plus 15" was developed in the late 1960s, at the beginning of a boom decade of building in Calgary that saw the city's downtown core almost totally reconstructed. The system, now an extensive, climate-controlled, pedestrian movement network, separates people on foot from vehicles on the street at least fifteen feet below. Mid-block corridors and bridges, required by

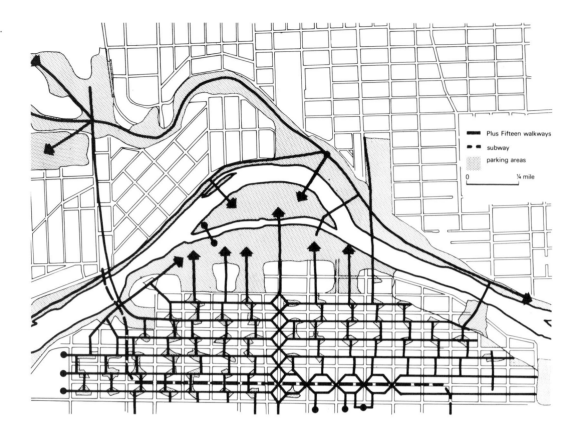

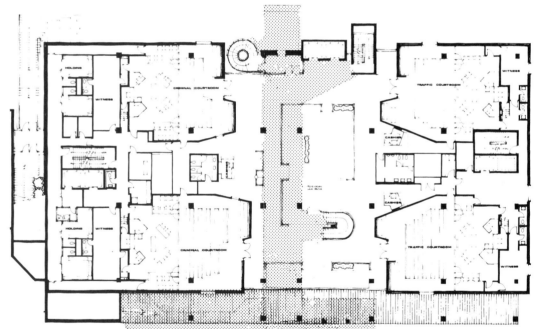

by-law in the central zone, link most of the city's new core buildings. Bonus building density is offered as an incentive to developers outside the core who integrate their structures into the system.

"Plus 15" can be criticized, however, despite its bold solution to traffic movement. For one thing, pedestrians still prefer the street level with its noise and hustle, its lively shops and restaurants, its confusion of cars and people; they stick to the lower sidewalks whenever the weather permits. Also, the design detail on the bridges and walkways is often crude and clumsy, giving them an air of oversimplified futurism straight out of an early sci-fi movie.

Calgary is a commuter city in which few inhabitants live downtown. Outside the few daylight hours when the core is active, the rigid and over-elaborate separation of traffic and pedestrians can seem all too radical. As the often dismal underground mall systems of Toronto and Montreal have shown, protection from weather can only be part of the solution for urban movement. The open street, for all its chaos and exposure, is still profoundly attractive to most urbanites.

A walkway links the Centre to entry point of "Plus 15" pedestrian system.

Heating and Cooling Plant

"Scale and a sense of place."

Architect: Clifford Wiens
Location: Regina, Saskatchewan
Completion date: 1967
Gross floor area: 28,000 square feet
Construction cost: $400,000
Client: University of Regina
Structural Consultants: H. H. Angus and Associates Ltd.
Concrete Contractors: Conforce Products Ltd.

"The grain elevator is one of the very few successful Prairie buildings," Clifford Wiens has said. "Construction was straightforward and honest, with the total organization functional in every way.... These structures functioned as symbols and beacons, giving scale and a sense of place."

The same honest Prairie vigour informs the design of Wiens's central heating and cooling plant for the University of Regina. In a wide, flat, treeless landscape the structure's strong shape is a direct expression of its industrial function.

The building houses a central steam and cooling plant and electrical distribution control for the campus. The firing floor is at grade level, surrounded by a sunken courtyard filled with crushed stone covering removable storage tanks. A mezzanine and a cooling tower complete the section.

The structure is precast, post-tensioned concrete on cast-in-place piling. The twenty-inch ribbed firing floor is tied to ten low reinforced concrete buttresses a hundred feet apart by Freyssinet post-tensioning cables. Precast A-frame units forty feet high at the peak were hoisted into place and anchored to the buttresses by post-tensioning. The A-frames are tied together at the ridge by the precast stem spine and brackets of the cooling tower.

Concrete was chosen over steel for the structure for its resistance to condensation, its fireproofing qualities, and its low maintenance. Vertical board-marks left in the finished concrete control the pattern of streaking. A crucial design consideration in the choice of concrete was its muscular strength of scale suitable to a vigorous visual statement.

Corner detail; precast A-frame anchored to buttress.

A-frame assembly.

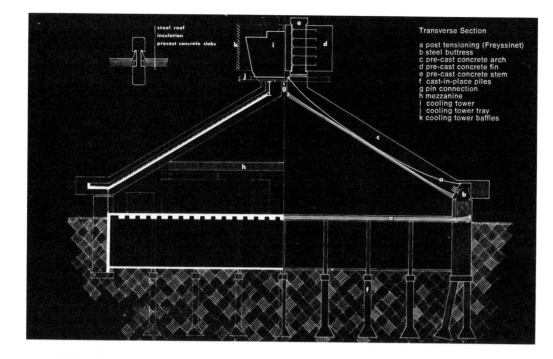

Transverse Section

a post tensioning (Freyssinet)
b steel buttress
c pre-cast concrete arch
d pre-cast concrete fin
e pre-cast concrete stem
f cast-in-place piles
g pin connection
h mezzanine
i cooling tower
j cooling tower tray
k cooling tower baffles

The triangular window walls at the ends are designed to dismantle to allow movement of heavy equipment in and out of the plant. The vertical mullions are slotted at the top for ease of removal and for thermal expansion. The mullions, roof decking, cooling trays, and screening louvres are of exposed, unpainted, low-alloy steel fabricated to oxidise in a corrosion process so dense it seals the surface with a rich brown patina which weathers gradually to a textured bluish grey. However, "client abuse or neglect of buildings is extremely high in Saskatchewan," Wiens complains. "The plant has large stained areas from bird droppings, easily prevented."

Despite this lament, the vigour and honesty of the structure shines in contrast to the other unimaginative precast concrete buildings on campus. The plant retains the courage of its convictions as a conscious act of design matching the symbolic energy of the Prairie elevator. On cold, stark nights the glazed ends glow like a furnace firebox potent with warmth and power, a beacon in the landscape.

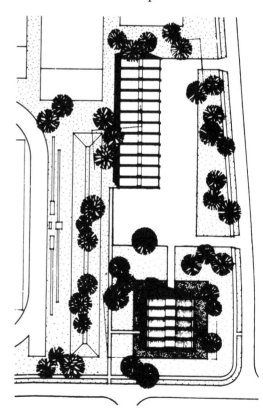

Opposite: site plan, interior; *Above:* precast stem spine and cooling tower brackets.

Architects' Office

Architects/Client: Wiens and Associates Ltd.
Location: Regina, Saskatchewan
Completion date: 1974
Gross floor area: 3000 square feet
Construction cost: $150,000
Structural Consultants: Reid, Crowther and Partners Ltd.
Steel fabrication and erection: Dominion Bridge Co. Ltd.

Office interior: view towards rear parking.

An architect's office is, apart from its purely functional aspects, "an advertisement for myself." It is, in Clifford Wiens's words, "a building that allows us to emphasize practical matters with our clients while they absorb the idea that we can be innovative."

This small office for two partners and four assistants occupies a 25-foot by 125-foot lot on Albert Street, one of Regina's main avenues. Empty "since the buffalo days," the lot is bounded by low brick buildings and has parking access at the rear.

IPSCO steel company offered the architects material at cost, which suggested an innovative design to them: a catenary, quarter-inch rolled-steel-plate roof suspended from a series of six "trees" constructed of twenty-four-inch-diameter gas transmission piping. The circular off-centre "trees" march the length of the building, forming cantilevered branches to support the concave steel roof and suspended light-gauge steel wall panels. The roof is insulated with sprayed polyurethane. Continuous hinged slip joints bolted to the structural brackets allow for movement.

The substructure is reinforced concrete slab on pilings with six-foot-high side parapets, off which the insulated interior wall panels are bracketed.

16 utility piping
17 bolted connection
18 structural pipe cantilever
19 structural pipe column
20 access panel to attic space above parking
21 insulated interior wall
22 lighting
23 fresh air intake
24 supply air
25 return air
26 heating / cooling unit
27 insulation
28 steel plate roof
29 slip joint
30 steel panel wall suspended from roof
31 hinge connection
32 structural concrete floor
33 structural concrete wall

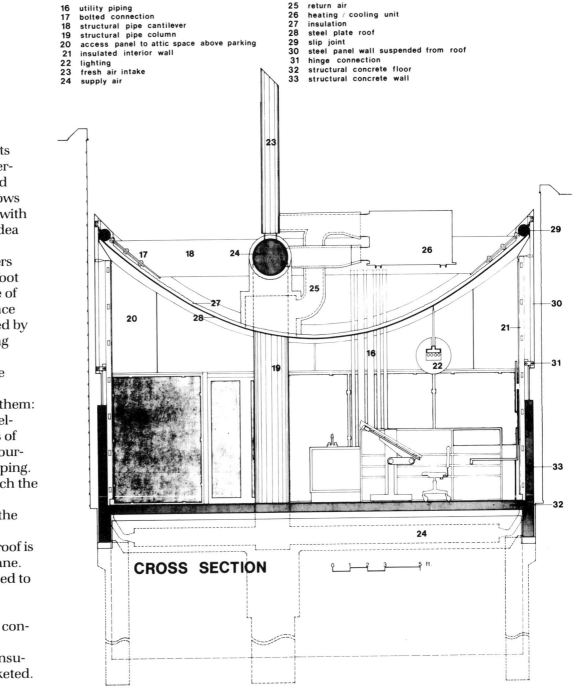

CROSS SECTION

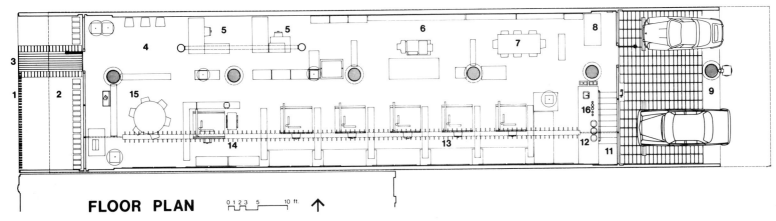

FLOOR PLAN

A partial basement at the rear contains washrooms. Storage space is provided by an attic over the parking bays. Two rooftop heating and cooling units supply air along the structural gas piping to an underfloor distribution with recessed baseboard vents.

The front façade, set in from the street line, displays the structural intent. The catenary curve is expressed in gun-metal painted steel panels, with the red pipe "trees" above. Narrow gaps are left between the building and its neighbours, accentuating its particularity.

Internally, the drawing boards are placed along the right-hand wall. A central corridor in the open plan divides the drafting space from the secretaries and client-consultation area. The open plan, though short on privacy, promotes an interchange of ideas and information. The office acts as a teach-ing studio for junior staff, who learn every aspect of architectural practise. A long suspended lighting unit with big circular white baffles runs the depth of the office.

High-gloss blood-red enamel dominates the colour scheme. The underbelly of the catenary, the steel columns, and the exposed utility pipes radiate its warmth. The curves mirror and articulate the strong colour tone, providing a relief from the flat white tracing paper on the boards. Light yellows and dark blues, chocolate browns and beige carpeting give contrast.

"We were the first architects to build our own offices in Regina," Wiens explains. "Although we could have built conventionally for less, the office, as an advertisement, has generated walk-in trade resulting in major commissions."

Below: view towards street;
Opposite: front entrance.

"The Prairie landscape requires strong silhouettes. . . ." Church entry under spiral skylight.

Precious Blood Church

Architect: Etienne Gaboury
Associate Architect: Denis Lussier
Location: St. Boniface, Manitoba
Completion date: 1968
Construction cost: $344,000
Client: Precious Blood Parish
Contractor: Bockstael Construction Ltd.

Light is the key to sacred architecture.

Function in church architecture is difficult to define in the secular spirit of the times. Spirituality is a slightly uncomfortable sentiment for the modern mind, yet it must remain crucial to any truly religious building that hopes to be more than a grandiose community centre.

In Precious Blood Church Etienne Gaboury strove to develop "a plan that resolved and clearly expressed the dynamic movement of the congregation around the altar," in the Roman Catholic liturgy, "while still acknowledging the symbolic and functional requirements of the sacramental spaces." The key to this fusion of function and feeling was — as it has so often been in sacred architecture — light. "The introduction of light must...be a result of the structure," Gaboury says. To achieve this result he examined a series of solutions, evolving towards a spiral: a spiral structure springing from a clockwise spiral plan to express the hierarchy of liturgical function, from holy water

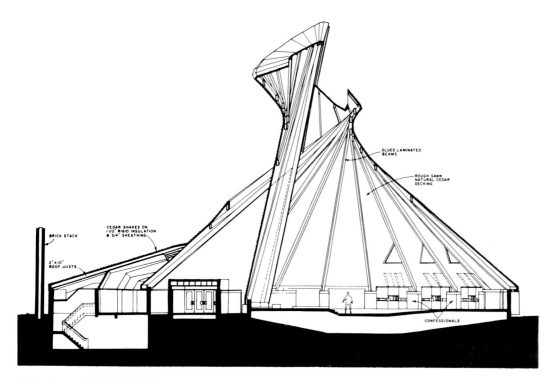

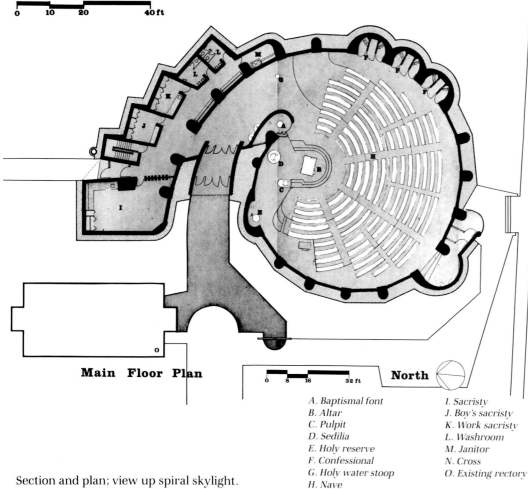

Main Floor Plan

0   8   16   32 ft   **North**

A. Baptismal font
B. Altar
C. Pulpit
D. Sedilia
E. Holy reserve
F. Confessional
G. Holy water stoop
H. Nave

I. Sacristy
J. Boy's sacristy
K. Work sacristy
L. Washroom
M. Janitor
N. Cross
O. Existing rectory

Section and plan; view up spiral skylight.

stoop to central altar in a heightening, unfolding sequence of continuous space.

The congregation of the suburban Winnipeg *Paroisse du Précieux Sang* is French-speaking and largely descended from the mixed-blood French-Indian Métis. The church's structural and spatial inspiration was that of a non-Christian but archtypally Prairie idiom — the native Indian tepee.

The structure is a swirl of twenty-five nine-inch glued laminated-fir struts seventy-two to a hundred feet long, enclosing a nave eighty-eight feet in diameter that soars eighty-five feet to the open skylight which echoes a tepee's smoke-hole. These wooden ribs are clothed externally in rough cedar shakes nailed to cross-joists and backed by rigid insulation, and they are finished internally with six-inch, rough-sawn, stained cedar decking.

The timber superstructure sits on a base of variegated clay glazed-brick walls, whose curves sweep and bulge to include the side sacristies and confessionals. The existing rectory on the site was integrated with the church by a subtle transition from the recti-linear to the curved, and by varying the height of the brick walls from the high level around the sacristy to the low screen at the sanctuary. The brick buttresses also vary in depth depending on the angle of the timber beams they support.

Wooden seating for 525 worshippers circles about the stone altar. The altar is raised several steps above the paved brick floor; sidelit from the inward fold of the spiral, and toplit from the apex skylight. The crisp, brittle Prairie light is softened and diffused by the cedar ceiling, and warmed by the beige brick-work. The confessional screens are flush with the curve. Inside each room priest and penitent sit face to face in armchairs; triangular openings in the main ceiling provide air and light.

A basement service room feeds a forced-air duct system for heating and ventilation. The freestanding, low, brick stack is a vertical accent, counter-pointing the irregular twisted cone of the church, swirling and swelling to terminate in the coiled peak sealed with stained glass symbolising Christ's sacrifice of "precious blood."

Space and sentiment are thus a unity. This is a true house of worship and awe, designed by a truly religious mind. The bravura gestures of the architecture are not merely clever; the vortex spiralling of the church's interior is spiritual without sentimentality of function or feeling. This building is that rare thing: a profoundly sacramental space that is unmistakably modern.

Gaboury House

Architect/Client: E. J. Gaboury
Location: St. Vital, Manitoba
Completion date: 1968
Gross floor area: 3700 square feet
Construction cost: $90,000
Contractor: Albert Roy

Rough-sawn cedar shakes and rustic shapes give a sense of shelter.

A house is a shelter and a refuge, and — particularly in an architect's design for his own family — an expression of a way of life.

Etienne Gaboury believes that, "If we accept architecture as an art form, a building must not only house man but transform him....A good house should ensure the fulfillment of all its inhabitants." At the same time the architect wanted a design that "belongs in the plains, that reaches out for the sun and turns its back on the cold winds of the north."

The Gaboury residence, in a suburb of Winnipeg, stands on an ample lot treed with oak, birch, and elm in a bend of the Red River. The site is typically flat, tiered on two levels at the riverbank, with superb western views of the sun setting on the water. The heart of the house is the south-facing family room linked to the kitchen, dining room, and living areas. The five bedrooms are half a floor up, over the basement garage; a studio sits on a mezzanine overlooking the central hearth.

The freestanding fireplace, built of clay tile and pipe, is the interior's focal point. Spaces and levels interlock around this pivot in a continuous flow whose fluidity is enhanced by the

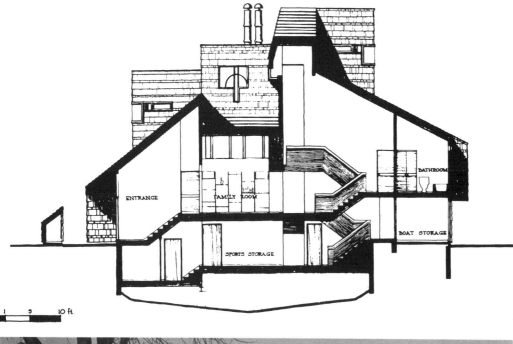

ENTRANCE

FAMILY ROOM

BATHROOM

SPORTS STORAGE

BOAT STORAGE

1   5   10 ft.

sensuous curves of the sloping, natural cedar, ceiling battens contrasted with off-white textured plaster walls. Rich brown floors, in carpet or cork, form a strong colour base for the family's taste in artwork.

The exterior of the house, constructed in standard western timber frame, is clad in rough-sawn cedar shakes bleached by weather to silver greys and rusty browns. Its vertical, slope-roofed composition recalls the traditional Prairie lean-to; the bellied curve of the living-room bow window conjures echoes of western grain elevators.

The wood-framed, double-glazed windows, seen by the architect as "a series of conscious events," are carefully considered perforations in this crustacean shell. A central stained-glass light over the high living room enriches the interior warmth.

Standing in deep snow among stripped branches in a stark landscape, the house signals a strong aura of ample shelter. Its shaggy cedar skin and steep slopes are at home among the white drifts. The architect has suppressed any urge to the spectacular so characteristic of some of his other designs, such as the Precious Blood Church in St. Boniface, in favour of a profound sense of family refuge in a cold climate, in a vernacular at once traditionally regional yet modern in its gestures.

Within, the house is serene and warm. Its flowing spaces enjoy a full range of the low winter sun, from morning light in the bedrooms to the marvellously glowing sunsets over the river, viewed from the diningroom, livingroom, and master bedroom. The neutrality of the interior, with its clean uncluttered details, provides a shelter for months of indoor living for a family's changing needs of privacy and community.

This is a house to last a man's life and, perhaps, to subtly enrich and transform him over many years.

Above: section; *Below:* snow softens the silhouette.

Living room fireplace and stair to upper levels.

Main floor plan.

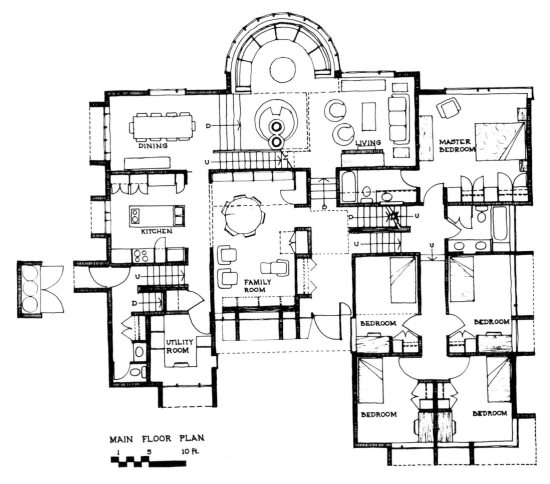

DINING

KITCHEN

UTILITY
ROOM

LIVING

FAMILY
ROOM

MASTER
BEDROOM

BEDROOM

BEDROOM

BEDROOM

BEDROOM

MAIN FLOOR PLAN

1   5   10 ft.

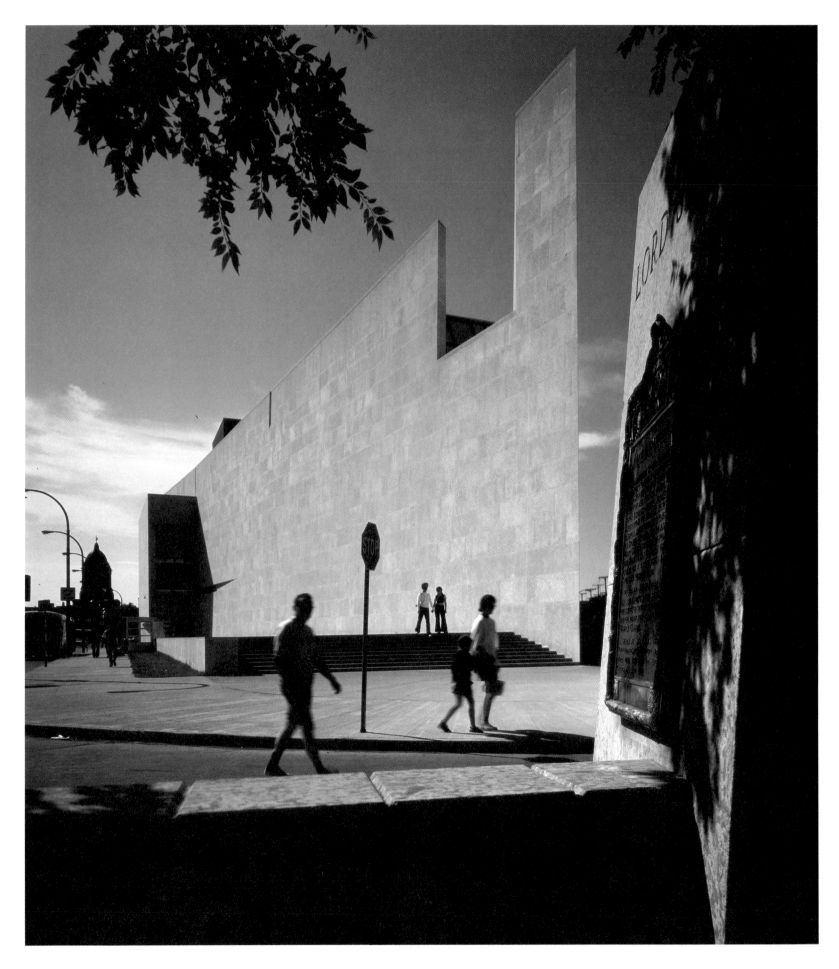

Winnipeg Art Gallery

Architects: Gustavo da Roza and
　　The Number Ten Architectural Group
Location: Winnipeg, Manitoba
Completion date: 1971
Gross floor area: 120,000 square feet, plus 25,000 square feet
　　in roof garden
Construction cost: $4.5 million, including fees and land
Client: City of Winnipeg
Structural Engineers: Read Jones Christoffersen Ltd.
Contractor: Bird Construction Co. Ltd.
Project Team: Gustava da Roza, Isadore Coop, Ludwig Bachmann

View towards main entrance.

Opposite: Building as sculpture.

The designer of a contemporary art gallery chooses between two basic options: building as anonymous art warehouse; or building as sculpture, complementing and perhaps competing with the artifacts it houses and displays. The Winnipeg Art Gallery, like Wright's Guggenheim Museum in New York, chooses the latter option.

The result of a 1967 competition, selected for its "brilliant symbolization of progressive Winnipeg," the gallery is a clean wedge of light grey sawn-cut Manitoba limestone four storeys high. The tight triangular site, which dictated the structural shape, points north — in the architects' words, "to crystallize the character of the Prairie environment."

So the gallery is a symbolic building, standing for the modernity of a provincial city, its hopeful commitment to culture, its identification with the stark landscape in which it sits. But it is also, within its high bastion walls, a showcase for artworks.

Transition between symbol and function is marked by the gallery's massive front door. This portal is a solid eight-inch-thick stone, eight feet tall and sixteen feet long. Its seven-ton weight is

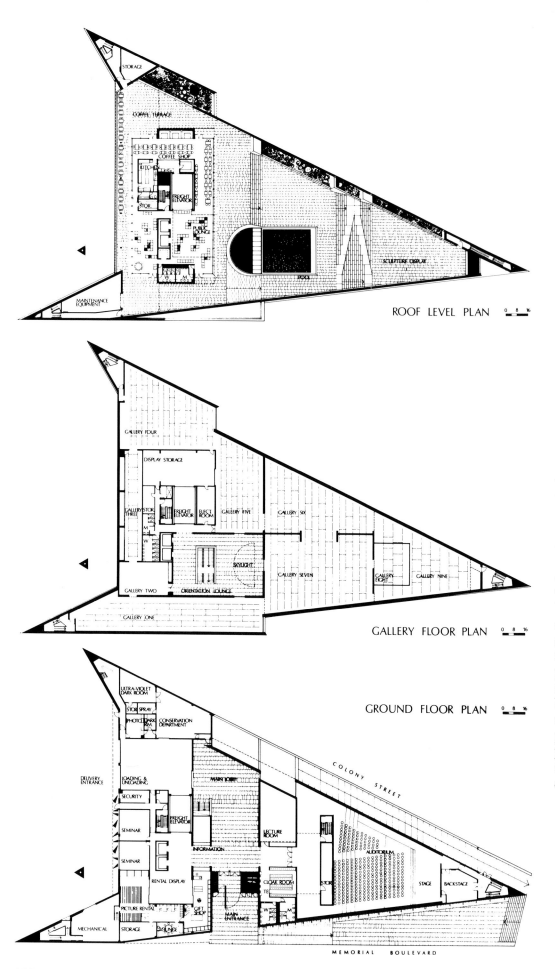

ROOF LEVEL PLAN

GALLERY FLOOR PLAN

GROUND FLOOR PLAN

pivoted one-third from its inner end, opening into a ground-floor lobby, lined with limestone, that also functions as a display space, giving a foretaste of the delights to come.

The interior stone finish leads up two grand flights of stone stairs to the third-floor main gallery level. The upper Orientation Lounge is lit by a semicircular rooflight — the only natural toplight in the gallery, apart from a clearstory at the apex of the wedge.

The ground floor houses an auditorium, seminar and lecture rooms, cloakrooms, delivery entrance, and rental space for "artists-in-residence." The basement contains mechanical plant, storage vaults, and a multi-purpose studio for children's art education, with a separate access off the street. The second-floor mezzanine level accommodates a library and staff offices. Roof level is given over largely to an outdoor sculpture display. A glass-walled restaurant and public lounge overlook this wide wedge, whose four-foot slope is ramped for easy wheelchair access and for forklifts moving heavy objects. A reflecting pool and planting make it an open-to-the-sky setting for the exhibition of large sculptures.

The structure is reinforced, *in-situ*, concrete bearing-walls and slabs faced with four-inch Tyndall limestone backed by rigid insulation. The galleries are finished internally with cream linen glued to plywood display walls and floored with neutral grey acrylic carpeting on felt underpadding. Bare concrete, where exposed, is sandblasted. The roof terrace is constructed on the "rain screen" method; concrete paving slabs on rigid insulation over pea-gravel fill are supplemented with drain weep tiles and undersealed with a waterproof membrane.

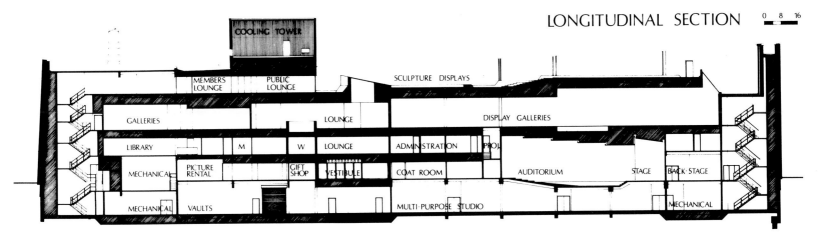

Left: gallery with sculpture display; *Below:* Roof level pool and outdoor exhibits.

The galleries are mainained at a year-round temperature of 70°F (plus or minus 2°F) and a constant relative humidity of 50% (plus or minus 5%). Recessed baseboards house continuous-return air-plenum extracts. Gallery ceilings have recessed double-circuited tracks for movable light fixtures.

Internally, the gallery provides flexible, neutral spaces for display. Partitions are movable; furniture is modular; ceilings are acoustic tile; function is all. Externally, the gallery is a clean, off-white wedge in the bright Prairie sunlight; "a brilliant symbolization of progressive Winnipeg"; a huge arrowhead pointing north.

Leaf Rapids Town Centre

Architects: Leslie J. Stechesen, Architects
Location: Leaf Rapids, Manitoba
Completion date: 1972
Gross floor area: 220,000 square feet
Construction cost: $8.5 million
Client: Leaf Rapids Development Corporation
Mechanical Engineers: A. E. Burstein and Associates
Construction Management: Northward Project Control
Project Team: Leslie Stechesen, G. M. Frederickson, D. G. Barry

Town Square.

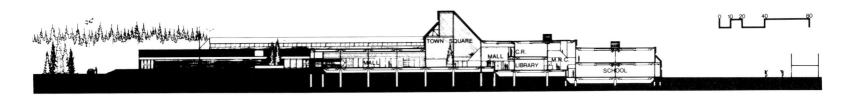

The vast majority of Canadians live below the fifty-fourth parallel, huddling as far south as they can get. North of that line, climate is extreme, reaching well below zero in winter, shooting up over 35°C in summer. The communities established in these harsh regions are usually specific to a purpose, such as mining, and require radically innovative solutions to town planning.

Leaf Rapids is a mining town of twenty-five hundred people, five hundred air miles north of Winnipeg. It is located on an esker — a ridge of post-glacial gravel — near one of the long lakes typical of the sparsely wooded, inhospitable landscape. The town was built in the early 1970s to a plan that separates cars and pedestrians. A perimeter collector road off the main highway serves bays of housing, none of which are further than half a mile from the town centre. Under this centre's one roof are all the social and commercial facilities a small town could need. The complex is comprised of a school for 625 students, a cultural centre, library, forty-room hotel, hospital, gymnasium, arena, rink, bank, post office, council chamber, bar, restaurant, supermarket, shops, department store, drug store, government offices, theatre, and crafts and hobby spaces. A swimming pool is planned.

The centre is laid out in quadrants on two levels about a cross-mall. The crux is the multi-level town square, on which the council chamber is located. All four internal streets feed into this focus, whose warm, local-pine walls and parapets, tile floor, and high, angled, toplit ceilings welcome crowds of townspeople.

The superb integration of the centre springs from the co-operation of many

A typical winter's day.

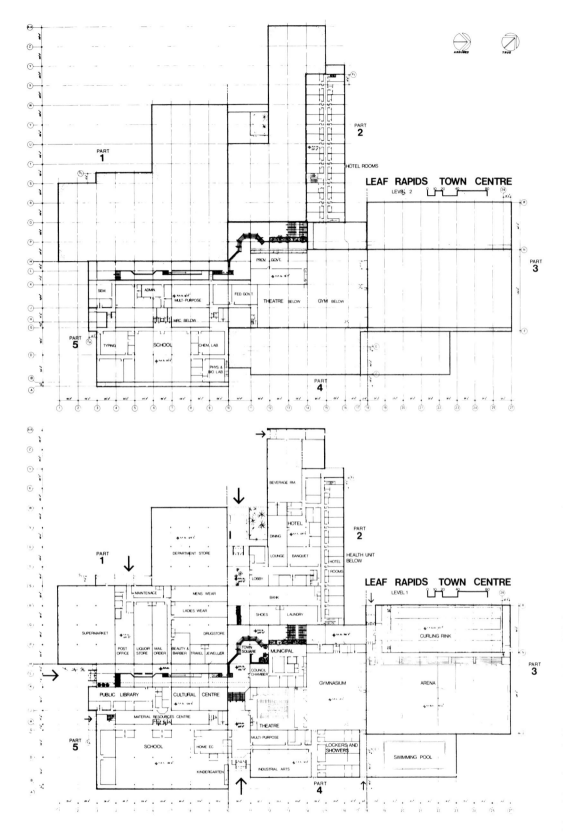

LEAF RAPIDS TOWN CENTRE

LEVEL 2

LEAF RAPIDS TOWN CENTRE

LEVEL 1

participants, including several governmental agencies and departments, the mining corporation, real estate consultants, mechanical services specialists, and the architects. Although Leaf Rapids is a company town, its planning was co-ordinated and expedited by a crown corporation under the direct supervision of a committee of the provincial cabinet.

All the elements of the centre are interdependent. The drug store supplies the hospital, which can expand into the hotel if extra beds are required. The school and public libraries share services. The hotel kitchen supplies meals to the health-care unit. Doctor, dentist, social worker, public health nurse, and family counsellor provide a comprehensive service to the small community.

Construction was carried out by project management on a basis of sequential tendering. Costs were high because it was necessary to ship in all materials and labour by helicopter and rail. The structure is a steel frame of light, portable, prefabricated components bolted to concrete piling. The frame is clad in insulated steel panels which weather to a patinated rust layer. The complex steps down the east slope of the esker and the roof levels are arranged to let in, through long clearstories, as much natural daylight as the low winter sun can offer.

Climate control in the main areas is provided by thirteen self-contained rooftop conditioning units, each with a direct-expansion cooling coil, compressor, air-cooled condenser, and electric heating coil. A further ten units service the smaller shops, office space, and the school. The mechanical system is governed by electronic controls with a central read-out. A calculated oversupply and interchangeable use is built into the system to cover individual plant breakdowns.

The landscape of northern Manitoba has a bleak beauty. Hard blue skies and bright silver snows make a blinding contrast for most of the year. In this severity, the centre is a refuge; a warmth to the blood and the eye, an imaginative, deeply thoughtful response to the social and climatic challenges of living in the cold North.

Views of Town Square.

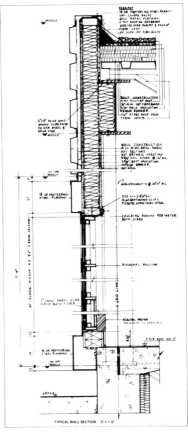

TYPICAL WALL SECTION 3"=1'-0"

Centennial Hall, University of Winnipeg

Architects: Moody, Moore, Duncan, Rattray, Peters, Searle, Christie
Location: Winnipeg, Manitoba
Completion date: 1972
Gross floor area: 250,000 square feet
Client: University of Winnipeg

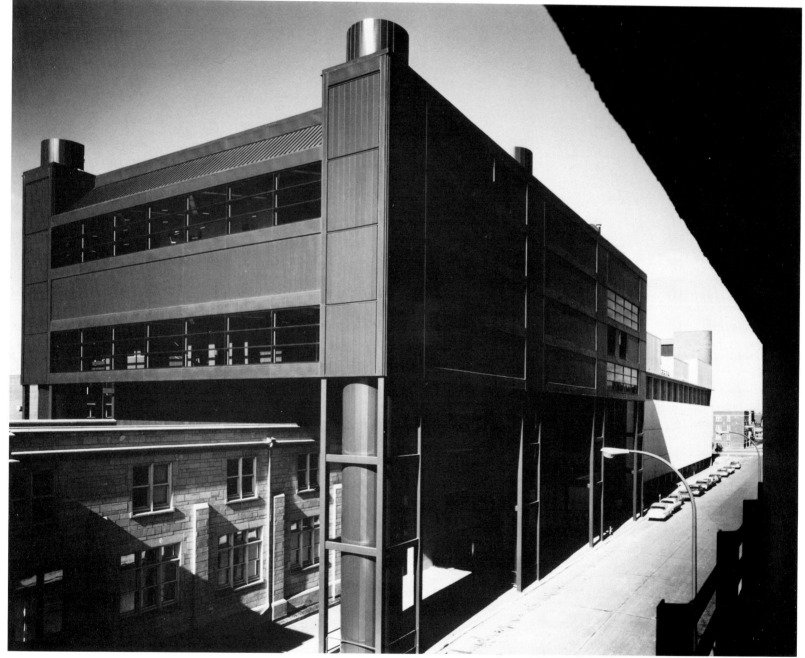

Centennial Hall integrated with existing structures on campus.

Interior pedestrian street.

In the late 1960s the newly independent University of Winnipeg needed extra space to house a library, lecture rooms, and laboratories for its rapidly expanding student body. It decided to develop on its existing campus rather than to purchase an adjacent and expensive downtown site. Major city roads surrounding the campus were also undergoing complicated outward expansion.

This left the university with two conventional options: to demolish and replace existing low-rise buildings, or to construct a highrise tower on the cramped and rather jumbled site. Another and more original alternative was suggested by the architects: to build over and between the existing build-ings, avoiding both demolition and the disruption of academic continuity, and the awkwardness of highrise circulation. This solution, though daringly simple in concept, involved complex structural and planning strategies. Centennial Hall had to be designed to rest lightly and independently on its base both to avoid extensive underpinning of the existing buildings and to keep to a minimum any interference with underground services. While achieving this light-footed dance on the crowded site, the hall had also to visually focus an unordered muddle of very commonplace structures of varying height.

Structurally, the hall sits on a series of square steel towers set among the

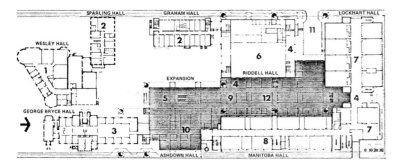

existing buildings. The towers are connected by floor-height, square-tube trusses varying in span from 40 to 70 to 120 feet. Precast, hollow-core, concrete floor units are supported on the trusses' top and bottom chords. The hollow sections of columns and trusses are packed with reinforced concrete to meet a one-hour fire rating.

The framework is clad in steel panels finished a dark bronze to harmonize with the solemn brickwork of the buildings it surmounts. The glazing is bronze-tinted. The authority of the exposed steel structure is carried through the hall's seven interior levels to unite the dispersion of its spaces among and above the existing structures.

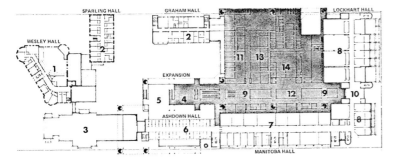

The library on the fourth floor, rising through three levels above, is the heart of the hall. Access to it from the first-floor entry level is by a series of escalators located in a pedestrian street. Adjacent lounges, laboratories, and cafeterias open onto deep courtyards in which children from the child psychology program slide and swing on playframes. Skylights and mezzanines add spatial variety.

Colour, in primaries of red, yellow, and blue, is used boldly to emphasize the structural clarity. Against the neutral grey of the acrylic carpeting and the white walls and ceilings, the vivid accents of red catalogue cabinets, bright yellow stair rails, and blue exposed pipework enliven the interiors, giving identification and coherence to an unavoidably complicated layout.

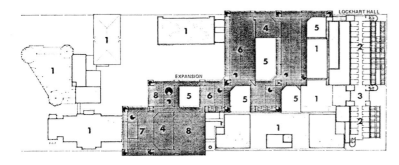

Despite the complex structural and planning strategies generated by the concept of building over and among the existing campus buildings, Centennial Hall presents a remarkable spatial simplicity. If there are minor lapses — areas where volumes are overscaled or oddly shaped; acoustical problems here and there — they do not detract from the masterful solution of an extremely awkward architectural brief.

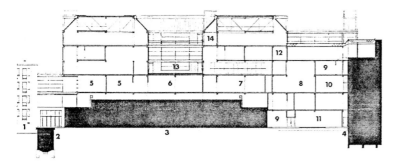

Primary colours emphasize structural clarity inside and out.

Architects' Offices

Architects/Client/Developer/Contractor: The IKOY Partnership
Location: Winnipeg, Manitoba
Completion date: 1978
Gross floor area: 11,000 square feet
Construction cost: $460,000

Drawing office.

Fascination with the idiom of machinery is one of the wellsprings of modern architecture. This fascination runs from Le Corbusier's bald metaphysical formulation of a house as a "machine-for-living" to the continuous delight of designers in structure as a statement of its own validity: a directly functional form with no need to present any credentials other than the simple fact that it "works."

The style known as "High Tech" derives from this long love affair with the machine. It expresses a kind of sophisticated poetry of technology, of machinery — in this instance off-the-shelf industrial building components — elevating bare functionalism to the realm of metaphor. What the style at its best says is: we live in a machine age, so let's enjoy it!

The architects of this brilliant High-Tech box describe it as "a factory for the production of architecture, a machine-for-designing." The fifteen architects who work in it, from partners to draftsmen, are all, in their own view, "machine-architects engaged in a collective and continuing discovery of new architectural knowledge."

The double-height "Big Room," as the architects call it, expresses this democracy of design. Set on a narrow city lot backing onto Winnipeg's Red River, the upper section, reached front and back by open steel stairs, is one large, open, double-cube volume, ninety-two feet long by forty-six feet wide. All the amenities, including studio space, conference rooms, reception, lounge, billiard room, and kitchen are exposed to one another. The only enclosed area is that of a glass-block-walled shower, steam, locker, and washroom set on the freestanding mezzanine level.

The structure is simplicity itself. Floors, roof and long side walls are precast concrete units finished, where exposed, a mottled light grey.

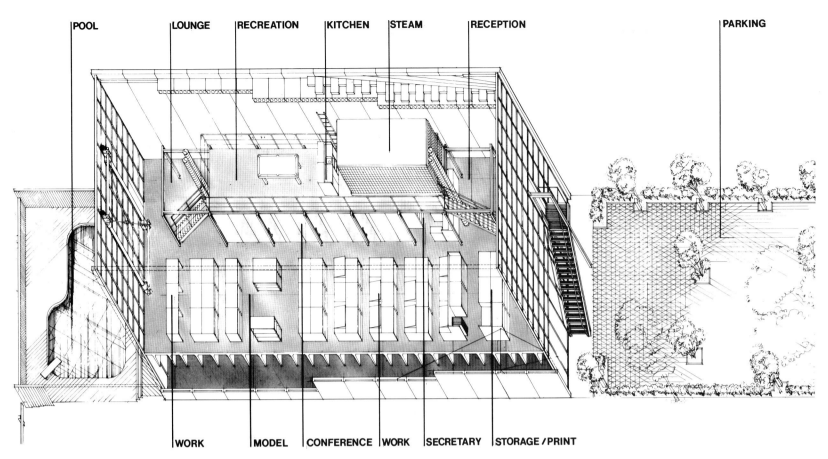

POOL | LOUNGE | RECREATION | KITCHEN | STEAM | RECEPTION | PARKING

WORK | MODEL | CONFERENCE | WORK | SECRETARY | STORAGE / PRINT

The mirrored glass end walls, opening on the street at one end, on a pool at the other, are stiffened by separate steel wind-bracing. The ground-floor podium on which the Big Room sits is leased out for offices. The building was erected in only three months using standard industrial components. The IKOY Partnership, a firm of architect-developers, specializes in such rapidly constructed buildings, and their own offices are a showcase of their talents.

The quality of a High-Tech design, so lucidly simple in concept, stands or falls by the verve of its detailing. As one IKOY partner stated, "a building is made up of so many connections. We think of each connection as a design." The IKOY offices display a superb bravado of connections. The flange assemblies anchoring the wind-braces are boldly detailed and painted bright yellow. Steel joists and beams are welded and bolted and coloured bottle green. Dark-blue steel stair-tread plates are topped with black rubber. Minimal pipe railings are connected by plasticized wire tightened by turnbuckles. Electric wiring winds between fluorescent fixtures like black spaghetti. Circular, gas-fired, forced-air

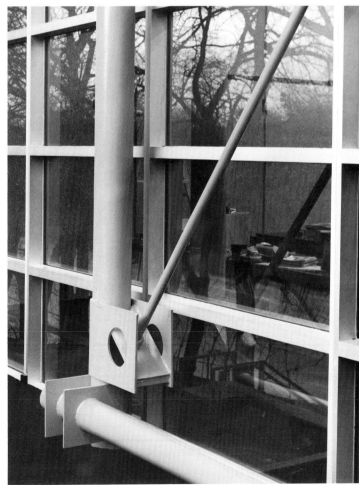

"Each connection is a design."

119

Front entrance: mirrored glass and crisp
mullions backed by wind-bracing.

Mezzanine lounge, looking towards entry.

ductwork is exposed and wrapped in silvered foil. Two horizontal exterior mirrored bands, picked out in contrasting grey, mark the floor and roof levels of the Big Room.

"You can't hide with your mind in the Big Room," a partner remarked. "Criticisms and disputes are extremely honest, even rude and crude."

In the IKOY "machine-for-designing" this rude honesty is made into an urbane style, a sophisticated metaphor for the poetry of technology, a sleek idiom of delight in the bald process of design and construction.

Modern Architecture in Ontario

John C. Parkin

Ontario, historically, has been blessed with good architects and a strong architectural heritage. Although traditionally eclectic, our approach has generally reflected a consensus; a delineation of and an adherence to the current mainstream of architectural thought, values, and concepts. Although this "mainstream" is always undergoing slow change, abrupt and radical digressions, whether they hark back to earlier and nostalgic forms or are based on new theories, have little impact on the continuum of our architectural history. The architecture of the post-Second World War period has proved no exception to this general rule. The progressive Modernism of this period did not spring into being overnight but slowly evolved during the first half of this century, only reaching pre-eminence in the mid-1950s.

Among the many early precursors of contemporary architecture, Eden Smith's Studio Building, built in Toronto in 1913, heralded Modernism in both its design and in its separation of load-bearing and infill elements. Traditional architecture, however, was still the mainstay until the mid-1950s. A general lack of confidence in things Canadian led in the 1950s and early 1960s to the most significant and influential commissions being awarded to contemporary architects of international reputation; Viljo Revell got the Toronto City Hall, Mies van der Rohe designed the Toronto Dominion Centre. However, commissions such as these, in conjunction with the work of Canadian architects, served to legitimize contemporary architecture.

The Ontario Association of Architects building, completed in 1954, the result of a competition held in the late 1940s, proved pivotal in the acceptance of contemporary architecture in Ontario. The Association, through its choice of a design in the contemporary style, gave its official imprint of approval to the movement and thus, symbolically, a respectability

to contemporary architecture. The Ortho Pharmaceutical building, completed in 1956, with its clear, classic, contemporary design influenced building not only in Ontario but throughout Canada and the United States. Victory had clearly been won for the progressive modern movement, and contemporary design became the "mainstream" of Canadian architecture.

If the 1950s and early 1960s witnessed a tentativeness in regard to contemporary design and to local architects, the late 1960s and 1970s saw a growth of confidence in both with most major commissions being awarded to Canadian designers working in the contemporary style — Ron Thom's design for Trent University, a contemporary interpretation of the Oxbridge tradition; Raymond Moriyama's Science Centre; and Eberhard Zeidler's Ontario Place and the Galleria in the Eaton Centre to mention but a few.

A commitment to contemporary design had been made, a commitment that has continued, and will continue despite the occasional advocacy of Post-Modernism, of the nostalgia of Neoclassicism, or of Gothic Revival. These digressions from the prevailing norm will have little, if any, lasting significance.

In the United States, major commissions have been awarded most frequently by private and highly competitive corporations, thus encouraging an architecture of personality with all its attendant emphasis on momentary, individual, and frequently jarring styles of building. Ontario's architectural clientele, on the contrary, is generally comprised of collective and highly regulated bodies. Our approach has consequently proved fairly consistent and subdued, preferring to rely on the formally neutral devices of proportion and scale with emphasis on basic building units for rhetorical effect rather than on the inclusion of highly individual and explicit symbols.

The post-war years in Ontario have witnessed a shift in the population base from rural to urban areas, from small cities and towns to large urban centres.

As well, under the additional pressure of significant immigration centred in Ontario, our cities have expanded rapidly during a very short period of time. This expansion led in the 1950s and 1960s to an explosion of building in our cities. Universities, hospitals, civic and public buildings, corporate offices, retail outlets, and housing — facilities of all types were required to meet an immediate and pressing demand. Yet from the vantage point of the 1980s, it is possible to survey the architectural results of the post-war boom years and take pride in the fact that our cities and their architecture are generally cohesive, pleasing, and harmonious. This result was not achieved spontaneously. Fortunately the post-war years also saw the birth and growth of municipal and regional planning boards which, in concert with good provincial legislation and concerned and active civic groups, have imposed some order and rationale during this period of burgeoning growth. For the first time in Ontario, architects and city planners have been compelled to work together, albeit at times to the mutual exasperation of both, to achieve a harmonious whole, with the result that our cities look more cohesive, urban, and urbane.

Nowhere has this trend been more obvious than in Toronto. The conservatism of the pre-war city has given way to a cosmopolitan, vibrant, and vital centre. Many factors have led to this transition; heavy post-war immigration, the national drift of the population into the urban centres, and the city's pre-eminence both as the business and financial centre of Canada and as the major centre for communication, performing, and visual arts. During this period of intense change and expansion, we have achieved a consistency in our architecture. However, even in those areas moulded now by contemporary architecture, we have the continuity of a Rosedale, an Annex, or the Beaches. This happy coincidence of the contemporary and the traditional has not come about without thought and foresight, without the interface between architecture and planning. No factor has been more important than the creation of Metropolitan Toronto in the early 1950s.

Although, of course, zoning regulations, both municipal and regional, have been and are very important, transportation is the principal ordering force of planning. Main arterial thoroughfares, in concert with the metropolitan subway system, defined the heartland of Toronto. The area bounded by the original subway line became the core of the main business, financial, and entertainment areas of Toronto, and of Canada. Major contemporary building has tended to cling to this area. Admitting on one hand that this concentration has caused the loss of some precious historical sites, it has also meant the revitalization of decaying residential areas such as the Annex as more and more of the population, attracted to the vibrancy of the city, made their homes close to the city centre.

On a somewhat more modest scale, the same forces have been at work in other Ontario cities: Hamilton — with concentration around Lloyd Jackson Square, an area which now encompasses new contemporary civic and public buildings as well as several restored historic sites — London, Ottawa, Kingston, and even smaller centres like Stratford.

The patriarchal influence of the provincial government has always been as a vigilant monitor not only of planning but of all aspects of municipal government, and this has proved especially fortuitous during this period of rapid expansion. It is always easy, of course, to criticize any level of government, but, by and large, we have been blessed with public officials, a civil service, and a responsible legislature which have made a better architecture not only achievable but, in the end, have also indirectly encouraged its development. Even though many complain of governmental interference, and those of us who design and build have all suffered from unfortunate and costly delays, this may well be a small price to pay for cities (and their architecture) which are pleasant to live in and increasingly attractive. The fact that Ontario is regarded elsewhere in

North America as an island of good planning and good architecture attests to the successful interaction between government and the private sector.

During this century the residential areas of our cities have taken on quite a separate character from that of the city centres; a character often not pleasing in its reliance on bourgeois forms, and more often designed at the caprice of the builder rather than responsive to the wishes of the purchaser. So many of our suburbs in the post-war period lack the essential unity and sensitivity which is to be found in some of our older residential areas. Some cities, among them London and Kingston, appear to have been blessed with such an inheritance of older residences that the centres of these cities have been relatively free of the surface urban blight that affected Toronto in the 1950s and 1960s.

During this period, the tendency was to segregate residential communities by the socio-economic status of the residents. The current trend toward people of quite different backgrounds living in relative proximity gives a much happier social balance to our city centres and incidentally causes interesting juxtapositions in urban scale and texture. The need for a meaningful interface between residential, commercial, and institutional architecture is becoming more and more important.

Years of affluence have allowed our cities, both large and small, to come to maturity. There are still countless examples of poor planning and poor design that must be addressed in the future. These range from relatively simple problems which are an embarrassing blight to cities of all sizes in the province — shoddy sidewalks, overhead wires, and urban arterial roadways — to more important issues — bestowing character upon certain suburban residential areas and reclaiming waterfront areas so as to restore an earlier, and more pleasing, relationship between man, land, and water.

The last decade has witnessed an upsurge in interest in our environment (built and natural), our history, culture, and heritage. There is an increasing awareness of social and cultural traditions, a new conservatism which, when taken to an extreme has, in isolated instances, resulted in the rather unfortunate mimicry of building styles of an earlier period. However, these same forces have, when taken as part of an evolving architecture, helped to enrich contemporary design. Thus, the architecture of Ontario is and will become increasingly sensitive to continuity in the use of materials; new brick buildings will be built in areas which are characterized by brick. The visual violations which were so often the case in the first sixty or so years of the century will give way to a harmonious palette of materials. Our architectural design will become increasingly responsive to the exigencies of our intemperate climate. Surface and underground malls, enclosed walkways, and atriums will be persisting effects common to many buildings.

The trend will continue toward placing important projects such as Nathan Philips Square and the Eaton Centre, in close proximity to the financial heart of Toronto, thus allowing intensely relating discrete units to function side by side in a contiguous relationship and resulting in a lively city, a city not separated into homogeneous areas. The introduction of housing into the heart of these areas is a happy event that will give credibility to urban spaces after dark on a winter's evening. The endless and mindless sprawl of our cities to exurban areas will be modified by the movement back to the centres; a movement which will add increased variety to the city centre. Spaces between buildings will be filled with the work of landscape architects, and the trees, shrubs, and flowers will beautify and help humanize our cities, offsetting the sometimes rigid nature of the architecture. New buildings will be increasingly discreet about the type of shelter they provide; a factor which will increase the challenge of urban design for architects.

Scarborough College

Junction of Science and Humanities wings from south.

Architects: John Andrews Architects; Page and Steele Architects
Location: Scarborough, Ontario
Completion date: 1965
Gross floor area: 400,000 square feet
Construction cost: $11.5 million
Client: University of Toronto
Contractors: E. G. M. Cape Co.
Project Team: John Andrews, Ed Galanyk, Jim Sykes,
    Michael Hough, Michael Hugo-Brunt

Authority of design: the College on the brow of the valley.

"Scarborough College is not only a building — it is an event, of significance for both the architectural profession and the public at large." "Scarborough College constitutes Canada's initial claim to the first rank of modern architecture. It radiates an impression of strength and an unimpeachable authority of design."

These comments by architectural critics hint at the impact of the design of Scarborough College. Along with Simon Fraser University, completed in the same year, it displayed a new style, both in education and in structure. John Andrews, the Australian-born architect who practised in Toronto in the 1960s before returning to Sydney, describes the college's design as "a common-

sense, problem-oriented approach. An architecture that derives its details from the way things go together."

Scarborough College is one of two satellite campuses of the University of Toronto, located in a suburban community twenty miles from the main downtown campus, at the eastern edge of Metro Toronto. Most of its five thousand full- and part-time students commute to the college by bus or car. Scarborough was instituted as one of the first units in a huge expansion of university enrollment, providing the promise of a college place for every qualified student in Ontario. It was an act of educational democracy, an attempt to supersede the exclusive elitism of pre-war universities.

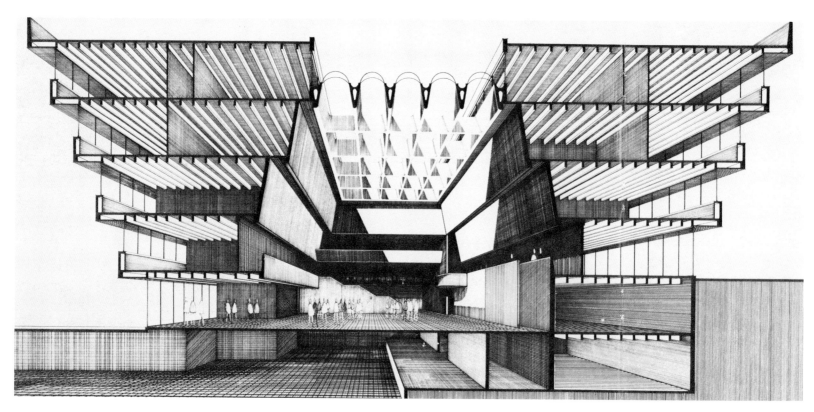

Ground plan

1 science storage
2 wet storage
3 storage
4 laboratories
5 preparation
6 lecture theatres
7 psychological laboratory
8 electrical
9 telephone equipment
10 washrooms
11 elevators
12 paint shop
13 garbage
14 workshop
15 receiving docks
16 lockers
17 kitchen
18 service road

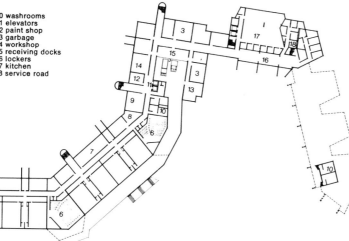

Above: section through central meeting place; *Below:* plan and sections.

The architects identified five basic determinants in the design: the site, the climate, the teaching philosophy, the construction process, and the capacity to grow. Their solutions to these factors, taken together, made the college an innovation in its time.

The site is a three-hundred-acre forested ridge and ravine designated as a conservation area. Its elevation provides splendid vistas to the south but also exposes it to harsh northerly winds. These geographic and climatic factors, along with a philosophy that sought to unite all disciplines under one roof, dictated the design of the

college: a single building set on the edge of the ridge along the spine of an internal, climate-controlled, pedestrian street.

The choice of reinforced concrete as the main structural material — because of its cheapness and because of the Brutalist fashion of the period — also shaped the building. The technique of pouring and forming *in-situ* concrete was integral to the design. A further factor was the serial contract system the speed of construction and the staged availability of funds made necessary. Sections of the structure were developed in such a way that design and construction ran in tandem.

The architects made a virtue of the determinants, transcending them with a design that "radiates authority." The college's plan was organized on the brow of the valley in two wings, one of five stories and one of six — humanities to the east, sciences to the west — joined by central administration offices planned around a common "meeting place": a spacious, square, four-storey atrium capped with a grid of concrete troughs filled with skylights.

The site's slope was exploited to allow entry to the complex at mid-level. The internal streets radiate from the "meeting place." From this mid-level

students can walk up or down to the laboratories, lecture halls, and seminar rooms. In the humanities wing, the streets themselves open up through stepped mezzanines to a complex interplay of levels capped by toplights.

Internally, the unpainted concrete is relieved by the use of open, pine ceiling slats and warm red-brown quarry-tiles. However, both inside and out, it is the bold modelling of concrete mass that gives the college its Brutalist distinction.

Raw concrete design involves shapes rather than surfaces. The architects of the college developed the character of concrete to contrive an almost mediaeval fortress wrapped protectively around the bowl of the southern terrace. Its masses interest the eye with a variety of slopes, steps, overhangs, angled terraces, and sculptured solids. These strong horizontals are set off by angled verticals in the Science Building's mechanical service shafts, and by the triple heating-plant chimneys that echo the upward thrust of some castle tower.

Scarborough, originally designed to take fifteen hundred students in the first phase and to grow to five thousand, has not expanded, as the architects had planned, along the spine of its internal streets. Expansion along the ridge's

Meeting place and Humanities wing: a Brutalist distinction in raw concrete strength.

edge was rejected as being too linear, and too costly for the extension of central services. The later additions, built in the 1970s to the north of the main building, are poor architecture.

Perhaps, with hindsight, the mediaeval Modernism of the college might seem to sit oddly with its democratizing aspirations. The building "radiates authority" in its design, while serving an anti-elitist educational ethos. Architectural dramatics rise up against such levelling sentiments. Distinction may be undemocratic, but it generates outstanding architecture.

Trent University

Architects: R. J. Thom Architects
Location: Peterborough, Ontario
Completion date: 1964-1968 (main complex)
Site area: 1400 acres
Construction cost: $23 million (main complex)
Client: Trent University
Structural Engineers: M. S. Yolles and Partners
Project Team: Ron Thom, Paul Merrick, D. M. Sai-Chew,
P. Bernard, P. Smith, A. Grant.

Trent University is mediaeval in inspiration, modern in style. It continues the cloister and quadrangle tradition of Oxford or Cambridge, the sense of scholars and students mingling in a "place of conversation" in a college system of seminars and tutorials, but it translates it into a contemporary idiom.

Unlike most of the other new universities built in Canada during the great national spurt of higher-education expansion in the 1960s and 1970s, notably Simon Fraser in British Columbia and Scarborough College in Ontario, Trent is not a mass campus. It is not a learning factory under one vast roof, but a low-key collection of small-scale colleges and residences linked by walkways and a unified architectural style, designed to achieve "a sense of repose which encourages scholarly application."

The architecture of Trent serves this conservative aspiration without condescension or false piety. The gently rolling semi-wooded site straddles the Otonabee River several miles outside the city of Peterborough. A boldly arched precast concrete footbridge links the banks.

The university, with almost twenty-two hundred full-time and two thousand part-time students, now consists of three residential colleges, a library, two science buildings, and recreational facilities. The original core, constructed in the 1960s was composed of the library, the Chemistry Building, and two colleges, Lady Eaton and Champlain. The original colleges and the library are finished in a grey *in-situ* concrete with a large-rubbled, exposed, local aggregate that harmonizes with the granite outcroppings of this edge of the harsh Canadian Shield. Weathered cedar and waxed pine lighten the interiors and exteriors of these dramatically sculpted structures that express that manner of dynamic conservatism inherent in the materials and mode of Sixties Brutalism.

The Bata Library, beside University Court, marks the southern point of the

Opposite: aerial view of campus on Otonabee
River with Faryon Bridge linking both banks;
Above: Champlain College from the river.

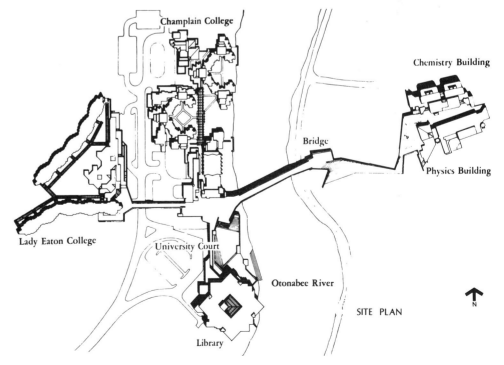

Champlain College

Chemistry Building

Bridge

Physics Building

Lady Eaton College

University Court

Otonabee River

SITE PLAN

N

Library

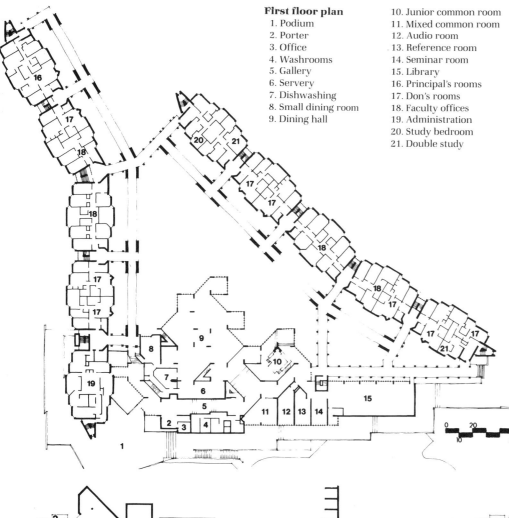

First floor plan
1. Podium
2. Porter
3. Office
4. Washrooms
5. Gallery
6. Servery
7. Dishwashing
8. Small dining room
9. Dining hall
10. Junior common room
11. Mixed common room
12. Audio room
13. Reference room
14. Seminar room
15. Library
16. Principal's rooms
17. Don's rooms
18. Faculty offices
19. Administration
20. Study bedroom
21. Double study

triangular master plan. Reflected in the river, its quiet interplay of vertical and horizontal planes act as an anchor to the campus. Its facilities are shared by all the colleges, linked by a system of pathways.

The residences, set among stands of sumach and pine, are organized on the traditional "Oxbridge" staircase system, each staircase serving a unit of ten to twenty rooms for students and staff. Serrated façades provide an almost private view for each chamber. Each college can accommodate up to 450 members, at least half of whom live in. Tutorial offices and seminar rooms are included, as well as dining and common halls. Students also visit other colleges for lectures, and so mingle across campus.

The Chemistry Building on the east bank houses laboratories, lecture halls, offices, and a coffee shop. Its concrete structural walls are straight out of the forms in a composition almost brutal in its bald planes. In the winter snows they seem like thrusts of the granitic Shield from which they spring. The coffee-shop annex, with its shingled roof a

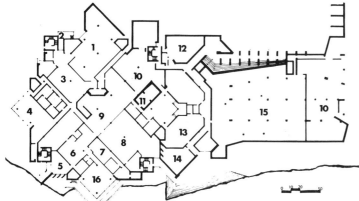

Third floor plan
1. Stack area
2. Lounge
3. Gallery

First Floor Plan
1. Workroom & stack storage
2. Service entry
3. Receiving
4. Staff lounge
5. Librarian
6. General office
7. Rare books
8. Government documents
9. Maps and microfilms
10. Storage
11. Recording studio
12. Film & slide theatre
13. Language lab
14. Listening room
15. Mechanical room
16. Conference room

Second Floor Plan
1. Cataloguing
2. Acquisitions
3. Bibliography
4. Reference
5. Catalogues
6. Reserved reading room
7. Circulation desk
8. Periodicals
9. University Court
10. Champlain College

splay of timber beams propped on a single concrete pier, is a counterpoint of playfulness. A skylight opens at the peak, drenching the rough concrete surfaces with light.

The more recent additions to the complex, particularly Otonabee College, designed (by other architects) as a painted steel and concrete block barracks, are less distinguished than the original core campus. They are either dull or quite out of keeping with the strong style of the 1960s' buildings.

Trent is a walking campus, intimate in its integration with the landscape, yet radically modern in its conservatism. It provides a "sense of repose" within a visual context that is coherent yet diverse, sheltering yet forcefully stated.

Left:
Library;
Below:
coffee shop.

Union Station

Architects/Engineers: John B. Parkin Associates
Partner-in-Charge: John C. Parkin, Gene Kinoshita
Location: Ottawa, Ontario
Completion date: 1966
Gross floor area: 96,000 square feet
Construction cost: $3.5 million
Client: National Capital Commission, for Ottawa Terminal Railway Co.
Contractor: Thomas Fuller Construction Co. Ltd.

Main concourse.

In the earliest days of the Rail Age, design engineers matched the excitement of train travel with an equal bravado of structure. The challenge to span a railway terminus with a bold metaphor of iron or steel in one superbly simple gesture demonstrating the reach of modern engineering technique inspired vaulted nineteenth-century train sheds such as Brunel's Paddington Station in London, and New York's Pennsylvania Station. The technical economy and sheer verve of these Victorian cathedrals of steam have seldom been matched in the age of the diesel. Train travel has become prosaic in its decline, superseded by the excitement of the airport, with its promise of almost instantaneous translation to far places.

Ottawa Union Station and Toronto International Airport's Terminal One were both designed in the mid-1960s by the same architects. The airport terminal is a clear-cut expression of the optimism of the new age of mass air travel. The station is almost an act of reminiscence, looking back to the heroic age of the railways. Airport and station have one theme in common: both are theatres of travel.

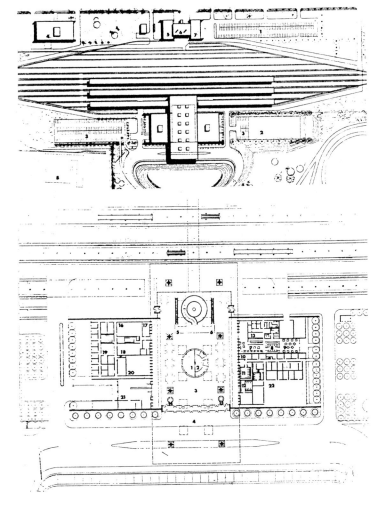

Above: steel canopy over passenger drop-off; *Left:* site and floor plans.

Site Plan
1. Employees' parking
2. Future parking
3. Parking
4. CN & CP building
5. Oil storage
6. Boiler plant
7. Car department building
8. Existing building

Floor Plan
1. Ticketing
2. Offices
3. Main concourse
4. Passenger area
5. arrivals
6. Departures
7. Coffee shop
8. Lounge
9. Dining
10. Barber
11. Men's washroom
12. Women's washroom
13. Kitchen
14. Red caps
15. Taxi
16. Engine and trainsmen's lockers
17. Train order office
18. Station staff lunch room
19. Recreation room
20. Public locker room
21. Baggage room
22. Administrative functions

Above: main elevation; *Right:* steel canopy rests on cruciform concrete columns.

Both buildings were designed in the same mainstream Modernist manner that marks three decades of the work of the Parkins. These designs include such seminal Ontarian modern structures as the 1956 Ortho Pharmaceutical factory and offices, and the 1964 Bata International Centre. As John C. Parkin has stated: "a building must honestly advise how its structure holds."

Ottawa Union Station embodies this ethos of honesty of function most clearly of all the Parkin architecture. Located just east of the federal capital, it relocated and consolidated all Canadian National and Canadian Pacific trackage in the area. The great national rail companies, now operating under the rubric of VIA Rail, operate twenty arrivals and departures daily.

The plan of the terminus is a cross. Parallel to the tracks are two wings of offices, telecommunications rooms,

cafeterias, and other amenities. At right angles across these is the main concourse. The two axes are structurally distinct. The administration and service wings are enclosed in one-storey buildings finished externally in grey precast concrete panels. The concourse is a glazed box eighteen feet high to the underside of its steel truss roof.

This soaring, black-painted, welded-steel canopy, spanning concourse, covered car entry, and part of the tracks, is the station's main feature. In length, 330 feet, in width 150, it rests on eight monolithic, cruciform, concrete columns. The roof is formed of an exposed two-way steel truss system in three main sections, cantilevered thirty feet on all our sides. The sub-trusses are spaced at fifteen-foot centres between the fifteen-foot deep major spans.

The entire roof rests on eight steel pins that allow for movement. The top transom of the concourse's glazed screen stops 1½ inches short of the bottom truss chord for the same reason. The rainwater downpipes are secreted in the screen mullions, an example of the scrupulous simplicity of detailing throughout.

The concourse floor is black terrazzo. A circular island ticket office sets off the angularity of the design. Four-foot square fluorescent fixtures are set in the steel deck ceiling.

Ottawa Station is serene and spacious, as filled with light as were the great Victorian terminuses. Its reminiscence is utterly Modernist, at once a gesture of respect for a heroic past and a lithe demonstration of contemporary structural technique. It is a splendid theatre of modern train travel.

Dow Corning Silicones Offices

Architects: Fairfield and DuBois
Location: North York, Ontario
Completion date: 1965
Gross floor area 15,000 square feet
Construction cost: $315,000
Client: Dow Corning Silicones Ltd.
Structural Consultants: M. S. Yolles Associates Ltd.

The small suburban office building, unpretentiously functional yet conscious of its company image, is a common architectural category seldom done with distinction. Low land costs and convenient commuting are countered by visual contexts often confused between subdivision domestic, light industrial, and super-highway megascale.

The context of the head office for Dow Corning Silicones Ltd. in suburban Toronto is particularly complex. To the south is the eight-lane Trans-Canada Highway and one of its sprawling spaghetti interchanges. To the north is the wasteland of Downsview Airport. To the east is a suburban development of 1960s bungalows, and to the west a large car-oriented shopping plaza served by a modern subway station. The irregular, narrow office site sits at the end of a cul-de-sac in a pocket of indifferent warehouses and small factories tucked into the expressway junction.

The building's design went through several more ambitious phases before cost factors dictated a simple, linear, two-storey structure parallel with the adjacent expressway and its intertwined interchange ramps. To match this mega-scale, the architects designed a strong and lucid statement easily read as one speeds by; an advertisement for the company, at once bold and dignified, that manages the difficult feat of relating both to the highway and to the suburban context at the building's back.

Lower level office floor.

The building's linear form echoes the highway's sense of motion. Its deep, rounded-end overhang roof, designed to screen the southern sun, seems streamlined to reduce wind resistance. The raised horizontals of its concrete-block cladding underline this motif of movement while giving the structure an earthbound solidity in tune with the materials and the scale of the expressway.

The entrance, on the north elevation, is marked by a blank screen wall enclosing the service ducts. This screen acts as a termination to the cul-de-sac. Discreetly monumental steps make some occasion of entry. The stripped key pattern of the three-foot deep concrete fascia acts as an effective lid to the design, set off by the continuous glazing underneath.

Interior scale and materials match the exterior. Columns constructed of four concrete blocks are turned at forty-five degrees. The office space is divided between a general open area to the north and private offices to the south, with a balcony at the upper level. At the east end large offices face the morning sun. At the west end the blank-walled conference room is turned at forty-five degrees to the line to give the building a distinctive stop. Natural wood, acoustic tile ceilings, and generous plantings offset the severity of the design.

Detailing is clean and crisp. The junctions of window mullions and blockwork are handled with simplicity. The surrounding landscape is treed and grassed up to the low ground-floor sills.

There is a deeply considered unity to all aspects of the building, a sense that its energetic simplicity has been achieved by careful consideration. In this it is an instance of a common but awkward category of building that manages a rare functional, unforced character.

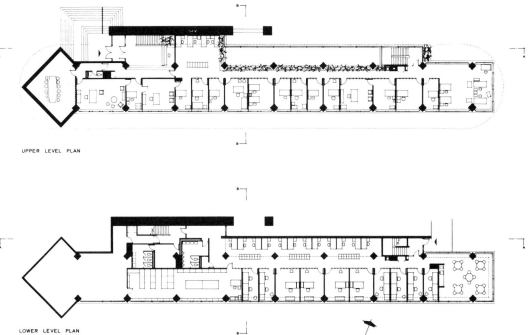

UPPER LEVEL PLAN

LOWER LEVEL PLAN

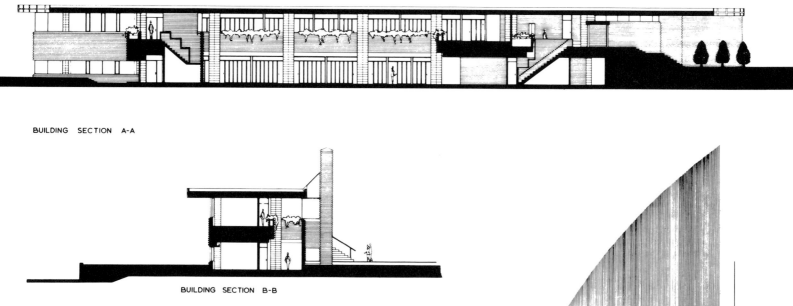

BUILDING   SECTION   A-A

BUILDING   SECTION   B-B

Sections and site plan.

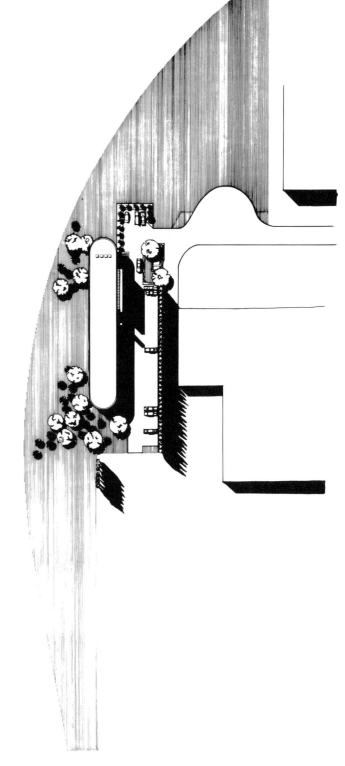

Above: east elevation; *Left:* the building in its context.

Greenwood: greenhouse.

Three Public Schools

Architects: Fairfield and DuBois; Dubois and Plumb

Location: Metropolitan Toronto, Ontario

Completion dates:

    Tecumseh Senior Public School — 1967

    Greenwood Vocational Secondary School — 1973

    Tom Longboat Junior School — 1982

Gross floor areas and construction costs:

    Tecumseh: 41,800 square feet; $1,100,000

    Greenwood: 84,500 square feet; $1,900,000

    Tom Longboat: 35,000 square feet; $1,200,000

Design Teams:

    Tecumseh — Macy Dubois, Andre LeRoux

    Greenwood — Macy Dubois, Sally Dubois, Andre Leroux,
        Gordon Rolleston

    Tom Longboat — Helga Plumb, Macy Dubois

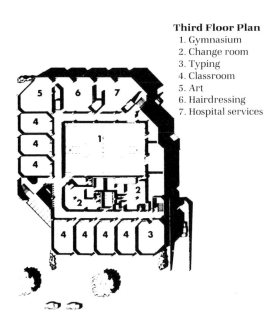

Third Floor Plan
1. Gymnasium
2. Change room
3. Typing
4. Classroom
5. Art
6. Hairdressing
7. Hospital services

Second floor plan
1. Upper cafetorium
2. Power operating
3. Remedial reading
4. Business machines
5. Classroom
6. Science
7. Limited vision
8. Static workshop
9. Sewing
10. Hard of hearing

First floor plan
1. Cafetorium
2. Library
3. Staff room
4. Health
5. Principal
6. Guidance
7. Restaurant services
8. Music
9. Cooking
10. Kitchen

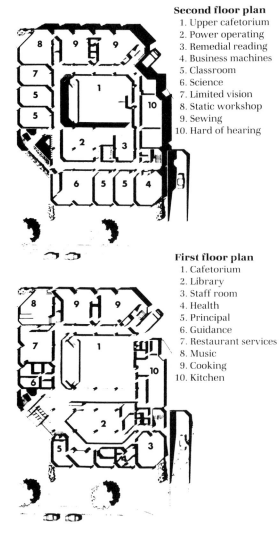

Greenwood: plans and entry.

Education at the primary and secondary levels has undergone a profound revolution in attitudes since the war. An almost Victorian institutionalism that persisted well into the twentieth century gave way to a more humane and relaxed ambience. At the same time facilities were expanded hugely to spread education across a widened social base. Experiments in teaching methods, tending toward a seminar style in flexible curricula, became common.

This is the social context which these three schools, designed over a fifteen-year period under the supervision of Macy DuBois, mirror in their architecture. All three, though serving different purposes, reflect the architects' humanity and restraint in meeting strict educational programs, political pressures, tight economics, and site limitations.

The key to good school design is a thorough analysis of the planning parameters. In many instances the local school boards provide detailed programs with well-defined requirements the architect must translate into a built form that yet expresses some imaginative visual coherence. Materials and standards of finish must be economical and hard-wearing to withstand the battering of generations of boisterous students.

All three of these schools share a common virtue of thoughtful planning given fittingly imaginative form.

Tecumseh School, the earliest building, was constructed adjacent to an existing junior public school on a site in a well-developed suburban area. Its plan functions were analysed to separate the noisy double-volume elements of the gymnasium and multipurpose rooms from the quieter needs of its fourteen classrooms and the central library and art space on two floors.

The plan of Greenwood Vocational is even simpler. Greenwood is a specialized vocational school for teenage girls,

mostly immigrant children who may also require remedial teaching. Situated on a tight urban site in Toronto's east end, its twenty-one classrooms fit in a neat three-storey hollow square around a central double-height cafeteria topped by a gym. The building's main external feature is its corner entry under a glazed two-storey greenhouse that lightens the blank look of the load-bearing twelve-inch stackbond blockwork walls. To minimize exposure to the south and west, the vertical classroom window slots are indented at forty-five degrees.

Tom Longboat is a small, standard, junior school in the newly-developed, open, northeastern edge of the City of Scarborough, not far from the Metro Toronto Zoo. The domestic, intimate scale of its twelve classrooms on two floors is enhanced by sloping ceilings, horizontal window bands, and stacked shingle roofs. Integrally coloured striated blockwork in a warm beige tone gives the Longboat school its cheerfully restrained atmosphere. The incorporation of heating and ventilating grilles in metal spandrels under the window strip contributes to the building's clean and modest lines.

Restraint is the architectural quality common to all three schools. An urge to monumentality, to design bravura, has been humanely resisted. The plans are lucid, easy for children to follow.

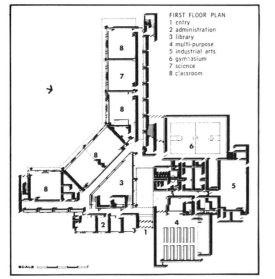

FIRST FLOOR PLAN
1 entry
2 administration
3 library
4 multi-purpose
5 industrial arts
6 gymnasium
7 science
8 classroom

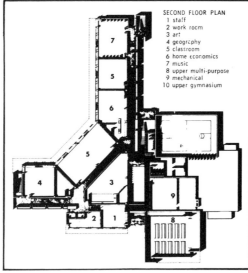

SECOND FLOOR PLAN
1 staff
2 work room
3 art
4 geography
5 classroom
6 home economics
7 music
8 upper multi-purpose
9 mechanical
10 upper gymnasium

Tecumseh: plans, section, and south elevation.

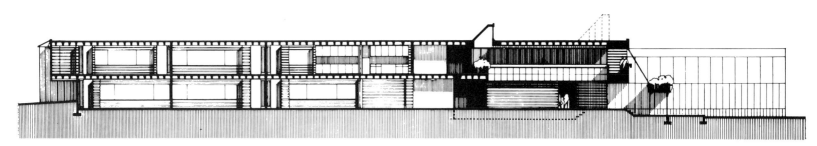

The materials, from the exposed concrete of Tecumseh to the blockwork of Greenwood and Longboat, are sturdy yet crisply detailed. Strong internal colours and well-considered artificial lighting enliven the architectural tonality. Despite these common features, each school has a distinctive character fitted to its function and context. Greenwood is compact and urbane yet uninstitutional. Tecumseh, with its wide overhangs and long, low concrete profile, is muscular and sheltering. Longboat hugs its grassy knoll in a relaxed suburban setting. Each building is thoughtfully planned, focused to a particular context, and executed in an appropriate manner.

This is educational architecture of a contemporary excellence that outlasts fashion. It is the built expression of a liberal humanity that can be lived with for generations. It is, in an unpompous sense, truly democratic.

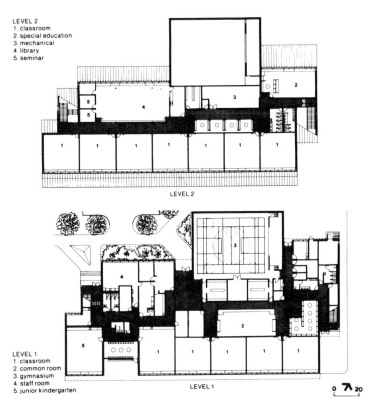

LEVEL 2
1. classroom
2. special education
3. mechanical
4. library
5. seminar

LEVEL 2

LEVEL 1
1. classroom
2. common room
3. gymnasium
4. staff room
5. junior kindergarten

LEVEL 1

0 20

Longboat: plans and south elevation.

143

Albert Campbell Library

Architects: Fairfield and DuBois
Location: Scarborough, Ontario
Completion date: 1971
Gross floor area: 26,700 square feet
Construction cost: $614,000, plus $84,000 for equipment
Client: Scarborough Library Board
Structural Engineers: Cazaly-Otter Associates
Contractors: Conasan Construction Ltd.
Project Team: Macy Dubois, Sally Dubois, Erdmann Knaack

This district library, serving a suburban Toronto community, transcends the limitations of a tight and narrow site set among the usual jumble of branch banks, apartment buildings, and shopping plazas to create an attractive ambience of what the architect terms "energetic repose."

The design of the Albert Campbell Library achieves this "energetic repose" by an imaginative articulation of space in plan and section. The three-quarter-acre site, further limited by a required sixty-foot setback from the street line and provision of on-site parking, dictated a compact building which could house up to a hundred and fifty thousand multimedia items, plus lecture rooms, display areas, audio-visual facilities, and storage stacks.

The dominant design motif is the curve of the roof and ceiling planes. This is at once visible in the approach to the library across a grassy knoll shaded with willows and maples. A bold earth-red fascia of rolled-steel strips stretching the width of the front elevation is suspended over a continuous glazed screen. The fascia flows into the lobby and rolls back to open up the library's main double-storied space.

The red metal strip ceiling is the building's unifying visual signature. Strip fluorescent lighting and electric force-flow air-diffuser units are integrated flush with the surface. Yellow-ochre carpeting adds warmth to the interior, complemented by the use of oiled oak in the stacks and study carrels.

The ceiling hangs between cavity walls of twelve-inch-square double bullnosed grey concrete block laid in stackbond, unpainted on the interior and exterior. The block walls are supported by poured concrete columns and slabs.

Left: side elevation detail; *Opposite:* main floor interior.

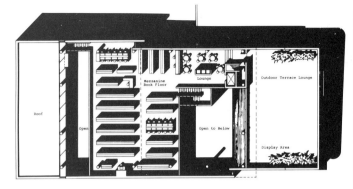

Mezzanine Floor Plan
0 5 10 20 40

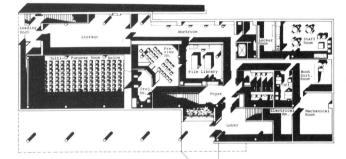

First Floor Plan
0 5 10 20 40

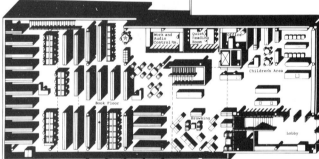

Second Floor Plan
0 5 10 20 40

Plans and interior looking towards street.

Library stacks, display areas, and a children's section occupy the upper two floors. The semi-basement lower level, exploiting a six-foot drop in the site from front to back, houses a multi-purpose meeting room equipped with film projection, a film library, and storage and sorting facilities. The upper mezzanine level opens out onto a terrace over the front entrance.

The curve motif is carried through in the design of the fixtures and furnishings, also the responsibility of the architects. "We tried to achieve the conflicting goals of a friendly, inviting space, clear comprehensible stacks, and continuous visual control," the designer says. Ends and edges on stack bases, carrel screens, seating, and counters are rounded. Vinyl fabrics and plastic laminates counterpoint the dominant red/yellow colour mode. Interior graphics are stencilled on rounded plexiglass panels.

The light values at desktop and stack levels have been criticized as being too diffuse and uneven. Pools of shadow haunt some corners. But overall the interior is an airy, cheerful, and popular space, serving its function as a library and community centre with a lively and unpompous grace.

The architects acknowledge the influence of Aalto and Utzon in the design. Macy DuBois is of the opinion that modern Scandinavian architecture has much to offer Canadian designers, due to a similarity of climate, landscape, and, perhaps, national temperament. Dubois promulgates the notion of an "elemental architecture" of "minimal means and maximum effect," of "a craft that uses technology artfully." This idea is well realised in this muscular yet playful structure.

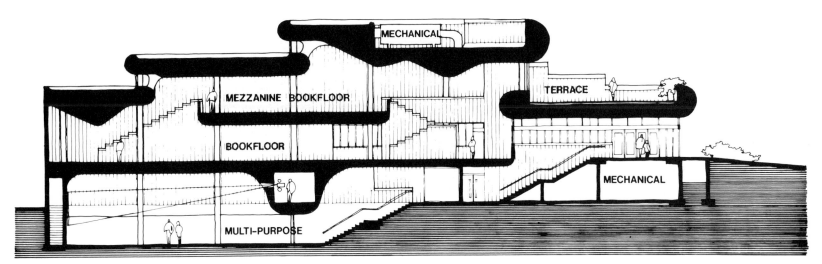

Section.

Fraser House

Architects: Ron Thom and Paul Merrick
Location: Toronto, Ontario
Completion date: 1967
Gross floor area: 3400 square feet
Construction cost: $108,000
Client: Donald Fraser
Contractor: George Slightham Ltd.

Textures and planes.

This house combines several unusual circumstances. First, the site: few cities can provide an acre and a quarter of forested hillside five minutes' drive from the downtown commercial district; a wooded promontory so protected by old maples that, in leaf, the trees screen the nearby urban buzz. Second, the designers: two young West-Coast architects who had recently arrived in Toronto planned a residence that subtly fuses a western domestic idiom and the local vernacular.

The Fraser house shares a small plateau sloping into a typical Toronto ravine; a headland just wide enough to hold five houses. Though the vistas are open to the south and east, combining the wildness of the Rosedale valley with a glimpse of urban expressways and office towers, the approach to the houses is secluded in a short cul-de-sac.

The body of the house is hidden from the lane by a double garage. A long, low, covered walkway of cedar shingles and timber posts, built on the edge of the slope, leads to the front door while it further distances the house from its urban context. The first impression of the house is of a sculptured geometry of odd-shaped roof planes, red-brown Pennsylvania brick panels, and angled skylights reflecting the surrounding foliage.

The brickwork echoes the upward thrust of the maples. The cedar-shingled roofs mimic the grassy slopes they almost touch with their eaves. Surfaces, planes, and textures seem random, almost as if they've grown out of the ground, yet the composition is subtly contrived.

The interior develops this organic inspiration. The three main levels are organized around the core of an eccentric open stairwell. Entry is at the middle level, into an open-plan living space that includes a dining area and a kitchen, both opening onto a deck cantilevered over the edge of the slope.

The study is up a flight. The main bedroom is on a mezzanine overlooking the living room. A bridge over the stair-well leads to a former nursery, now a guest room. On the lowest level are three bedrooms for the owner's daughters, and a recreation room.

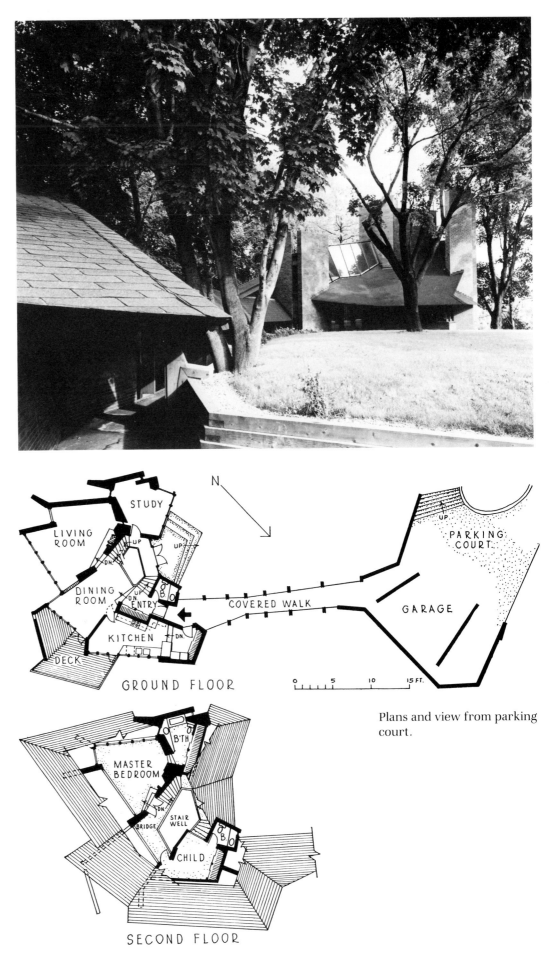

Plans and view from parking court.

149

The materials are the same inside as out: semi-glazed red-brown brick and waxed cedar ceilings steeply sloped. The floors are cork tiles. The easterly window walls and clearstories open onto an enclosure screened by leaves and branches. All cupboards are built in under the angled soffits.

None of the walls are parallel; there are no right angles in this house, either in plan or section. Wherever you stand, the orientation is to the space as a whole rather than any small compartment.

The Fraser house is aligned east and west, along the run of the ravine. South light penetrates only through clearstories. The natural illumination of the interior is always muted, even in high summer. Inwardly, the space is a constantly modulated play of shade and surface, an interaction of enclosures and exposures.

"This house is its own world," says the owner, who has lived here with his growing family since the house was built. "The architect made us a perfect and very personal place to live."

Opposite: stair well looking up to skylight.

Elevation from the ravine.

Myers House

Architects: Diamond and Myers; designed by Barton Myers
Location: Toronto, Ontario
Completion date: 1970
Gross floor area: 2500 square feet
Construction cost: $55,000
Client: Barton Myers
Structural Engineers: M. S. Yolles and Associates
Contractor: McMullen and Warnock

A downtown courtyard.

Berryman Street, on which this radically modern house is located, is a lane of old, working-class, semi-detached cottages in a downtown district of Toronto that has become fashionable. In this thoroughly urban and traditional context, Barton Myers has inserted an uncompromisingly contemporary residence that preserves the street pattern without condescension.

Myers develops a philosophy of urban infill that strives to "conserve and build upon the existing fabric." This house, designed for the architect and his wife and daughter, fulfills an intention of radical conservatism and sensitivity to an inherited urban tradition.

On a small city lot, 25 feet by 118 feet, the interior seems spacious. The house is planned on two floors around an internal courtyard glazed with a fibreglass greenhouse roof. The living areas and main bedroom open, through a full-height glass screen, onto a walled garden with a fountain, trees, and sculpture. The garage and mechanical service space border the vestibule on the street frontage, with two secondary bedrooms above. The two sections of the house are linked by a second-storey bridge.

The front elevation is an abstract geometry that springs from the cornice and eaves lines, the vernacular of the street. The simplicity of the structure — concrete-block, cavity side walls spanned by open-web steel joists — echoes the traditional modes but in a modern manner.

Internally the house is filled with light and is totally "High Tech" in its detailing. The gas-fired, forced-air cylindrical heating and ventilating ducts are wrapped in silvered sheathing. The flooring is grey cement, the ceilings exposed aluminum corrugated decking. The staircase is ship-like in its welded I-beam strings and sheet-steel-plate treads. The retractable canvas sails that screen the greenhouse roof over the courtyard add another jauntily nautical note.

The house is not solemn, despite its stark Modernism. An antique Franklin wood-burning stove with brass knobs enlivens the living area. A pine four-poster fills the daughter's bedroom.

Section and internal court with greenhouse roof.

Dining in the courtyard.

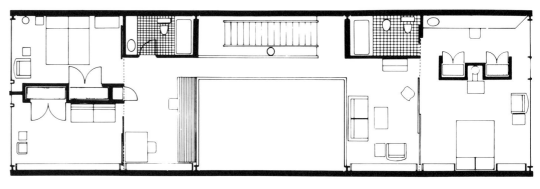

Second Floor

First Floor

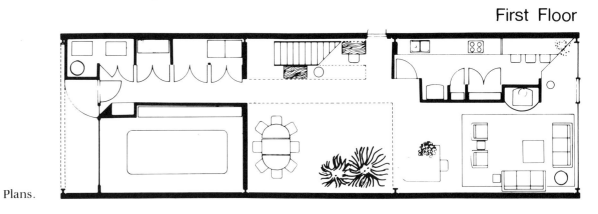

Plans.

Privacy is somewhat sacrificed to the sense of spaciousness. The bedrooms are separated by sliding space dividers. One bathroom, under the main roof, is covered by a plastic bubble dome. The entire interior space is accessible to eye and ear from the central atrium.

Myers, born in Virginia, worked in Louis Kahn's office in the 1960s. From Kahn he learnt an architecture in which "buildings and details are expressive of how they are put together." From American designers like Charles Eames he derived the use of off-the-shelf components and standard industrial systems in domestic and other non-industrial contexts. Yet at the same time Myers is open to historical and vernacular references, to the continuous urban fabric. He calls this "an architecture of accommodation."

It is this freedom from ideology, this energy of many sources, that characterizes Myers's designs. It is a form of energetic eclecticism that promises a true sophistication for architecture's Post-Modern era.

Street elevation: enhancing the urban fabric.

Ontario Place

Architects: Craig, Zeidler, Strong
Location: Toronto, Ontario
Completion date: 1971
Site area: 96 acres, including 51.4 acres of landfill
Construction cost: $29 million, including site works
Client: Ontario Department of Trade and Development
Structural Engineers: Gordon Dowdell Associates
Landscape Architects: Hough, Stansbury and Associates
Contractors: Secant Construction

Pavilion pods.

Theme parks became popular in the 1970s. They derived, in recent times, from temporary events such as Expo '67 or the 1939 New York World's Fair, made permanent. The modern tradition of such popular mass mechanistic diversions goes back to Victorian models like the 1851 Great Exhibition at London's Crystal Palace. Some theme parks, like the commercial Disneyland, are playgrounds pure and simple. Others, like the government-funded Ontario Place, have a double function: to entertain and to raise civic consciousness.

Ontario Place was funded by the provincial government as a permanent showcase. It operates with an annual subsidy. It is Ontario on display, as well as an amusement park with boats, slides, concerts, cinema, a highly imaginative Children's Village designed by Eric MacMillan, and a one-ton iron temple bell housed in a modern glass-roofed pagoda designed by Raymond Moriyama.

The park was constructed on landfill claiming an area of Lake Ontario along Lakeshore Boulevard. Three old Great Lakes freighters were sunk on a stone bed and covered in concrete to form a fifteen-hundred-foot breakwater. Within this perimeter, three artificial islands were formed, comprising fifty acres.

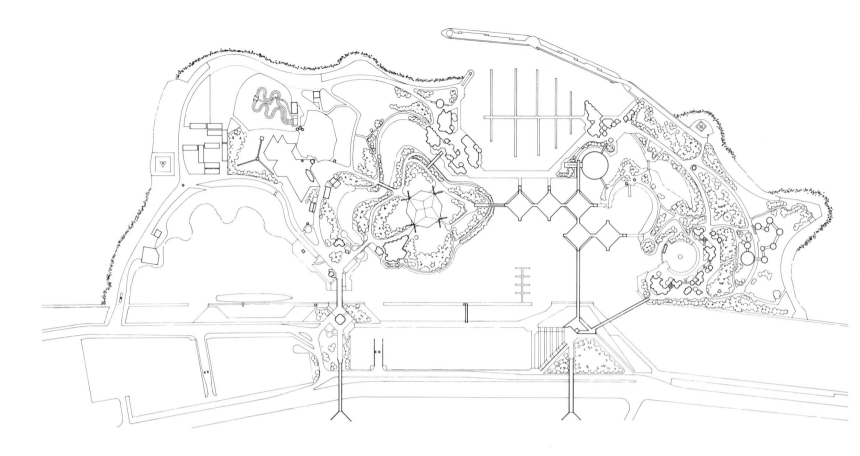

Above: site plan; *Right:* section through Forum; *Below:* pod structure.

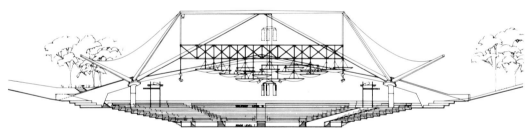

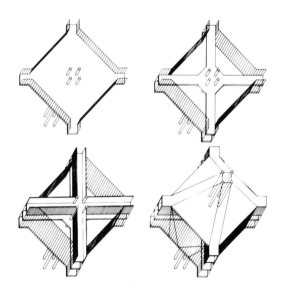

The main built structures are the five pavilions, the Cinesphere, the Forum, and, completed in 1981, eight mini-pavilions and a small geodesic dome making up a group on the West Island entitled "Ontario North Now."

The five pavilions and the Cinesphere are the park's focus. They were constructed by driving concrete-filled caissons thirty feet into the lake's bedrock. Upon these bases a series of steel and aluminum superstructures were erected, linked by glazed steel bridges to one another and to the land.

Each eighty-eight-foot-square pavilion pod is supported on four central pipe columns rising 105 feet from the lake. Tension cables support short-span trusses welded to these shafts. The trusses house all the mechanical systems.

The Cinesphere is an 800-seat cinema with an eighty- by sixty-foot curved 70mm IMAX screen equipped with a "total sound" system. It is housed in a spherical triodetic dome of sixty-one-foot outer radius. A fifty-six-foot-radius inner dome of prefabricated steel tubing supports the outer shell of extruded aluminum alloy tubes erected on the geodesic principle.

The Forum is an open-air auditorium seating three thousand. The roof is constructed of copper-sheathed tongue-and-groove plywood formed into a hyperbolic paraboloid supported on concrete bastions. The sixty-eight-foot revolving stage is set on three concentric wheel rings attached to a concrete sub-floor.

Ontario Place exploits a system of flexible functional modules providing a wide variety of elements. The structures are designed, in the architect's words, "to give an illusion of dimensionless space, exploiting technology to shape the society of tomorrow."

The detailing, with its cables and shackles, its tensed-wire railings and welded, white-painted piping, is pop-nautical. Zeidler enjoys the jauntiness of ship's tackle, the sense of hovering lightness it induces, the festival of mock-departure such stationary "boats" conjure up to the eye and mind. The three-hundred-boat marina, the cruising Showboat, the anchored naval destroyer, the gulls and geese all enhance the park's nauticality.

As the musical clock trills out the "Theme from Ontario Place" and fireworks burst in the summer's night sky, the theme park celebrates the province, entertains its citizens and visitors, and, it is hoped, enhances Ontario's image.

Cinesphere at night.

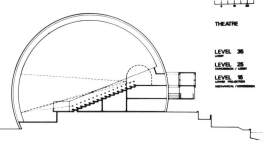

Above: section through Cinesphere; *Left:* view from a bridge.

A "ring street."

McMaster Health Science Centre

Architects: Craig, Zeidler, Strong
Location: Hamilton, Ontario
Completion date: 1972
Gross floor area: 1,761,500 square feet
Construction cost: $61,400,000, plus $10.5 million for equipment
Client: McMaster University
Structural Engineers: John Maryon and Partners Ltd.
Mechanical Engineers: G. Granek and Associates
Contract Management: Doyle-Hinton Contract Services Ltd.
Project Team: E. H. Zeidler, H. Banelis, R. H. Jacobs, F. Kulcsar, A. Roberts

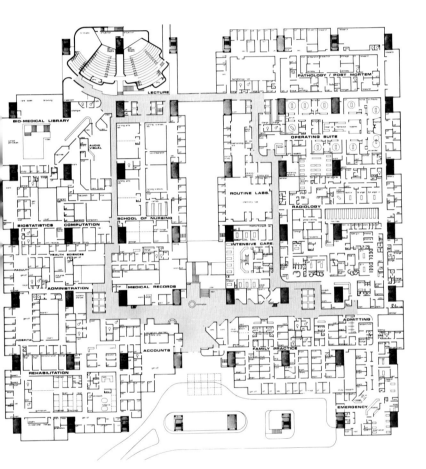 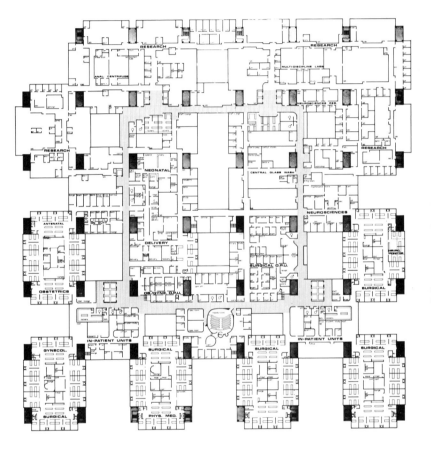

Left: entry level floor plan; *Right:* upper floor.

The design of a conventional hospital, with its complexities of circulation and services, its requirements of flexibility, change, and expansion, is one of the most testing of architectural challenges. In a facility like McMaster, which incorporates a radical concept of total health care, the designer's test is fundamental.

The McMaster Health Science Centre combines a 400-bed university teaching hospital, a research facility, a nurses' training school, and a regional health centre caring for over four hundred thousand out-patients annually. More profoundly, its ambition is to reverse the increasing fragmentation of modern medical practice by the total integration of every level of health care both within the hospital and in the community it serves.

Put simply, McMaster is founded on teamwork; a recognition that complex social necessities such as medicine can be adequately coped with by co-operation rather than specialization. This teamwork extends to the design and building process; the architect was as deeply involved in the evolution of the content as he was in the building

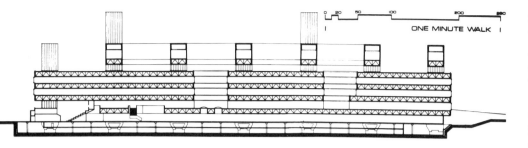

ONE MINUTE WALK

Top: section;
Middle: nursing station;
Bottom: cafeteria overlooking central court.

form. "McMaster changed my approach to architecture," writes Eberhard Zeidler, the principal designer. "It showed me the way to a new architecture that has no end and no beginning."

The radical architecture of the centre is a result of this five-year planning process. The need for a building with "no end and no beginning," capable of being expanded or adapted for any change, led to the development of a structural system cellular in concept, based on a service framework that is both constant and flexible, which the architect terms the "Servo System." It expresses the idea that "architectural form can never be final, but must constantly evolve to suit changing needs."

The centre's "Servo System" separates the structure and services of the four above-grade levels into permanent and impermanent elements. The permanent elements include the structural framework and the mechanical-electrical spines. These elements are combined vertically in steel towers, twenty-one feet high by ten and a half feet wide, separated by clear spans of seventy-three and a half feet. The towers are linked by a system of steel space-frame trusses eight and a half feet deep, providing a walk-through ceiling space. This open-web structure allows for the flexible threading of services and accepts a wide range of point and wall loads. The towers extend above the main roof in mechanical penthouses holding thirty airconditioning units with an individual capacity of 80,000 cubic feet per minute.

The external cladding is precast, smooth-finished concrete units in four different sizes, three with windows, one blank, backed with an air barrier of urethane insulation and a foil vapour seal. The glazed towers are clad in anodized aluminum framing, the penthouses and elevator shafts in pre-finished galvanized steel.

The floor plans are organized on a "ring street" pattern. Each "ring" on the upper two in-patient levels is a nursing unit with thirty-six beds, divided into single, two-bed, and four-bed rooms. The rooms are grouped around a nursing station with intimate visual and physical supervision over the unit.

Corridors in a large hospital can

be long and tedious, but these are enlivened with skylights, bright colours, and sculptured block walls. Four banks of elevators serve the "rings." Bulkveyor units — service elevators — serve all floors from a central dispatch.

The lower two levels contain the teaching and research facilities with a direct student entrance through a wide esplanade. A biomedical library, food assembly, and preparation, storage, administration, and reception are on these lower levels, above a thousand-car below-grade garage.

The centre's interior is as bright, airy, and humane as any hospital's can be. The confusions of orientation in a complex institution are handled adroitly and cheerfully. Modern medicine's image is increasingly that of the monitor screen and the technical machine rather than the friendly caring face. In McMaster both doctors and designers strive to counter such impersonality with concern.

Yet an architecture with "no end and no beginning," while true to the program and the spirit of the times, can seem makeshift, a series of expediencies both visual and social. The centre has some aspect of a technological process evident in the very success of its solution to a context that "must constantly evolve to suit ever-changing needs."

Elevation: precast cladding and glazed towers.

Eaton Centre

Architects: The Zeidler Partnership and Bregman and Hamann, with E. L. Hankinson and Parkin Millar Associates
Location: Toronto, Ontario
Completion date: 1977
Gross floor area: 3 million square feet
Construction cost: $300 million
Clients: Cadillac Fairview Corp. Ltd., Toronto Dominion Bank, and the T. Eaton Co.
Structural Engineers: C. D. Carruthers and Wallace Consultants
Contract Management: The Foundation Co. of Canada Ltd.; Eastern Construction Co. Ltd.

The galleria: *Below,* section; *Opposite:* view looking north.

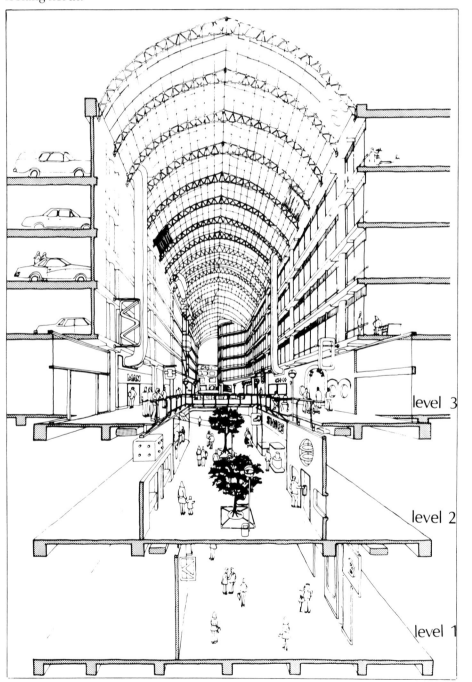

level 3

level 2

level 1

"I'm like a shipbuilder," says Eberhard Zeidler, chief designer of the Eaton Centre. "I build the ship; someone else sails it away." The metaphor is apt for a structure as large as the centre, which is equal in size, scale, style, and cost to a transatlantic liner.

Three main elements comprise the centre: a 900-foot, three-level gallery accommodating two hundred fifty thousand square feet of retail space; a ten-level department store containing a million square feet of floor space; two office towers at each end of the block-long fifteen-acre site — the north tower twenty-six storeys high, the south tower thirty-six storeys.

The centre stretches along Yonge Street, Toronto's main downtown shopping strip. It is served by two subway stations and has site parking for two thousand cars. Two historic buildings — Old City Hall and Holy Trinity Church — are immediately adjacent.

The massive financing of a megaproject of this scale required three sources of funding: a major developer, a major bank, and Canada's main department store chain. Financial feasibility was concerned with the efficiency ratios of gross-to-rentable floor areas in this prime and expensive central location. Traffic of up to one million shoppers a week, with a gross sales turnover in excess of $500 million a year, was projected. The Eaton Centre was, when opened, the largest indoor shopping complex in the world.

The centre, for all its claim to historical reference in nineteenth-century urban models such as Milan's Galleria,

is, in effect, a suburban shopping plaza with a downtown location, served by rapid transit rather than the car. Its ethos is mass-marketing and fast-food servicing. Its design is an alliance of the German-born architect's Bauhaus training and cheerful North American vulgarity, of Germanic severity and streetwise jazz.

The heart of the centre is the "galleria," a linear atrium or internal street with a curved glass roof 127 feet above the lowest of its three main shopping malls. This 900-foot-long gallery accommodates hundreds of stores and restaurants in a climate-controlled environment and acts as a fresh-air plenum which, with the use of a heat exchange system, balances the energy requirements in the complex.

The galleria's nautical ambience, of a liner on a perpetual cruise, is enhanced by the functional detailing in welded-steel handrail piping, exposed duct-work, and glassed elevators. The revealed deck structure of flat-slab column caps adds to the air of sailing, as do the flock of fibreglass Canada geese suspended from one end of the long glass arch.

On the street façades the gallery's floor levels relate to the sidewalks. The elevation is kept low to the three-storey idiom of the thoroughfare, and tries to acknowledge its scale by skilful detailing that echoes the traditional cast-iron fronts that once existed there. The office towers have curved corners and sleek, flush, glazed skins that extend their visual metaphor as liner "funnels."

Original fears that the centre would drain the vitality from the Yonge Street strip still persist, despite the fact that the complex's huge popularity has acted as a magnet for many new downtown visitors of all ages and conditions, who travel in from the suburbs to shop and meet in its great gallery, around the focus of a spurting fountain. And, for all its megastructural scale, the centre's visual impact on the street is remarkably discreet.

"Architecture is a fusion of functional logic and cultural memory," Zeidler has said. "It operates by a kind of informed intuition, an emotional instinct derived from an understanding of structure and social necessity. It is, at best, an art derived from technology, yet free to express feeling. I feel that buildings should be joyful, happy places to be."

In the Eaton Centre, as in his design for Ontario Place, Zeidler has skilfully and subtly fused "functional logic" and "cultural memory" in a great liner of a structure that sails the street carrying its thousands of happy spenders.

Main entrance on Dundas Street West.

Yonge Street elevation.

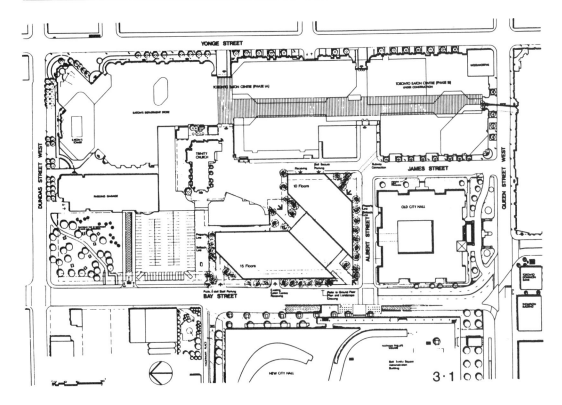

Site plan.

Scarborough Civic Centre

Architect: Raymond Moriyama
Location: Scarborough, Ontario
Completion date: 1973
Gross floor area: 335,629 square feet
Construction cost: $10.5 million
Client: Corporation and Board of Education, Borough of Scarborough
Structural Engineers: Robert Halsall and Associates
Management Consultants: McDougall Construction Management Ltd.
Project Team: Raymond Moriyama, Ted Teshima, Jim Wilkinson,
    David Vickers, Clarence Freek

Main entrance.

The Borough of Scarborough is, to a large degree, a dormitory suburb comprising the eastern sector of Metro Toronto. Its major growth in population and development has occurred since the Second World War, accommodating both native Torontonians moving away from the city's downtown, and many new immigrants.

In the late 1960s the Scarborough corporation commissioned a new civic centre to include offices for the municipality and the Board of Education, a council chamber, and various allied facilities on a 170-acre site the official plan intended as a focus for the borough. The civic centre is linked to a town centre consisting of a large enclosed shopping mall. Later residential, commercial, and government developments are planned.

The site is an open, partially wooded tract of former farmland situated south of a major expressway. The civic centre is designed as a symbol of Scarborough's particular identity as well as a functional official building. The program was developed in a process of exhaustive consultation between the architect and all levels of public employees and elected representatives. In this process the consciousness of the centre's practical and symbolic functions was clarified for all participants.

The design developed as an enclosed multi-storey circular central space or atrium eighty feet in diameter, with the two office segments — five floors for the municipality, four for the Board of Education — arranged as mezzanined wedges on opposite sides. On the borough side the floor levels step back in a regular structural bay of fifteen feet. On the board's segment the floors cantilever out at intervals of six, eleven, and sixteen feet from the column line. The two segments are linked by bridges that function as rest areas. Two freestanding concrete elevator towers complete the structural system.

The council chamber, or "Meeting Hall," is set down half a level off the central space overlooked by the office tiers. The core atrium, sixty-seven feet high, is the main public area and design feature, throwing the philosophical emphasis of the complex on its social rather than its official function.

Above: aerial view from north; *Below:* floor plans.

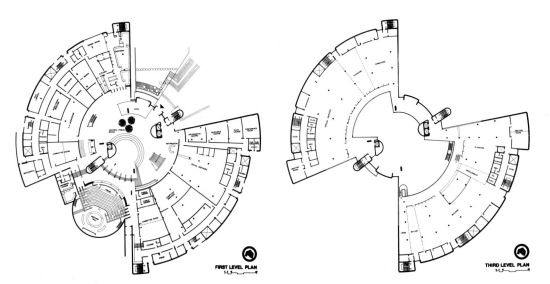

FIRST LEVEL PLAN

THIRD LEVEL PLAN

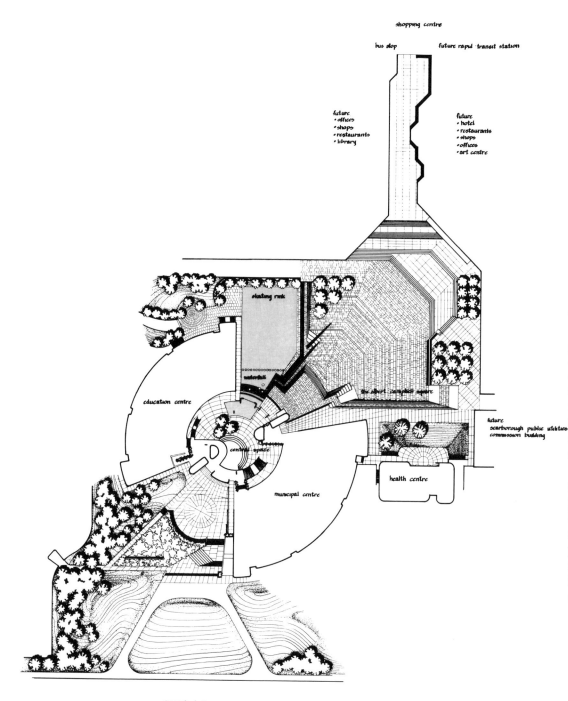

shopping centre

bus stop   future rapid transit station

future
• offices
• shops
• restaurants
• library

future
• hotel
• restaurants
• shops
• offices
• art centre

skating rink

education centre

waterfall

the albert campbell square

central space

future
scarborough public utilities
commission building

municipal centre

health centre

borough drive

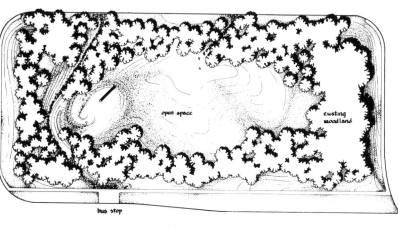

open space

existing woodland

bus stop

ellesmere road

0   50   100

Site plan.

The central space is capped by a flat-slab roof. The attached segments are sculpturally articulated by triangular forms in dark reflective glass and white aluminum siding with a fluora-carbon finish, forming a light-weight skin. This sheathing is self-cleansing and forms crisp outlines defining the centre's distinctive geometry.

The contract was carried out under a project management team system with multi-package bidding by contractors. This required the architects' close supervision but ensured that the contract was completed well within the schedule and the budget.

The interiors are designed on a basis of white on white, with a counterpoint of strong colours in the carpeting and office partitioning which allows various government functions to be easily located. Reflecting pools inside and out and a waterfall add an air of tranquility, enhanced by planting. An open square to the north is landscaped for public functions and is served by a stainless-steel pylon housing light and sound systems.

"The architect taught the borough something crucial about the nature of participatory democracy expressed in a building," a local official declares. "The centre is immensely popular with the people, who use it for functions and to meet and mingle. It has created an identity for Scarborough that I hope we can all live up to."

Steps, east elevation.

The central space with
balcony office levels.

171

Metro Library

Architect: Raymond Moriyama
Location: Toronto, Ontario
Completion date: 1977
Gross floor area: 364,000 square feet
Construction cost: $30 million
Client: Metropolitan Toronto Library Board
Structural Engineers: Robert Halsall and Associates Ltd.
Contract Management: Charles Nolan Co. Ltd.
Project Team: Raymond Moriyama, Ted Teshima, A. Finlay

Architects, for all their preoccupation with structure, materials, building systems, costs, and function, are often moved by metaphor, both visual and literary. A kind of poetry of space compels them, where the program allows such vision.

A project such as the Metro Library, the million-book central reference facility in Toronto's city-wide system, encourages such image-making. A central library is an occasion for civic grandeur. It is a public claim to reverence for knowledge, to cultural sophistication; a kind of palace of books.

Moriyama, who has long felt that "a man should be an artist of his own life," grasped this metaphorical necessity. When his team had completed complex studies on the library project, which took seven years from feasibility to completion, he searched for an image to express its social poetry. The metaphor that organized the design of the library is that of the "empty cup." The architect perceives our society as one in which "we focus on the empty cup, forgetting that the essence is the emptiness inside ...so the mind must be a bridge making linkages." So the core of the library evolved as a five-storey toplit atrium around which the floors of open mezzanines curve like the rims of cups. Into this huge hole all the interior space flows, to fill "emptiness."

Opposite: the "empty cup;" *Right:* main entrance and sections.

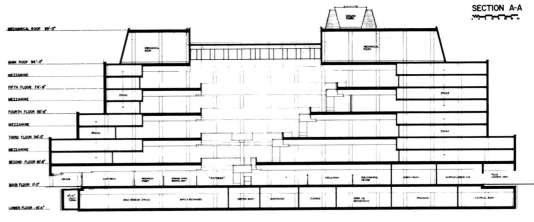

SECTION A-A

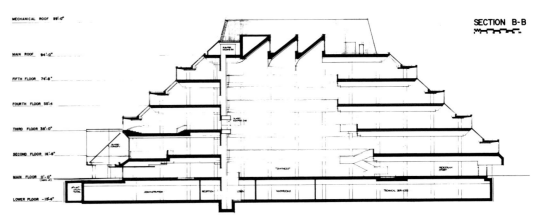

SECTION B-B

The structure is based on a grid of circular reinforced concrete columns at thirty-by-thirty-foot centres. In the designer's original concept, this skeleton was to be enclosed in a translucent glass box. However, the local planners were concerned with the scale of such a large structure on the street. They insisted upon confusing the clarity of the design by sloping two of the corners on the main axis, and clothing the building in a more conventional red-brown brick vernacular stepped back from the frontage. Only the angled triangles of skylights over the entrance and at the rear remain to hint at Moriyama's first idea.

The main entry to the library is kept low, with sound-deadening pools giving an almost Oriental hush to the lobby. Beyond the security barriers the atrium opens; the hundred-foot high "empty cup" is dramatically revealed. Long curving ramps and a pair of curved glass elevators link the floor levels.

Colour is used both for warmth and for direction to the various departments. Hard-wearing synthetic fibre carpeting in earthy rust and orange shades is glued to the screed and rises up over balustrades and parapets. Vinyl asbestos tile is used in the mezzanine and stack areas, ceramic tile in service and washrooms. On the ground floor, where traffic is heaviest, exposed aggregate blocks and terrazzo are laid. Heating is provided by an internal-source heat pump.

Lighting is a fusion of daylight, fluorescent, and mercury vapour, with incandescent accents. It is designed for two levels of ambient illumination, general and localized. Fixtures in the work areas are mounted above suspended, cloth-covered, fibreglass sound baffles.

Study carrels, stack ends, card file cabinets, and desks are bleached oak.

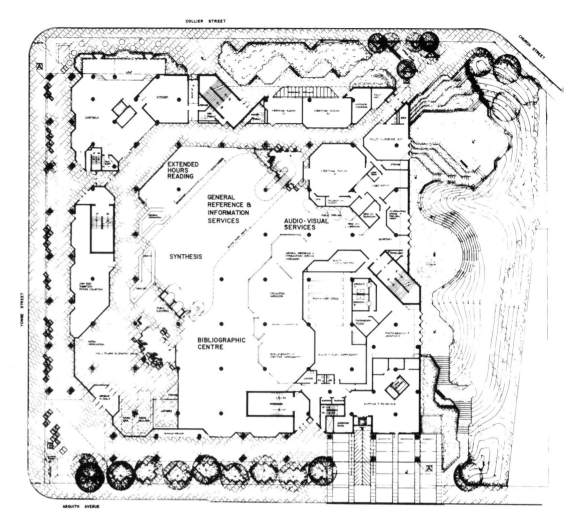

Ground floor plan and balcony patterns.

Planting is used extensively to soften the sightlines. There is a large film library and a "talking book" service of cassette tapes. The seating, in secluded lounge areas under the glass skylight slopes, is in comfortable armchairs. The view from these lounges over the city's skyline is exhilarating, a relief from close concentration.

Metro Library is highly popular with users of all ages, as a meeting place as well as a reference source. Whether many of these visitors perceive the metaphor or not, Moriyama's "empty cup" is always well filled.

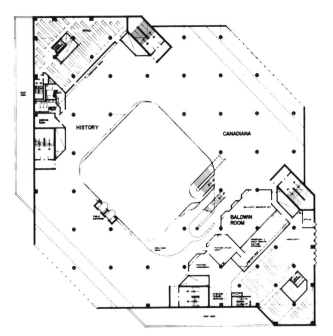

Upper floor plan and view from elevators.

Home for the Aged

Architect: Jerome Markson
Project Architect: Paul G. Harasti
Location: Toronto, Ontario
Completion date: 1973
Gross floor area: 129,500 square feet
Construction cost: $3.5 million
Client: Department of Social Services, Metro Toronto
Contractor: Vanbots Construction

Front elevation overlooking valley.

The accommodation and care of elderly people, those without adequate family resources, is a growing public concern as the median age of populations in advanced industrial countries moves steadily upwards.

Opinion varies as to whether "senior citizens" should be integrated in mixed-housing developments with residents of all ages, or separated in special environments with people of their own condition. The advantage of the latter option is that elderly people can be brought together round a focus of appropriate health care and services.

The disadvantage is that such "homes for the aged" can be seen as social ghettoes.

True Davidson Acres, in Toronto's Borough of East York, is perched on a hilltop overlooking a river valley. Four floors of bedrooms project on either side of the wooded knoll, propped on slim circular columns. The ground level, accommodating the main rooms and including everything from a hair salon to a chapel, a library to a laundry, forms a self-sufficient miniature "downtown" extended by four extensive quarry-tile-paved, shaded terraces.

Each living floor is planned as an "internal street." The bedrooms are served by communal washrooms, nursing stations, and dining areas that open onto terraces. The interior finishes of composite wood tiles and ceramic wall linings in the public areas, with birch rails and skirtings to protect surfaces from wheelchairs, are both durable and bright.

The bedrooms sleep two, either a married couple or two people of the same sex. Their 200-square-foot space is articulated by a thirty-degree angled splay that gives privacy and window-space for each occupant, and takes advantage of the long valley views. Having another person in the room provides company and eliminates the sense of loneliness or institutionalization single rooms or wards might have induced.

The average age of the 280 residents is eighty-seven for women, seventy-eight for men. The staff ratio is one for every two residents. Subdued lighting offsets the bright colours and the warmth of brick, tile, and wood. Main services, including a mortuary, are in the basement, along with a garage for staff and a service yard.

Externally, the rusticated orange, silicone-faced, clay brick is modulated by the angled, flush, bedroom windows above ground floor. The windows are fixed, with vent panels, to prevent suicides. Floating above the perched columns, the long façade has a pleasantly unstressed rhythm against the wide southern-Ontario sky.

The building exploits the drama of the site, which may at the same time underline the sense of isolation from the rest of humanity its aged occupants might feel. To soften this, the architect has sensitively planned and detailed the place to a gentle scale. This community of the elderly is a sweet haven and next-to-final resting place.

South elevation.

Main terrace.

"Downtown" meeting place.

178

Main floor plan.

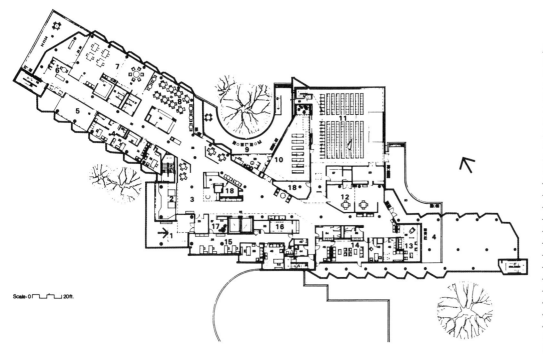

Legend

10	West terrace	36	Administration office
11	Library	37	Reception
12	Crafts room	38	Assistant administrator
13	Adjuvant room	39	Storage
14	Storage	40	Administrator
15	Health club	41	Washroom
16	Washroom	42	Coat room
17	Washroom	43	Garbage room
18	Examination room	44	Janitor's room
19	Doctor's office	45	Supervisor's lounge
20	Doctor's washroom	46	Staff lounge
21	Central nurses' supply	47	Women's auxiliary
22	Corridor	48	Laundry
23	Nurse	49	Beauty salon
24	Waiting room	50	East terrace
25	Super nurses' office	51	Storage
26	Servery	52	Barber
27	Cafeteria	53	Washroom
28	Tea room	54	Washroom
29	Family room and sacristy	55	Corridor
30	Central terrace	56	Day care centre
31	Tuck shop servery	57	Kitchen
32	Tuck shop storage	59	Storage & dressing
33	Lobby	60	Auditorium
34	Gift shop	61	Vestibule
35	Vestibule	62	Chapel
		63	Storage

Scale·0 ⌐_⌐_⌐ 20 ft.

Bedroom level plan.

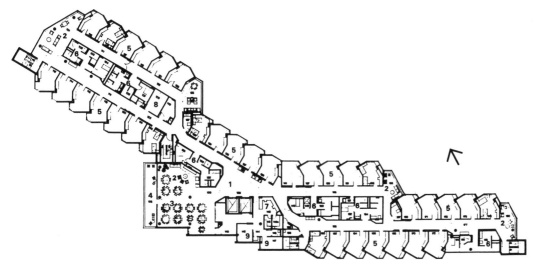

Legend

101	Lounge	142	Infirmary
102-7	Washroom facilities	143	Nurses' station
108	Janitor	144	Corridor
109	Clean linen	145	Drug room
110	Soiled linen	145a	Treatment room
111	Corridor	146	Washroom
112-21	Living units	147	Infirmary
122	Corridor	148-50	Washroom facilities
123-4	Living units	151	Janitor
125	Lounge	152-4	Washroom facilities
126	Living unit	155	Corridor
127	Utility	156	Garbage room
128	Bathroom	157	Living unit
129	Living unit	158	Washroom
130	Shower	159-64	Living units
131	Living unit	165	Lounge
132	Washroom	166	Living unit
133	Lobby	167	Utility room
134	Balcony	168-73	Living units
135	Living unit	174	Bathroom
136	Lounge	175	Living unit
137	Living unit	176	Shower
138	Dining room	177	Corridor
139	Living unit	178	Washroom
140	Servery	179	Living unit
141	Living unit	180	Lounge

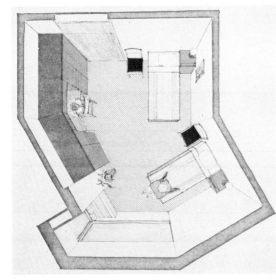

Typical bedroom sleeping two: angled for privacy.

Metro Zoo

Architects: R. J. Thom, Clifford and Lawrie, Crang and Boake
Location: Toronto, Ontario
Completion date: 1974
Site area: 710 acres
Construction cost: $40 million, including landscaping
Client: Municipality of Metropolitan Toronto
Structural Engineers: M. S. Yolles and Associates

Africa Pavilion.

Zoological parks are theatres of nature: contrived recreations of wildness for our diversion and instruction. There is a modern tendency to make zoos look as "natural" as possible — in a word, *ecological.*

Metro Zoo was the first major ecological animal park in the world. The concept is to show off the four hundred species each in its own native environment, complete with appropriate flora and fauna. To that end, the four thousand animals are grouped in pavilions that recreate, as scrupulously as pos-

sible, the major zoographic regions of the planet.

The site is an open plateau surrounded by deep, wooded ravines, divided by a mature deciduous forest covering a sharp change of level. The four pavilions, representing the regions of Africa, Indo-Malaya, Eurasia, and North America, are dispersed around the plateau. Two more pavilions, representing South America and Australasia, are projected in the master plan, plus a large aquarium and auditorium complex.

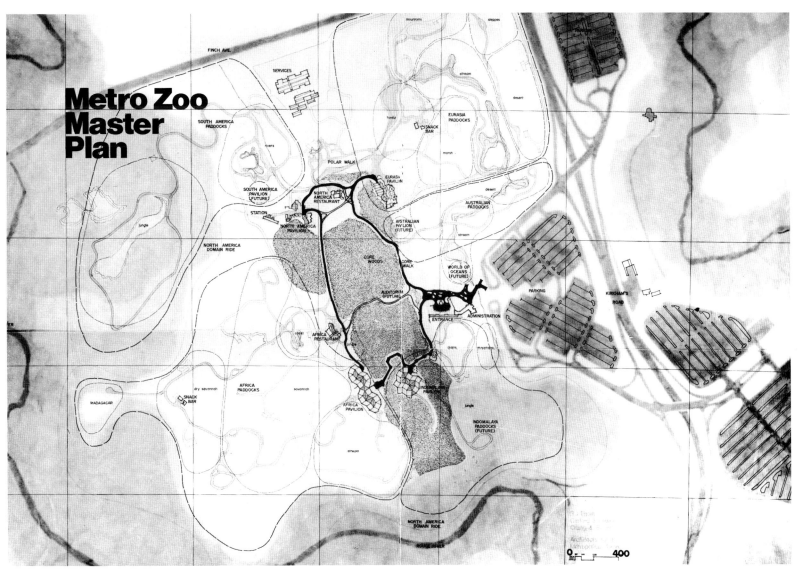

Site plan and section through
Indo-Malayan Pavilion.

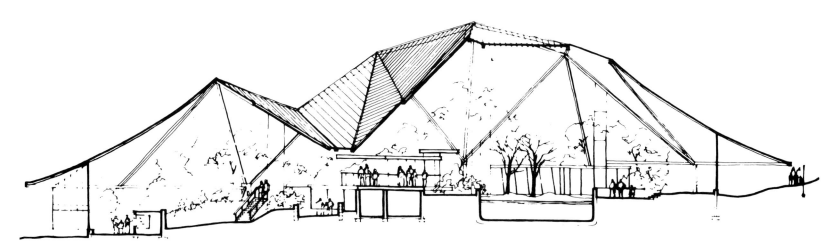

The North American and Eurasian pavilions are fairly conventional structures of reinforced concrete and steel with skylights and greenhouse glazing. The African and Indo-Malayan pavilions are more original in concept. They were conceived as "non-architecture." That is, they are enclosures that strive not to impose upon their environments. As visitors stroll through habitats that resemble jungle paths or tracks in the bush, separated from the animals by water barriers, planting, and level changes, the structures do not disturb this careful illusion.

These two pavilions are designed as a series of light and airy hyperbolic paraboloids with a forty-two-foot grid of squares and rhomboids. The grid is canted at angles of ninety, sixty, and thirty degrees, to provide a flexibility of enclosure in plan and section. The roofs are partly solid, partly glazed, with extensive opening sashes for natural summer ventilation.

The Hypar shells use a steel tubular triodetic system with two-inch cedar decking and shingle surface. Tripod steel and concrete buttresses support the point roof loadings. The roofs are high enough at the peaks for tall trees to grow, providing patches of light and shade.

Heating and ventilation is supplied through a system of buried trans-site ducts with flexible air module supply units. The underground ducting can be locally regulated to each particular zone and habitat. Extracts are carried to the animal holding areas to reduce the pungency of odours in the public areas. $5 million worth of services are buried, including sewers, water mains, telephone, and power lines.

The pavilions range up to 54,400 square feet in gross floor area. The paraboloid form is free-flowing, light as tenting, graceful as a series of canvas marquees, yet permanent. In summer the pavilions are open and airy, filled with birdsong and animal grunts,

Hyperbolic paraboloids.

snorts, and cackles. The architecture serves this carefully presented strangeness with discretion and grace.

The landscaping has been designed to preserve this naturalness, and at the same time protect both animals and human spectators. This landscaping flows in and out of the pavilions, and links them to the site with its rock formations, waterfalls, and twenty thousand planted trees and shrubs. An electrically powered rubber-tired train makes a 4.8-kilometre circuit of the outdoor Canadian Animal Domain.

A zoo should also be a serious research facility for studying animal behaviour. Among Metro Zoo's one million yearly visitors are a number of zoologists from all over the world. But this zoo's main function is as a theatre of nature with an illusion of audience participation. It is a nicely contrived drama-in-the-round where human beings are both spectators and actors in this display of nature's diversity.

A theatre of nature.

Royal Bank Plaza

Architects: Webb, Zerafa, Menkes, Housden Partnership
Location: Toronto, Ontario
Completion date: 1976
Total rentable area: 1,250,000 square feet
Construction cost: $100 million
Client: Royal Bank of Canada
Structural Engineers: Nicolet Carrier Dressel and Associates
Contractors: V. K. Mason Construction Ltd.
Project Team: Boris Zerafa, Bernie Himel, Rolly Sweetman

Banks have been a major element in Toronto's civic style for a century and a half. Toronto is a banker's town, the headquarters of powerful institutions which, unlike banks in the United States, are chartered to operate across the nation.

The focus of Toronto's prime financial district, and therefore Canada's, is the Toronto Stock Exchange on Bay Street. Since the mid-1960s four tall bank towers have been built in a cluster around the exchange, transforming the city's downtown skyline. Each of the four, by curious chance, is sheathed in a different colour. The 1967 fifty-six-storey, three-tower Toronto Dominion Centre, designed by Mies van der Rohe, is black. The fifty-seven-storey Commerce Court, designed by I. M. Pei, is silver. The 1975 First Canadian Place for the Bank of Montreal, designed by Edward Durell Stone, is white. The Royal Bank Plaza is golden. Together, all four bank buildings, each the regional headquarters of its own system, make a brilliant statement about the variety and vigour of cash.

The Royal Bank Plaza is the only one of the four to have been designed by Canadian architects. It is also, by no chance, the most imaginative solution to the construction of a massive downtown office tower that embodies the image of its owners yet enhances the urban fabric.

Left: aerial view from the east; *Opposite:* close-ups of serrated aluminum curtain walls with golden skin.

Rather than compete in a pointless height race, the plaza was organized as two triangular towers, forty-one and twenty-six storeys tall, set 110 feet apart on either side of a central 130-foot-high "urban room," banking-hall atrium. Below the banking hall is a two-level shopping concourse linked to the subway and to neighbouring buildings by underground tunnels.

The plaza's diagonal design takes account of pedestrian street patterns in the geometry of street intersections and counterpoints the dull squareness of the surrounding towers.

The structure of the office towers consists of forty-by-forty-foot reinforced concrete column bays around central shear-wall cores. The floors have a structural thickness of twenty-four inches with five-inch slabs and a mechanical system space beneath, resulting in a thirty-six-inch-deep sandwich. The use of high-strength fly ash concrete, with tolerances calculated by computer, reduced and simplified the column reinforcement. The glazed, unit space-frame that encloses the ends and roof of the atrium is constructed of steel box-girders assembled on the ground and hoisted into position by lifting jacks.

Mechanical rooms on the twelfth floor of each tower contain air-handling equipment serving the atrium and offices, with a central service area on the forty-first floor of the south tower housing a high-pressure water-chilling plant and heat recovery units. Computer consoles regulate the high velocity airconditioning systems and fresh-air intake to the underground garage holding six hundred cars.

The serrated aluminum curtain walls that enclose the triangular towers, breaking up the surface of the massive buildings with brilliant reflections, incorporate 2500 ounces of gold coating on the outside face of the inside panes of double glazing set between stainless steel mullions. The "urban room" is a boldly modelled space, dramatized by a suspended sculpture consisting of 8600 twenty-foot aluminum tubes painted white and yellow — like a packet of giant needles frozen in the act of falling.

The Royal Bank Plaza is architecture as abstract artwork — a vivid volume to be walked around and through, or to be dazzled by as the sun glitters on its golden skin. It is a palace of money graced by a certain visual wit, welcome in Toronto's long and rather solemn tradition of banking.

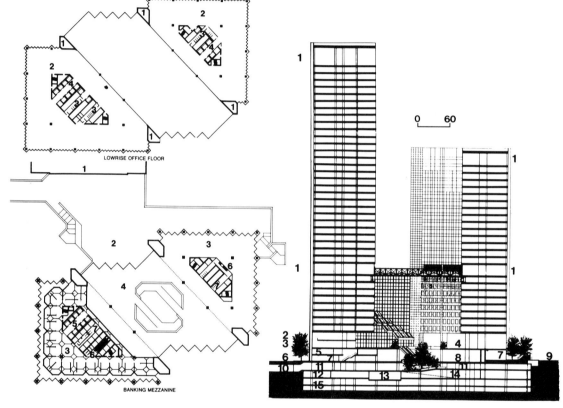

Plans and sections.

Central Banking Hall.

North York Municipal Building

Architects: Adamson Associates
Location: North York, Ontario
Completion date: 1978
Gross floor area: 555,333 square feet
Construction cost: $16,164,000
Client: North York Borough Council
Engineering Consultants: Reid, Crowther and Partners
Construction Management: Milne and Nicholls Ltd.
Project Team: John Bonnick, Gar MacInnis, David Cody, George Nash

Main elevation on Yonge Street.

North York, one of the five municipalities that, with the city, comprise Metropolitan Toronto, was incorporated a city in 1980, in an act of self-identification. To establish its own local focus, against the centrifugal pull of the of the downtown urban core, North York is in the process of constructing a civic centre complex.

The Municipal Building, housing the council chamber, committee rooms, and borough offices, is intended as the nucleus of a grouping linked to the neighbouring Board of Education building, and to a future library and cultural centre planned around a civic square. The location, near a major crossroads where extensive commercial and residential development is in progress, is intended as North York's own urbanized "downtown" in a borough with a suburban history.

The Municipal Building is conceived as an internal street that will be extended, above and below ground, to link all the public and private elements in this development with one another and with the adjacent main subway route. The bold simplicity of this concept is expressed in the vast glazed atrium onto which the main floors of the building open.

This is "visible government" vividly translated into architecture. The official departmental offices are located on mezzanines open to public view. The council chamber has a curving glass wall that is accessible directly off the lowest level of the "street." The chamber is a subdued and intimate space, carpeted in a chocolate brown weave that also covers the built-in public seating.

The structure, of reinforced concrete flat-slab with drop panels and circular columns, employs a thirty-by-thirty-foot plan grid, flexible for office partitioning.

Three glass-enclosed elevators in the centre of the plan serve the office floors and the underground parking for 565 cars. Open stairways link each level.

The interior finishes include beige brick, blond oak, carpeted floors, exposed sandblasted concrete columns, painted plaster, and acoustic tile ceilings. Vivid colour accents are provided by the furnishings and by the primary colours painted on the exposed ductwork.

Internal street.

Section through Council Chamber
1. Parking garage
2. Council chamber
3. Mechanical
4. Politicians' lounge
5. Reception dining
6. Central records storage
7. Information Services Department
8. Alderman's office
9. Controller's office
10. Bylaw Reinforcement Department
11. Personnel Department
12. Parks and Recreation Department
13. Public Works Department

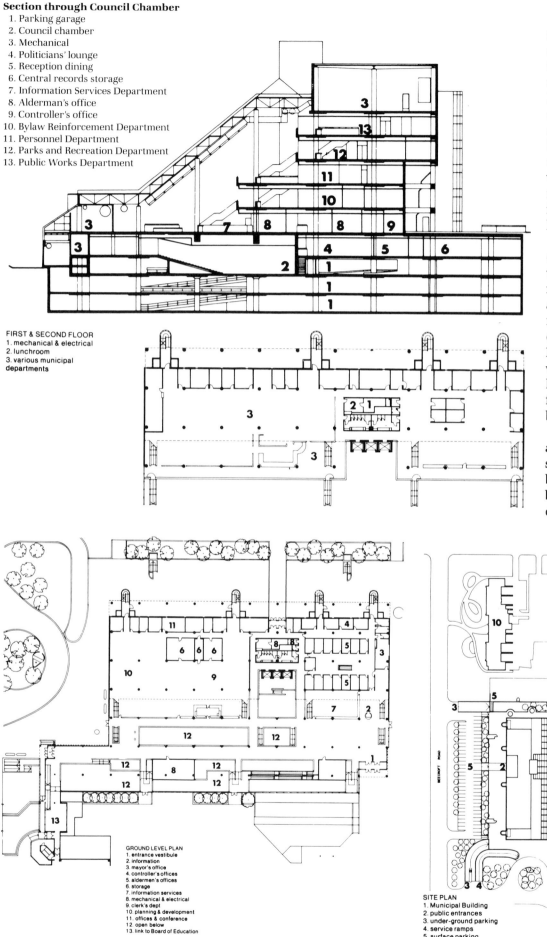

FIRST & SECOND FLOOR
1. mechanical & electrical
2. lunchroom
3. various municipal departments

GROUND LEVEL PLAN
1. entrance vestibule
2. information
3. mayor's office
4. controller's offices
5. aldermen's offices
6. storage
7. information services
8. mechanical & electrical
9. clerk's dept
10. planning & development
11. offices & conference
12. open below
13. link to Board of Education

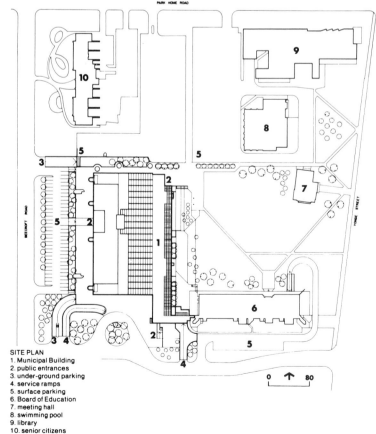

SITE PLAN
1. Municipal Building
2. public entrances
3. under-ground parking
4. service ramps
5. surface parking
6. Board of Education
7. meeting hall
8. swimming pool
9. library
10. senior citizens

0   80

The unifying and distinctive visual feature of the building, internally and externally, on the main elevation, is the sloping, shop-assembled, steel, roof-truss system five floors in height. Horizontal bands of vertical glazing alternate with inclines of bronzed aluminum sheathing to form a 300-foot long skylight with triangular glass screens at each end. Mechanical services, located at ground level beside the main entrance, are expressed on the front façade as a louvred feature in the lower glazed slope.

This skylight roof system unifies the design inside and out. It dominates what will be the future civic centre's main plaza, boldly stating North York's ambition to be a major city in its own right. By contrast, the rear elevation, designed for expansion, is a 1980s Art Deco exercise in abstract geometry with circular glazed staircase towers, horizontal bands of brickwork, and freestanding grids for columns and beams.

North York's Municipal Building is an imaginative act of architectural self-identification. It is a suburban borough's brave leap of faith that it can become a self-centred urban entity in its own right.

190

Lower level cafeteria.

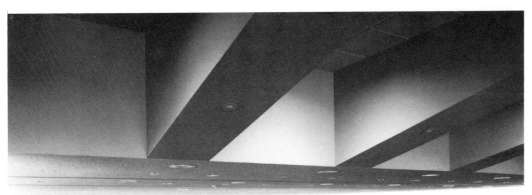

Council Chamber.

Bedford Glen Housing

Architect: Ernest Annau
Location: Toronto, Ontario
Completion date: 1979
Gross floor area: 306,000 square feet
Construction cost: $12 million
Client/Developer/General Contractor: Cadillac Fairview Corporation
Project Teams:
   Architects: Ernest Annau, Steven Kirsheblatt, Luciano Di Carlo, Stuart Piets
   Developer: Samuel Kolber, Jack Marshall

View from ravine.

Bedford Glen is a rare example of a medium-density development integrating into a suburban single-family residential neighbourhood and enhancing, rather than disturbing, the scale of its surroundings.

The Bedford Park district, on the boundary between the cities of Toronto and North York, was developed in the 1920s along the edge of one of Metro's deep ravines. It is characterized by two-storey porched houses on leafy side streets near the junctions of several main road arteries. In this quietly domestic context, Bedford Glen, with its greater density of thirty-seven units per acre, fits with remarkable ease.

This integration is accomplished by a subtle adaptation of the local domestic vernacular to a larger scale. The two blocks containing the 158 condominium units are set on either side of the ravine along the main roadway. Though seven and six storeys high respectively, these blocks read as five storeys from the street level. The buildings are linked by a glued timber bridge with curved support arches over a pool edged with paving and planting.

Beige clay brick and sloping, cedar-shingle roofs are articulated to domesticate the scale of the blocks. Chimneys enhance the idiom. Sundecks, floor-to-ceiling glazing, and plant-boxes create an intimate openness. The forty-nine rather less distinguished three-storey townhouses at the rear of the site form a transition between the residential neighbourhood and the terraced condominiums.

The condominium units are two-storied on the lower tier, with single-level one-, two-, and three-bedroom apartments above. Double-storey penthouses, with splendid views east and west, occupy the top level. All units have deep decks lined with planters and living rooms with cathedral ceilings. Two and three levels of parking for 303 cars accommodated underground, plus indoor recreational facilities and locker rooms.

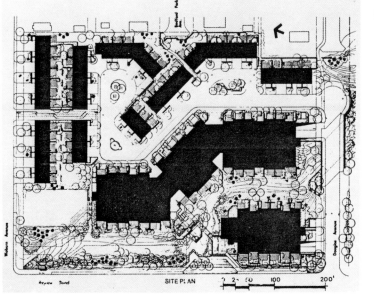

Site plan.

Condominium units.

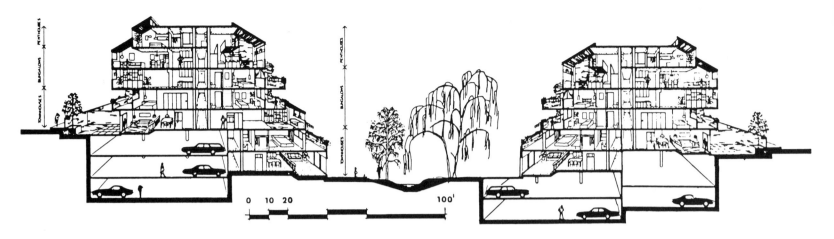

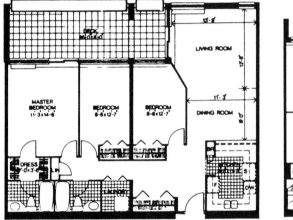

3-BEDROOM

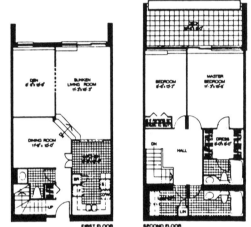

2-STOREY, 2-BEDROOM WITH DEN

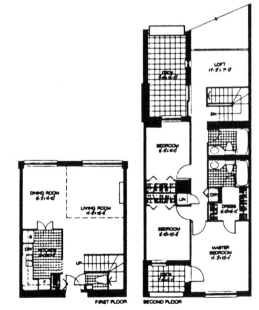

2-STOREY, 3-BEDROOM PENTHOUSE

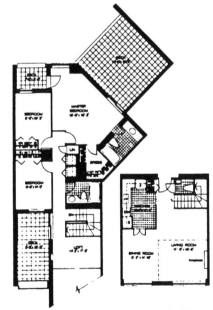

2-STOREY, 3-BEDROOM PENTHOUSE

The structure is mainly load-bearing brickwork with a playful use of flying buttresses deriving from the Victorian Gothic common in Toronto. The use of white trim on windows and projecting balconies is also traditional, and lightens the solemnity of the local clay brick.

"Architecture's first principle is the harmonious integration of a new structure in its context," says Ernest Annau. A vital factor in the successful integration of Bedford Glen is not visible, but it was crucial. This was the involvement of the local community in the planning process. When, in the mid-1960s, the developer proposed a high-density complex on this choice ravine site, neighbourhood residents' associations protested vigorously. Nine years of infighting, between the borough officials, the developer, and the community, followed.

Annau's contribution, apart from his qualities as a designer, was to evolve the project in partnership with both residents and developer. "It was like walking on eggs," he comments. "A kind of shuttle diplomacy was needed." The architect's talents as a diplomat, more crucial to the design process than is often acknowledged, were as necessary in achieving the excellent result as any other professional gift.

Sections and typical condo plans.

194

Above: entrance hall; *Below:* decks.

Bank of Canada

Architects: Arthur Erickson, with Marani, Rounthwaite and Dick
Location: Ottawa, Ontario
Completion date: 1979
Gross floor area: 600,000 square feet
Construction cost: $66,800,000
Client: Bank of Canada
Structural Engineers: C. D. Carruthers and Wallace Consultants Ltd.
Contractors: Ellis-Don Ltd.
Project Team: Arthur Erickson, Ronald Dick, J. Strasman, K. Loffler, F. Allin, P. Chau

Elevation on Wellington Street: reflections of Parliament.

If a commercial bank's headquarters is perceived as a palace of money, the nation's central bank is clearly money's temple. The design of the Bank of Canada's head office in the federal capital is informed by this worshipful solemnity.

The mandate of the Bank of Canada, established in 1934, is to "regulate credit and currency in the best interests of the economic life of the nation." The central bank issues the country's paper money, defends the dollar on foreign exchange markets, and controls monetary policy by manipulating the bank rate and restricting the supply of credit. The bank's shares are wholly owned by the federal government, but the governor and his board have a wide degree of independence from ministerial control.

This complex relationship between the bank and government is mirrored, literally, in the architecture. The bank's skin of light- and heat-reflecting glass mirrors the green copper mansards and rough Victorian Gothic ashlar of the Confederation Building across Wellington Street. Oxidized copper, used in the bank's floor bands, narrow window mullions, and louvres, reflects the traditional idiom. The symmetry of the bank's twin office towers, flanking the 1938 silver-grey granite Beaux Arts bank building, acknowledges the bank's place within Ottawa's solemn bureaucracy, yet at the same time stands brilliantly alone.

The bank's plan is simple: two new twelve-storey office towers accommodating sixteen hundred employees are linked by a full-height atrium that incorporates the old bank. Three basement levels provide space for parking, services, and storage. At ground level the plan provides pedestrian links between Parliament Hill and the Sparks Street shopping mall.

The central atrium is the key to the design. Within this tall greenhouse, luxuriant with pools and planting, the five-storey façade of the old bank is used as a stage set, a metaphor of granitic solemnity. Externally, fronting the Sparks Street mall, five freestanding copper-clad columns rise 140 feet to form a colonnade that mimics the classicism of a Greek or Roman temple.

This visual wit, is developed in the

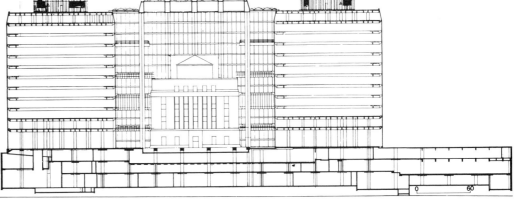

Main floor plan and long section.

interplay between transparency and reflection in the clear and mirrored glass panels. The building alternately allows itself to be seen through or throws back a reflected neighbour. It is at once opaque and penetrable, its taut skin modulated by chamfered corners and indented bays.

The office blocks are constructed on a thirty-foot-square reinforced concrete grid in a series of "trees," each centred on a three-foot-diameter column supporting a twenty-five-foot-square capital constructed of three-foot-deep ribs cantilevered from the central drophead. The mechanical and electrical systems are integrated in the column caps, connected by raceways in each ceiling coffer, powered by in-floor ducts. This system, which supports the acoustic ceiling panels, allows for the provision of flexible floor-mounted power and telephone outlets.

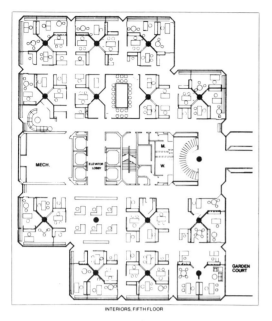

INTERIORS, FIFTH FLOOR

1. Electrified acoustic ceiling panel
2. Lighting fixture air supply & return
3. Suspended ceiling between module-edge beam's return air plenum
4. Communication underfloor duct
7. Power & telephone to work station
8. Perimeter induction system
9. Copper spandrel
10. Window mullions at 2'6" centres
11. Curtain wall

The offices are arranged in a cluster pattern with six-foot-high furniture acting as divisions. Full-height partitions slot into the concrete coffer ribs for maximum sound proofing. Furniture, services, and structure are thus integrated in the cohesive "treed" pattern that derives from Wright's Johnson's Wax offices.

The board room and other executive offices remain in the old bank building, whose entrance, flanked by granite Grecian urns and copper doors representing ancient coins, leads into a superb marbled hall with a coffered and gilded ceiling. A numismatic museum opens off the atrium. Flying bridges connect the upper floors of the old and new blocks. Rustic slate surfaces the ground floor, and the entire pedestrian podium on which the bank rests.

As a temple, the Bank of Canada head office is solemn yet ironic, its symmetries lightened by a subtle visual wit that avoids coyness or self-mockery. It is that rare phenomenon: a thoroughly modern design that expresses dignity without dullness.

Above: office floor layout and section; *Left:* central atrium.

Office floor showing concrete "tree."

Central atrium, looking up.

Wandich House

Architect: Jim Strasman
Location: Peterborough, Ontario
Completion date: 1979
Gross floor area: 6120 square feet and 2675 square feet of deck
Construction cost: $500,000
Structural Engineers: Robert Halsall and Associates Ltd.
Contractor: West End Construction Ltd.

A promontory on the lake.

The bridge linking buried bedrooms.

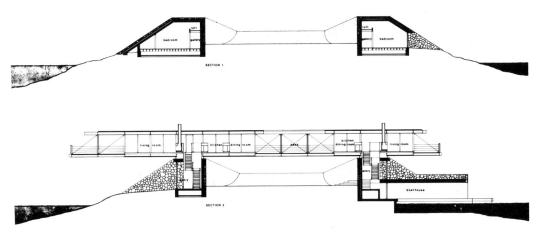

A small granite peninsula, spotted with pine and birch, slopes into the iron-blue waters of Stony Lake, one of the Kawartha Lakes near Peterborough, Ontario. To the south is green hillside farmland; to the west, rocky islands where turtles sun their backs in a stretch of open water; to the east, a still run, filled with waterlilies, between the peninsula and an islet. In the setting of this southern Ontario idyll, architect Jim Strasman has designed a house for all seasons.

The client desired a year-round second residence for his family of four, with separate guest quarters for friends and their children. Further space was needed for extra weekend visitors, along with a boathouse, parking, and storage space. A large sundeck, cooled by lake breezes, was also requested.

The designer's challenge was to provide all this accommodation without overwhelming the small headland, while, at the same time, exploiting every exposure of the site. And, as this was a year-round house, it had to be sheltered from winter snows yet open to the summer air.

Strasman's solution to both these challenges was superbly simple. He buried the bedrooms in two separate cave-like concrete bunkers covered with granite stones blasted from the site to form a base to build upon. The gaps between the stones are packed with earth and planted wih the native grass and scrub. The lakeside elevation of these bunkers is sloped to follow the rise of ground up from the water's edge, thus appearing to be an almost natural feature.

Each of the six bedrooms in the bunkers, four facing west, two east, has a tall slot of a window or a glass door looking onto the lake. The sloping ceilings are bush-hammered concrete, the walls are four-inch rough-sawn cedar boards laid diagonally. Carpet is laid on a suspended timber floor.

Burying the bedrooms under stone keeps them warm in winter, cool in summer. The boathouse, laundry, and mechanical service room are also concealed in the substructure.

Bridge deck.

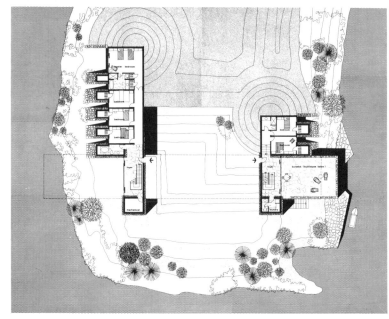

Lower level plan.

Upper level plan.

Having hidden half the house in the shelter of grassed granite, Strasman boldly linked both bunkers with an airy steel bridge. The 4000-square-foot bridge — a rolled-steel I-beam truss in twelve-foot bays braced with crossrods — is 170 feet long, 23 feet wide, and flies 22 feet above the waterline. Bolted to concrete benches, painted a flat charcoal brown, the ten-foot-high bridge projects over the lake. It houses on its long deck two fully glazed enclosures containing separate living, dining, and kitchen areas for the host family and its guests.

The deck, floored with two-by-six-inch pressure treated cedar planking, connects with the stone-floored lower level by means of two open-tread staircases. Steel and cedar, stone and glass, play off against one another with great delicacy of detailing. Under the bridge, in the paved area between the bunkers, cars park, and kids play on rainy days.

The elegant simplicity of the design, its light and airy frame, is visible from every aspect. For such a spacious house, its impact on the site is minimal. The horizontal lightness of the steel trusses counterpoints the slim vericals of the tree trunks in an interplay of the natural and the machined. The transparent glazing allows the landscape to visually flow through. At night, with the lights on, the glass becomes solid.

A relaxed sophistication, serene yet skilfully contrived, is the hallmark of this lakeside house for all seasons.

The master bedroom.

Xerox Research Centre

Architects/Engineers: Shore, Tilbe, Henschel, Irwin, Peters
Project Architects: Steve Irwin, Alf Tilbe
Location: Oakville, Ontario
Completion dates: Phase 1, 1980; Phase 2, 1983
Gross floor area: 130,000 square feet
Construction cost: $14,600,000
Client: Xerox Canada Inc.
Contractors: Milne and Nicholls Co. Ltd.; Jackson Lewis Ltd.

Phase One, entrance.

New technologies spawn new building types. The pace of modern industrial advance is rapid, the techniques inventive, the categories constantly splitting and specializing with an ever-intensifying ingenuity. The architect is challenged to invent new images to reflect this fact; a fact that has such a crucial, if often obscure, effect on contemporary life.

Industrial technology has fascinated architects for a century. Modern architecture springs from a kind of poetry of the machine. Designers have been influenced and even awed by the purity of industrial procedures, where "form follows function" with such seeming clarity.

The industrial research facility is the advance guard of technology. The quality of research and development can make or break a company — or a country. It is no great fancy of the architects of the Xerox Research Centre to describe it as "a machine for research ...dynamically expressive of attitudes of innovation which put the company in the forefront of its field."

The Xerox Centre is situated on a slightly sloping, featureless, twelve-acre site within the Sheridan Park Community. The first and second phases of the complex house a staff of over two hundred. The complex, when fully complete, will contain three hundred thousand square feet of research facility.

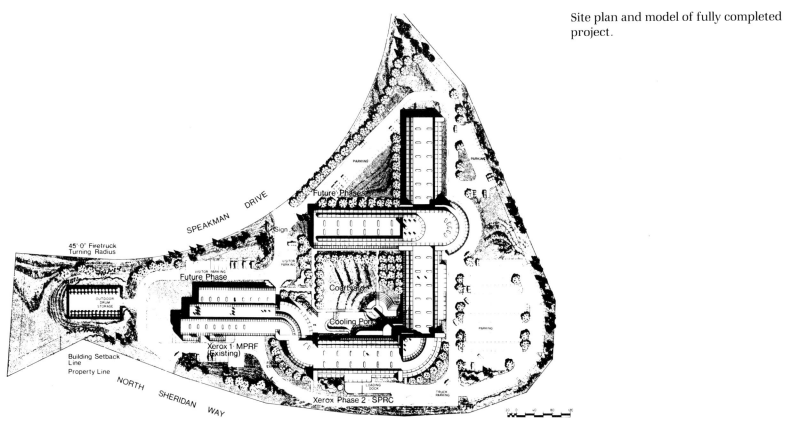

Site plan and model of fully completed project.

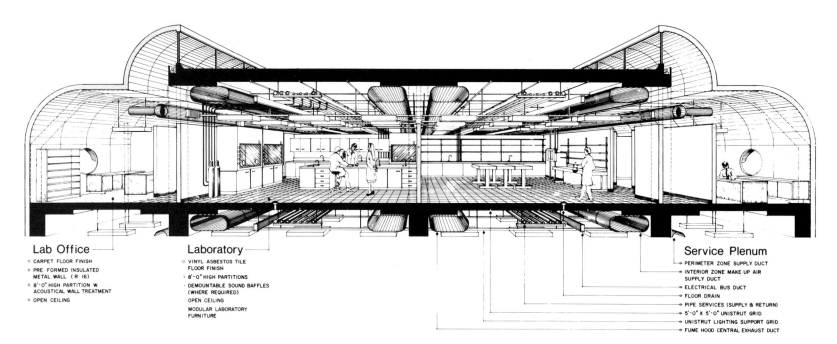

Lab Office
- CARPET FLOOR FINISH
- PRE-FORMED INSULATED METAL WALL (R-16)
- 8'-0" HIGH PARTITION W. ACOUSTICAL WALL TREATMENT
- OPEN CEILING

Laboratory
- VINYL ASBESTOS TILE FLOOR FINISH
- 8'-0" HIGH PARTITIONS
- DEMOUNTABLE SOUND BAFFLES (WHERE REQUIRED)
- OPEN CEILING
- MODULAR LABORATORY FURNITURE

Service Plenum
- PERIMETER ZONE SUPPLY DUCT
- INTERIOR ZONE MAKE-UP AIR SUPPLY DUCT
- ELECTRICAL BUS DUCT
- FLOOR DRAIN
- PIPE SERVICES (SUPPLY & RETURN)
- 5'-0" X 5'-0" UNISTRUT GRID
- UNISTRUT LIGHTING SUPPORT GRID
- FUME HOOD CENTRAL EXHAUST DUCT

Cross-section and part-plan.

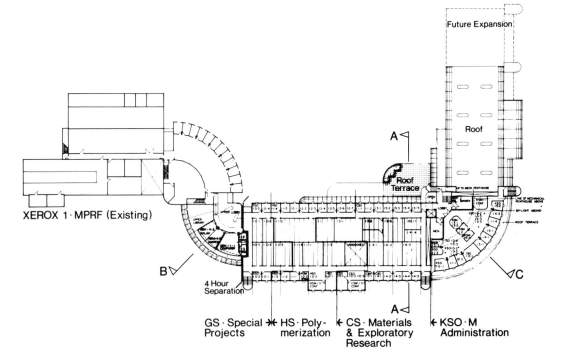

XEROX 1 · MPRF (Existing)

Future Expansion

Roof

Roof Terrace

4 Hour Separation

GS · Special Projects ⟶ HS · Poly-merization ⟶ CS · Materials & Exploratory Research ⟶ KSO · M Administration

Two major laboratory types make up the centre. Phase 1 is a pilot process plant with test labs, related support functions, and office space. Phase 2 includes smaller analytical laboratories, offices, support facilities, and public areas such as lunch rooms, lounges, libraries, a gymnasium, and a conference and exhibition space.

The complex is planned on three sides of a landscaped court with stepped pools and planting. The pools provide chilled water for cooling the building. A bank of trees screens the open side of the court from parking space linked to the nearby expressway.

The materials-processing laboratory is structured around a central elevated service spine that feeds out to the large labs and down to the control areas. This achieves an economical three-way system. easily capable of expansion. The analytical labs are serviced by a large horizontal duct supported by a unistrut grid that allows for a flexible attachment of fume hoods. High levels of energy conservation are insured by the constant recirculation of heat. A single central exhaust stack is designed to comply with stringent environmental pollution standards.

The "machine for research" image is expressed in the exterior design. Slim, fibreglass-insulated, porcelain-enamelled, steel sandwich panels, glossy grey in finish, tautly sheath the concrete and steel skeleton. These prepainted self-cleaning panels provide an insulation factor of R=15.

The flexibility of prefabricated steel allows the building's forms to be moulded into a complexity of counter-pointed curves, sleek and almost poetically "functional." Windows are held to a minimum, with curved clear-stories and banks of glass block. Lidded portholes add a jaunty touch.

The architects have designed research facilities for a number of clients over the past two decades, including oil and steel companies and the federal government. In the process their capacity for industrial imagery has grown more subtle and sophisticated, in keeping with the advance of modern technologies.

Entry detail.

Cladding close-up.

207

St. Fidelis Church

Architect: Rocco Maragna
Assistant Architects: Miltos Catomeris, Craig Lowery
Location: North York, Ontario
Completion date: 1981
Gross floor area: 12,500 square feet
Construction cost: $450,000
Client: Parish of St. Fidelis
Structural Engineers: M. S. Yolles and Partners Ltd.

"Symbolic intervention"...bell tower,
cupola, canopy.

"Renovation" is too pale a term to describe the birth of this charming little church out of the bones of a construction company's old garage. The apt epithet is surely "transformation."

The transformation is social as well as architectural. The Roman Catholic congregation in this suburban pocket of Toronto is largely first- and second-generation immigrant, mainly Italian and Polish. The fathers toiled in the construction industry the old garage represented. Many were injured, some were killed. Now, in better times, fathers and sons have raised the funds to transform an emblem of their suffering into a place of worship.

The congregation asked Maragna to keep within the walls of the existing building, which was a hybrid structure of concrete, steel, and block. A deep oil trough gouged the cement floor. Roof levels varied. With a tight budget, alterations had to be kept to a minimum. In this context, the architect opted for what he calls "symbolic intervention." He simplified the three main elements of traditional Catholic architecture — bell tower, cupola, canopy — and applied them to transform the old building.

The cupola is raised above the altar as a triangular skylight cut in the old, flat, steel-decked roof. Beneath the cupola a series of suspended baffles made out of drywall on metal stud diffuses the natural daylight.

The external canopy derives from the Italianate *baldacchino*: a suspended or supported porch that signals entry into sacred space. It is constructed out of blue-painted metal cladding slit by skylights, hovering over a flat brick arch, and makes subtle shadows on the simple oak church door in the white-washed wall.

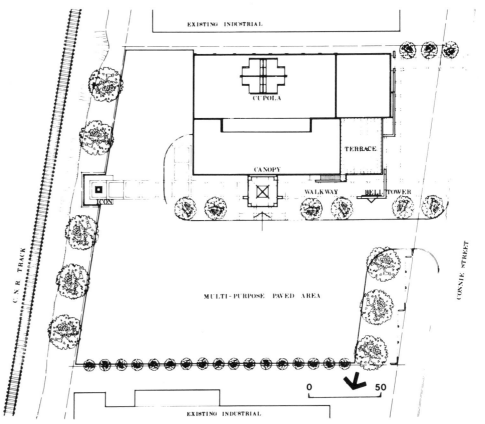

Sanctuary and altar.

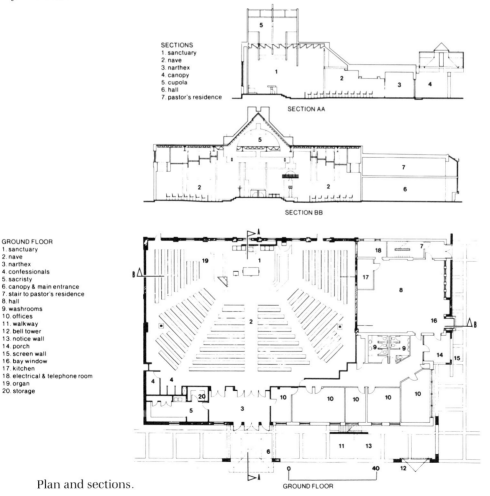

SECTIONS
1. sanctuary
2. nave
3. narthex
4. canopy
5. cupola
6. hall
7. pastor's residence

SECTION AA

SECTION BB

GROUND FLOOR
1. sanctuary
2. nave
3. narthex
4. confessionals
5. sacristy
6. canopy & main entrance
7. stair to pastor's residence
8. hall
9. washrooms
10. offices
11. walkway
12. bell tower
13. notice wall
14. porch
15. screen wall
16. bay window
17. kitchen
18. electrical & telephone room
19. organ
20. storage

GROUND FLOOR

Plan and sections.

The bell tower is the most abstract gesture of the three "symbolic interventions." Built out of red-brown semi-glazed Belden brick with integral iron spots, it straddles the corner flanking the entrance to the roadway. Its three-legged angle-arched form, offset by an Art Deco metal cross, is a symbol at once Post-Modern and ironically historical.

Apart from the bell tower, canopy, and cupola the exterior of the old building is largely untouched. The blocks are stuccoed and, with the brickwork, painted over in crisp white. The roof fascias are deep blue. Both together offer a Mediterranean simplicity.

The narthex is a cool, tile-floored space with a low ceiling. Through glass doors is the nave and the double-height sanctuary. Aisles lead through oak pews for 550 worshippers towards the tabernacle, raised four steps above the wine-coloured carpeting.

A ninety-foot-long, eight-foot-deep steel truss, which is the only major structural intervention, opens up the two halves of the old building, turning nave and sanctuary into one continuous space. Painted deep blue, supported on two steel piers, it echoes the industrial idiom of the garage in a new context.

Light illuminates the Carrara marble altar, lectern, and font from above and behind. A screen wall backing the tabernacle is set in from the southern windows, spreading out the daylight, filtering it through an abstract crucifix of blue-white stained glass. Along the side walls, lights create a sequence of shadow arches, adding one more element to reinforce memories of meditation.

A remarkable marriage of sacred and profane elements distinguishes St. Fidelis. The recent, industrial past shines through the church's symbolic transformation like a peasant bride's stark face through a wedding veil. The bride's origins are sturdy and proletarian, and not to be denied. In its overlay of the spiritual and the mundane, St. Fidelis transforms an old workaday building into what the architect describes as "religious space in which man can celebrate his presence on earth."

Main entrance.

Modern Architecture in Quebec
An Introduction

Raymond Affleck

My intimate involvement with architecture in Quebec over the past thirty years has been concentrated on Montreal, perhaps at the expense of smaller centres throughout the province. But the metropolis has played an overwhelmingly predominant role in the development of modern architecture in Quebec.

Montreal's predominance in this respect derives from a variety of factors: location, climate, history, concentration of capital, and, above all, the dynamic interaction of French and English cultures.

In the decades since the war the English community has become increasingly heterogeneous and mobile. The word *anglophone* now includes members of most European and many Asian cultures. On the other hand, as the 1950s opened, French culture was still largely homogeneous, stable, and conservative.

French Quebec is changing radically, becoming at once more typically North American and distinctively Québecois. The effect of this evolution upon the province's architecture is not yet quite clear; but, given the social nature of the art, its impact will most certainly be felt in the coming decades, in the city and in the hinterland.

An important aspect of Montreal's unique role in the development of modern architecture during these years was the role of McGill University's School of Architecture. This school was directed by John Bland for thirty-one years, from 1941 to 1972 — a remarkable record of dedicated service to the teaching of architecture in Canada. These years covered both the formative and the mature periods of modern architecture; years during which the school consistently turned out graduates of high calibre, as well as frequently serving as a focus in the community for architectural and environmental issues.

The third influence I would like to mention is the gradual replacement of European and British influences by American. This was by no means a complete turnaround, but by the mid-1950s, American models in architecture and urban design had become prevalent, far outweighing the earlier tendency to turn to Britain or France for inspiration and precedent.

The development of modern architecture in Quebec can be conveniently divided into three decades — the 1950s, the 1960s, and the 1970s. This division is, of course, somewhat arbitrary. It does, however, help to structure three discernable periods in the overall process.

The 1950s were not a period of great creative activity in architecture in North America, and Quebec was no exception. However, by mid-decade a number of young Montreal architects had begun to experiment with the modern idiom. Included in this early work was the Town of Mount Royal Post Office, the Beaver Lake Pavilion, Mount Royal Park, and more important, the Salle Wilfrid Pelletier, Place des Arts. The latter project has considerable importance in that it signalled a reawakening of the traditional concern for significant public architecture. During this decade there were also some beginnings in the field of modern domestic architecture, largely in the suburbs or vacation areas, often considerably influenced by American or West-Coast Canadian models.

One early modern building of great significance in Montreal was Central Station, designed by staff architects of the Canadian National Railway. This large terminal is an early example of Montreal's pre-eminence in the architecture of movement. Its spacious concourse was destined eventually to play a key role in the development of that city's celebrated weather-protected pedestrian network.

In marked contrast to the stolid 1950s, the 1960s in Quebec, particularly in Montreal, was a decade of incredible creativity and achievement in architecture. In the downtown core it marked the completion of Place Ville Marie and Place Bonaventure, as well as a major segment of the weather-protected network linking these projects to Central Station and the Bonaventure Metro Station.

Place Ville Marie had a great impact on downtown Montreal. Built on air rights over the mainline of the CNR, it is a fine example of high modern style as well as of large-scale comprehensive planning. Place Bonaventure, also built over the railway tracks, provides an interesting contrast to Place Ville Marie's clearly defined geometric forms and paved plaza. This project contains within a unitary form a great variety of urban uses and transportation facilities. The roof-top hotel is notable for the manner in which it weaves together built form and natural landscape.

One of the more innovative developments of this era was the design and gradual implementation of Montreal's weather-protected pedestrian network (sometimes referred to rather misleadingly as the "underground city"). I feel that this system, pioneered in Montreal in the early 1960s, is a genuinely original contribution to the urban architecture of northern cities. Similar systems based on a combination of underground, ground level, and "Plus 15" levels are now widespread in other northern cities in Canada and the United States. The system was first introduced by the CN architects to connect their new Central Station, located in the centre of a downtown block, to surrounding streets. It was vastly expanded and given more class by the designers of Place Ville Marie and subsequently Place Bonaventure.

Another important achievement of this era was the completion of the first stage of the Montreal Metro or subway system. From its inception the Metro Authority followed the policy of commissioning different architects to design individual stations. This resulted in an interesting variety of station architecture. Peel Station and Bonaventure Station are two excellent examples.

This remarkable decade also saw the creation of Expo '67. This World's Fair was unique for its commitment to high-quality planning, landscape design, and architecture. Many individual pavilions were designed with excellence and flair. More important, however, was the achievement of the overall environment; the weaving of landscape and water, the creation of pedestrian systems of great variety and charm and the skilful introduction of innovative transportation systems. In many ways Expo '67 was a microcosm of the creative energy that characterized Montreal during the 1960s. It can also be seen as an advance image of the city of the future — a city designed to cater to the needs of a society whose business is primarily service, communication, and learning.

After the creative high of the 1960s a let-down in architectural achievement was predictable. The 1970s can be characterized more as a period of consolidation than of advance. New structures in the downtown core were generally undistinguished. An exception was Complex Desjardins, a large office-hotel complex organized around a huge enclosed urban room or winter garden; a significant addition to Montreal's weather-protected space. Complex Desjardins also initiated a second north-south pedestrian system including an elegant link to Place des Arts cultural centre and Metro station to the north and a planned connection to the government offices and Convention Centre to the south. In the institutional field two significant projects were completed, the Grand Théâtre at Quebec City and the Montreal campus of the University of Quebec. The latter project provides an interesting example of a compact downtown university connected directly to the Metro. It integrates into its design two historic church façades.

Also during the 1970s Montreal continued its pre-eminence in the architecture of movement. The extension of the Metro produced several excellent new day-lit stations such as Angrignon and Préfontaine, while the new airport at Mirabel provided a cool, elegant environment for harried international air travellers.

This decade also saw the development of a strong commitment to the conservation of the province's fine architectural heritage. This has resulted in the preservation and recycling of many fine buildings as well as the emergence of several projects that combine conservation with new infill structures.

Finally, the late 1970s and early 1980s witnessed the emerging influence in Quebec of that critique of modern architecture generally referred to as Post-Modernism. The concern of this movement for the language of architecture, historic continuity, and context can be seen in the striking ski centre at St. Sauveur in the Laurentians. Also of great significance both for the profession and the public has been the long standing Alcan architectural lectures, a series that has, over the years, brought to Montreal outstanding practitioners and theoreticians from all over the United States and Europe.

Place Bonaventure

Street elevation; rooftop hotel.

Architects: Affleck, Desbarats, Dimakopolous, Lebensold, Sise
Location: Montreal, Quebec
Completion date: 1967
Construction cost: $80 million
Client: Concordia Estates Ltd.
Structural Engineers:
    R. R. Nicolet and Associates;
    Lalonde, Valois, Lamarre, Valois and Associates
Contractor: Concordia Construction Inc.
Project Team: Ray Affleck, Eva Vecsei, J. E. La Riviere, D. Lazosky,
    H. K. Stenman, N. Holloway, R. Khosala, H. de Konig

Place Bonaventure was hailed, upon its completion in the mid-1960s, as representing "a new scale and a new maturity in Canadian architecture." It was welcomed as a break from "the overworked cliches of arbitrary formalism and exotic expressionism which plague architecture today."

Central to the "new maturity" of this massive complex was the collaborative process by which it was designed and constructed. From the project's inception, the architects, engineers, client, and contractor developed the building program as a team. The form of the structure, unusual for its time, arose out of this integrated procedure.

This collaboration covered all the elements of construction. Computer-ised critical path networks, study models, cost analyses, bid packages, and site mock-ups of structural segments such as merchandising corridors and complete hotel rooms were developed collectively. This alternative to the linear procedure of commission-design-construction encouraged what the architects describe as "an extremely rapid, often unpredictable, but most creative mode of clarifying problems and finding solutions."

Place Bonaventure occupies six acres in eastern downtown Montreal, filling a wide railroad cutting at the foot of Mount Royal. The Canadian National Railway Central Station is one block north. Rail tracks and a subway line run under the building. The complex was a key unit locking together the development of this section of the city as part of Mayor Jean Drapeau's ambitious Expo '67 vision.

The seventeen-storey complex is composed of two floors of street-level shopping served by a subway station and pedestrian links, an exhibition hall, a five-level merchandising mart, and a 400-room rooftop hotel. More than a million square feet of office and display space is provided. A plaza, built over an underground garage, opens up the west frontage.

The construction is reinforced concrete frame and cast *in-situ* exterior panels developed as a double-skin "rain screen" wall. The inner skin is aerated concrete block with vertical cavities acting as air chambers to inhibit

Rooftop hotel and section.

capillary suction through the hairline construction joints.

The exposed concrete surfaces inside and out have a variety of finishes — from heavy sandblasted vertical ridging to light sandblasting and smooth ribbed runs. Externally the complex is sculpted with a forceful virility into modulated vertical planes with minimal glazed areas as relief.

The 250,000-square-foot, mezza-nined exhibition hall is structurally dramatic. Thirty-six columns, each nine-by-five feet, at fifty- and seventy-five-foot centres, are connected by deep box-beams and winged ribs. Coffered concrete ceilings, thirty feet above the floor, provide powerful linear visuals to articulate the vast open space. Metal pan drop panels create a full-height service space above the perforated coffers.

The rooftop hotel garden is land-scaped with pools and planting. De-signed to grow mature trees, the slab

is topped with soil and gravel on rigid insulation, fibreglass-reinforced asphalt, and drained concrete fill. Two floors of hotel rooms overlook this garden in the sky with its winter snowscapes and year-round waterfalls.

"We must be able to deal with a pro-gram...in a way that is open-ended and really communicates change — not the static composition which is death to urban design," Ray Affleck has said. "Our concern is with the quality of spaces we experience with all our senses." If Place Bonaventure, a decade and a half down the road, seems a touch dour, its plaza windy and un-peopled, its virile "new maturity" yet endures beyond the fashion of its daunting Brutalist idiom.

Exhibition Hall.

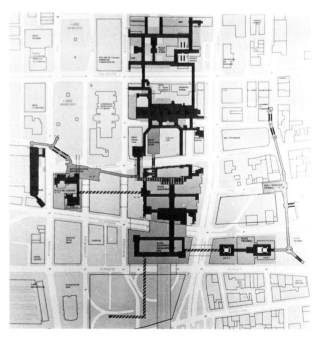

Downtown Montreal: underground linkages.

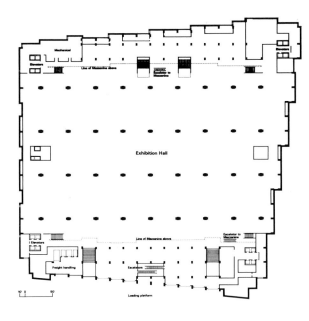

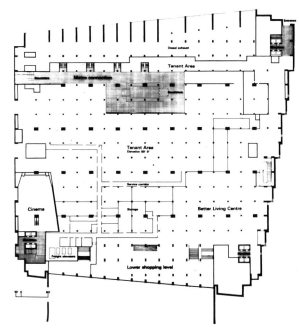

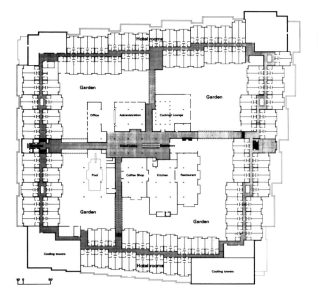

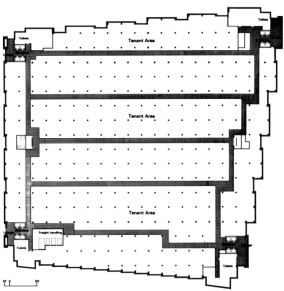

Floor plans and close-up of concrete cladding.

217

Habitat

Modular logic.

Architects: Moshe Safdie; David, Barrott, Boulva
Location: Montreal, Quebec
Completion date: 1967
Construction cost: $22 million
Client: The Canadian Corporation for the 1967 World Exhibition
Structural Consultants: Dr. A. Komendant; Monti, Lavoie, Nadon Associates
Contractor: Anglin Norcross Quebec Ltd.

Construction persists as one of the very few major idustries that remains essentially unindustrialized. Despite the constant proliferation of new products and technologies, building is still largely a process of on-site assembly. Many of the elements are unstandard. If automobiles, for example, were not mass-produced but were put together in the individual and trade-oriented manner most buildings are, Chevrolets would cost as much as houses. This awkward fact has bothered many modern architects. Attempts have been made to mechanize the building process, to mass-produce standard components on factory assembly lines in the hope of reducing unit costs and the need for costly on-site labour.

The results have been too often disappointing. Economic prefabrication, of standard elements or of complete modules, requires long production runs. But buildings are not Chevys, to be stamped out by the thousands. Sites differ, often drastically, and the adaptation of standard units often proves prohibitive. The technology of assembly in place, though considerably mechanized, remains essentially pre-industrial.

Yet, in the 1960s and early 1970s, hopes ran high. The belief that technology could solve urgent urban housing needs, could upgrade standards while reducing unit costs, was buoyant. The vision that mass-production could, by turning out thousands of cheap prefabricated units, free the designer's imagination was central to modern architecture's yearning for an egalitarian yet esthetic Brave New World.

Habitat, part of the development for Montreal's 1967 World Exhibition (Expo '67), was one of the most radically imaginative designs in this hopeful canon. Yet it has, in effect, become a kind of monument to its failure. Like the hopes for Montreal's future, trumpeted in Expo '67 and in a contemporary municipal plan bravely titled *Horizon 2000*, Habitat in the words of a local commentator, actually "masked the reality of approaching decline."

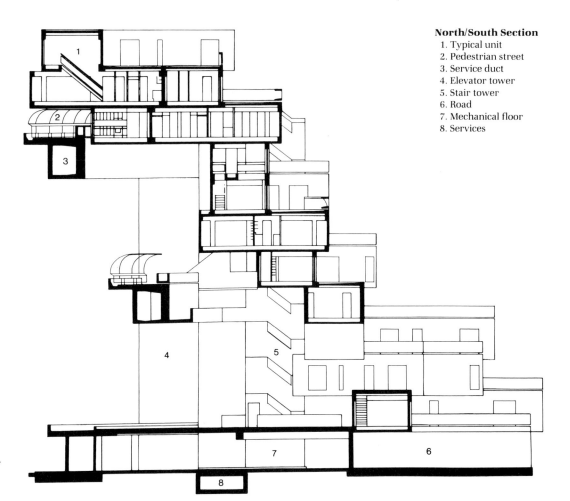

North/South Section
1. Typical unit
2. Pedestrian street
3. Service duct
4. Elevator tower
5. Stair tower
6. Road
7. Mechanical floor
8. Services

Section and aerial view.

219

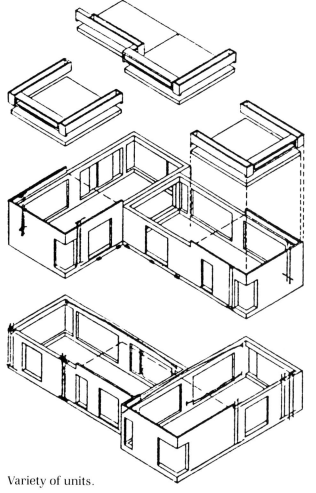

Variety of units.

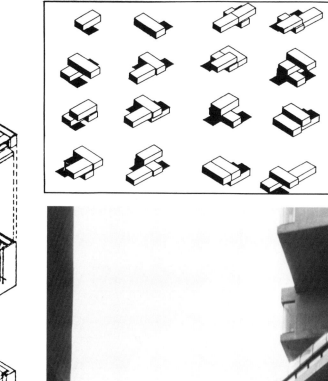

Building modules.

Interior streets.

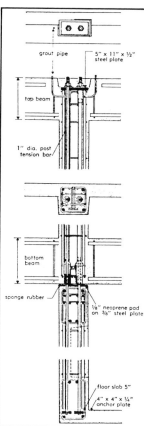

Modular structural
connections.

Habitat is situated on the St. Lawrence River south of downtown Montreal, opposite the Expo '67 site. It comprises 158 dwelling units on eleven levels in three clusters, separated by common entrance gardens. Interior streets at the fifth and tenth levels, combined with horizontal service ducts, link the clusters. Vehicular access and a mechanical plant are on a subfloor.

The basic building module, mass-produced in a temporary on-site factory, is a reinforced concrete unit with out-side dimensions of thirty-six by sixteen feet by twelve feet high. Three hundred fifty-four of these modules are combined in fifteen different housing units, from a 600-square-foot single-bedroom to a 1700-square-foot four-bedroom. Each of the three clusters is arranged around independent stair and elevator shafts. The elevators serve every fourth floor.

The load-bearing modules, manu-factured at a rate of one every two days, were cast complete with floor and walls in hinged steel casting moulds. Rail-riding derricks lifted the precast boxes into position, and kitchen and bathroom units and roofs were dropped in place. All modules were constructed with connection tolerances of plus or minus one-eighth of an inch. The units contain a mechanical sub-floor one foot deep with all services installed, but for plumbing and wiring. The rainwater drainage system is internal.

The modules are interlocked with one another, and with the rigid internal street system that braces against wind and earthquake stress, by post-tensioning. The streets, sheltered by curved acrylic covers, are ten-foot-high girders constructed of precast concrete sections connected by high-tensile cables, grouted and dry-packed at the joints.

Sub-zero temperatures during construction created several problems: prefinishing the modules on the ground required complete weather protection; grouting would not set in extreme cold; localized heating presented major difficulties. Above all, such sophistica-tion of pre-assembly called for an advanced degree of structural analysis and organization. Rigid barriers be-tween trades had to be breached to

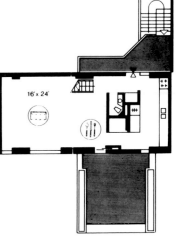

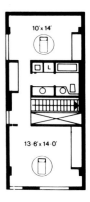

Typical apartment and view over river.

achieve new patterns of labour-man-agement collaboration. As Safdie commented, "the traditional linear, non-overlapping approach [to construction] is as outdated as the piano roll."

Safdie's ambition for an economi-cally mass-produced solution was modified by several factors. Most crucially, the size of the project was cut drastically from 1000 units to 158. Schools, shops, and offices were origi-nally to be included in a self-sufficient urban unit. On account of this radical size reduction, the capital outlay on fabrication machinery represented an abnormally high overhead.

In contrast to the then-prevailing rate of $14 per square foot for multi-storey housing, Habitat's units averaged $140,000 apiece. However, Habitat must be considered as a prototype.

The design resembles a stack of children's play blocks balanced randomly. This loose pattern allows gaps and overhangs and provides each unit with privacy and varying views over the river and the city. Extra modules could have been added for expansion, though this has never happened.

The idiosyncrasy of the design, derived from Mediterranean village models, required many structural modifications. Large overhangs neces-sitated individual reinforcing. Concrete balcony railings and planting boxes added extra loading.

Habitat avoids the monotony of most mass housing. Today it is an up-market condominium complex, much prized by its owners for its quirky chic. It seems at once a visitor from an exotic culture, from a more cheerful climate, and a monument to a now rather faded faith in a Brave New World of egalitarianizing industrialism, the mass-production of popular housing.

The Grand Théâtre

Architects: Victor Prus and Associates
Location: Quebec City, Quebec
Completion date: 1970
Gross floor area: 350,000 square feet
Construction cost: $10 million
Client: Ministry of Cultural Affairs, Government of Quebec
Structural Consultants: Vandry, Bergeron and Associates
Mechanical and Electrical Consultants:
    Paquet, Dutil, Potvin, Trépanier and Masson
Acoustical Consultants: Bolt, Beranek and Newman Inc.
Contractors: Komo-Janin Construction Ltd.

Salle Louis Fréchette.

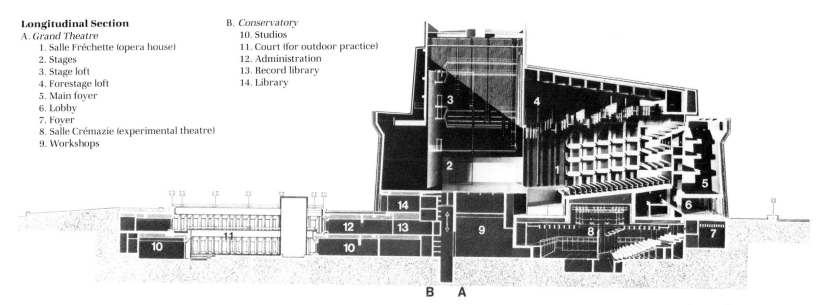

Section and mezzanine foyer.

A major arts complex, funded by government, is as much a statement of official cultural confidence as it is a performing space pure and simple. It is a deliberate act of policy, an attempt to institutionalize a national or regional character, to celebrate a society's aspiration to cultural sophistication.

This aspiration is nowhere more deeply felt than it is in French Canada. In the 1960s Quebec's "Quiet Revolution," spurred by Premier Jean Lesage, coincided with the centenary of Canadian Confederation. Given Quebec's apparent desire for special status in Confederation, cultural projects like the Grand Théâtre, funded jointly by the federal and provincial governments, marked a double celebration — of Canada and of Quebec.

The Grand Théâtre is, in effect, Quebec's national cultural centre. It houses, on a small site on the western edge of downtown Quebec City's parliamentary precinct, a 1900-seat opera house/concert hall/theatre, a smaller 400- to 900-seat performing space adaptable for drama, chamber music, and recitals, and a conservatory of music for 350 students. An evening in the theatre in Quebec City, a provincial capital proud of its long history as the focus of French culture in North America, is, in the architect's words, "a special occasion to be attended with ritualistic decorum."

The theatre's design, which won a national architectural competition in 1964, is suitably decorous and self-aware. The two performing spaces,

223

named for nineteenth-century Quebec poets, are stacked one upon the other to form a block 240 feet long by 180 feet wide. This 60-foot-high temple of culture, with its inwardly inclined, blank, precast concrete walls and columns topped by a pediment of skylights, sits on a podium created by sinking two levels 26 feet below grade. The conservatory of music, added in 1973, has fifty studios arranged around a sunken, open-air practice court with a pool; it is completely below grade, complementing the classic simplicity of the concept.

Patrons enter the temple at its recessed glazed corners. From lobby level visitors go up to the large Salle Louis Fréchette or down to the smaller Salle Octave Crémazie. Stairs and elevators lead to four levels of cantilevered mezzanine foyers wrapped around three sides of the main auditorium. The foyer balconies, which serve the various seating levels within the Salle Louis Fréchette, are enclosed by a 12,000-square-foot concrete relief sculpted by Jordi Bone.

The reinforced concrete proscenium wall of the Salle Louis Fréchette divides the structure vertically. The main auditorium is square in plan. Seating in the balconies and in thirty boxes provides each spectator with a sense of being close to the stage. The space is designed, as Victor Prus explains, "to impart to the audience a sense of self-awareness." Its ceiling is a vast chandelier of transparent, suspended, acrylic tubes topped by small light bulbs. These are interspersed with shallow, acoustic reflector discs. Theatre and foyer walls are finished in sandblasted exposed concrete with ribbed terra cotta block panels between columns.

A twenty-eight-foot-deep forestage, which can be hydraulically lowered to create an orchestra pit for 120 musicians or raised to add 200 extra house seats, forms a transition between the audience and a series of main stages occupying an area three times as large as the auditorium. Equipped with complex mechanical, electrical, and electronic systems, the stages are flexible for the production of operas, concerts, or dramas.

Glazed screen close-up.

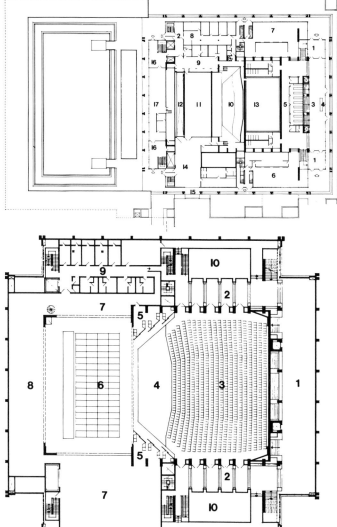

Legend:
1. Public entrance
2. Stage door entrance
3. Lobby
4. Ticket counters
5. Cloakroom
6. Cafe
7. Exhibitions
8. Administrative offices
9. Musicians' dressing rooms
10. Orchestra pit — opera house
11. Trap space — opera house
12. Stage lift — opera house
13. Stage loft — experimental theatre
14. Receiving area
15. Receiving dock
16. Conservatory entrance
17. Library

Floor plans.

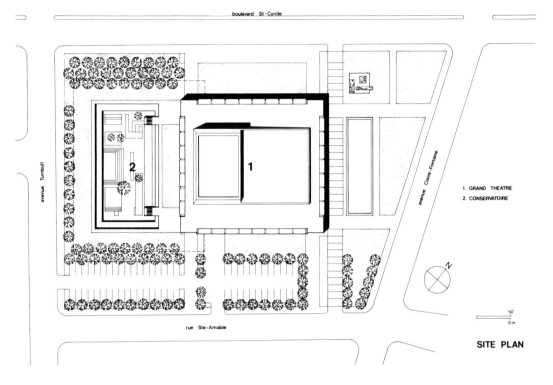

1. Grand Theatre
2. Conservatory

The Salle Octave Crémazie is a much simpler volume approximately a hundred feet square. It has a level floor surrounded on four sides by a continuous mid-height gallery. Above the central stage is a lighting grid with catwalks and a shallow loft for flying minor props. This theatre-in-the-round is adaptable for proscenium productions or for integrated dramas with the adjustment of movable modular bleachers which can be rolled away into storage under the gallery.

Quebec's Ministry of Cultural Affairs is, as Prus writes, "committed to the policy of defending and nourishing French-Canadian culture by all the means at its disposal." Surrounded as it is by a continental sea of anglophones, Québecois society has some sense of being besieged. It is not surprising, therefore, that this temple of official culture has the air of a castle, of a rock-ribbed keep proclaiming, despite the muscular refinement of its design, a somewhat solemn dedication to Quebec's national survival.

Precast concrete walls and columns.

Stairway,
Administration Building.

Hoffman-La Roche Complex

Architects: Marshall, Merrett, Stahl, Elliott and Mill
Location: Vaudreuil, Quebec
Completion date: 1972
Gross floor area: 450,000 square feet
Construction cost: $16 million
Client: Hoffman-La Roche Co.
Structural Engineers: Shector, Barbacki, Forte and Associates
Mechanical Engineers: Keith Associates Ltd.
Contractors: C. M. L. Enterprises Inc.
Project Team: M. N. E. Stahl, M. C. S. Nicolaidis,
    M. H. M. Schauenstein

Main lobby.

A facility producing modern pharmaceuticals must present an image of absolute cleanliness and efficiency. The manufacture of medicines involves such complex chemical processes, fraught with risk and worrying to the consuming public, that a builiding in which drugs are made must look most reassuring.

The buildings designed for this Swiss-based company on the mainland across the St. Lawrence River from Montreal Island are as crisp and white as Aspirin tablets. Situated on a 250-acre site, in a new industrial park surrounded by farmland adjacent to the Trans-Canada Highway, the complex is uncluttered and cleanly profiled.

Four distinct structures make up the first phase of the complex: a fourteen-storey administration building; a three-storey, 230,000-square-foot pharmaceutical production facility including laboratories, packaging, and shipping; a one-storey chemical production unit with control labs; and a 44,000-square-foot power and mechanical service building.

The administration and production buildings are clad in crisply detailed, off-white, precast concrete panels with a smooth exposed aggregate finish. Tinted windows are deeply recessed, the horizontal and vertical planes are boldly articulated to produce strong modelling with deep shadows. By contrast, the mechanical service unit is fully glazed, exposing the complexity of its functions and adding a needed touch of openness. The administration building is constructed of reinforced concrete frame with columns at thirty-six-foot centres on pile foundations. Walls, windows, partitioning, and

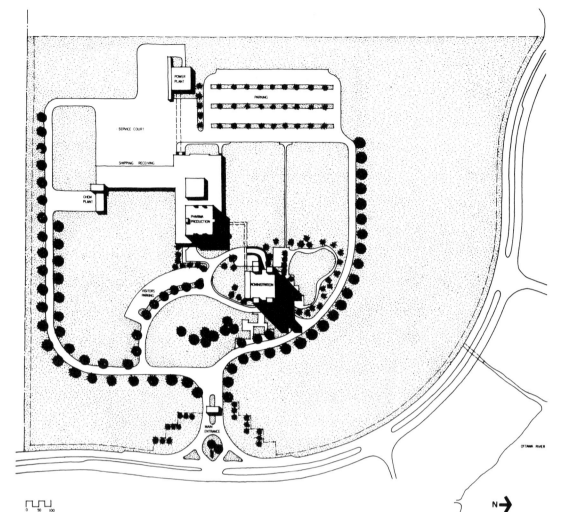

Site plan and general view.

acoustic tile ceilings are designed on a standard five-foot module.

The lower three floors are arranged in mezzanines, as are the top two floors housing a medical library and a conference room. A computer facility, insulated with copper, is situated on the ninth floor. Four elevator, stair, and service towers, expressed as separate elements, free the floor space for flexible office layouts.

The pharmaceutical unit is laid out on a vertical production system. Raw materials, finished products, and waste are moved by elevators, conveyors, and chutes. Laboratories, cold rooms, and warehousing are located on the ground floor. All mechanical services are concentrated underground, connected by service tunnels to the mechanical power house. The flooring in the production area is a jointless epoxy surface.

The three-level power house encloses a boiler room, electrical substation, refrigeration plant, emergency generators, fire protection system, anti-pollution air scrubbers, a dust-extraction system, maintenance shop, and ambulance unit. Steam, chilled water, glycol solution for low-temperature cooling, compressed air, hot water, and power are all distributed throughout the complex from this central control.

Flue gases from the scrubbers are discharged through three freestanding stacks extended twenty-five feet above the power house roof. The stacks, which are insulated to prevent excessive cooling of exhaust air, are enclosed in orange porcelain-enamelled sheet metal. The scrubbers ensure a very high level of pollution control.

Perky metal lamp standards with bulbed heads offset the severity of the architecture. Internal finishes in the reception areas are unfussily detailed, exposed concrete, slotted metal ceilings with flush air diffusers, and glued carpeting. Horizontal and vertical expansion of office and production space is planned.

The architecture of the Hoffman-La Roche complex is simply and strongly stated. It is, in its crisp image of modern pharmaceutical manufacture, both handsome and reassuring.

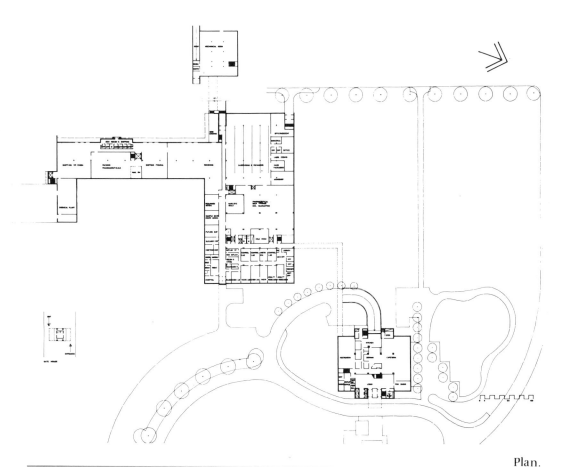

Plan.

Administration Building.

Molson House

Architects: Victor Prus and Associates
Location: Mont Tremblant, Quebec
Completion date: 1974
Gross floor area: 7400 square feet
Construction cost: $350,000
Clients: Mr. and Mrs. Peter Molson
Structural Consultant: Z. Zielinski
Landscape Architect: Maria Prus
Contractors: Rosario Lacasse Inc.

View over the Laurentians.

In a landscape at once gentle and dramatic, Victor and Maria Prus designed what they describe as "a cluster of pavilions to signify settlement in a wild terrain."

The wooded site in the Laurentian Mountains, sloping toward a lake, looks eastwards to the shimmering poplars of Mont Tremblant. Five interlinked pavilions provide a year-round shelter for a family of four. The house, running across a ridge, is approached by a driveway to the south. The land drops away to the lakeshore.

The pavilion roofs are open, boarded pyramids supported on bolted, laminated, cedar "trees" propped on steel pipe columns and brick piers. Their shingled slopes are slight to retain snow for added winter insulation. Continuous copper flashing strips above the eavestroughs help to support the snow load and minimize icing damage. The eaves overhang the fully glazed walls by four feet to shut out the high summer sun and to throw rainwater well away from the house. Each pyramid is capped by a central skylight, or lucerne, that illuminates the interior space.

The five pyramids shelter independent zones for living, for dining, for the master bedroom, for children, and for an open, wire-screened belvedere that juts out into space to catch the summer breezes and give four-way views of water and mountains. An open sculpture court and an enclosed atrium with a cascading ornamental pool fill the inner spaces.

To protect the interiors from harsh winter winds and subzero temperatures, all windows, sliding and fixed, are double-glazed and thoroughly sealed at the junctions. The roofs are packed with six inches of fibreglass mat insulation. Heating is forced-fan electric with flush floor vents. The system switches over to summer cooling.

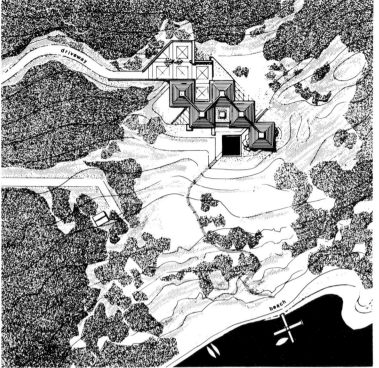

Site plan.

Belvedere.

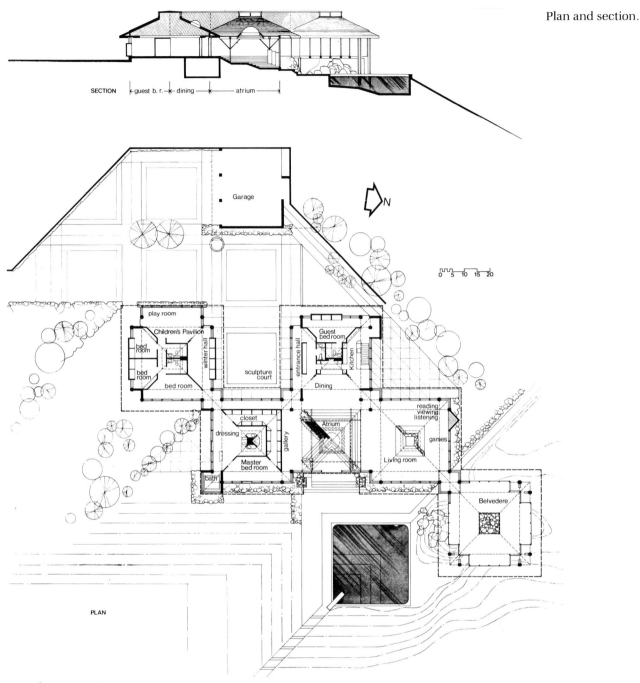

SECTION ⊢guest b. r.⊣ dining ⊢ atrium ⊣

Garage

N

0 5 10 15 20

play room

Children's Pavilion

bed room

bed room

winter hall

Guest bed room

entrance hall

Kitchen

sculpture court

bed room

Dining

closet

dressing

gallery

Atrium

reading viewing listening

games

Master bed room

Living room

bath

Belvedere

PLAN

The central living room fireplace is sunken with surrounding seating. Floors are semi-glazed brick and carpeting. The dining room overlooks an atrium, which can be used for dancing. The long white wall screening the master bedroom becomes a gallery for displaying tapestries, prints, and paintings. The children's pavilion opens onto a sheltered, level, outdoor play space.

The almost Japanese character of the pavilions, which are mutually braced at roof level, is remarkably in tune with this most un-Oriental large-scale landscape. Sensitive siting makes the cedar pyramids seem to float above the slope like a group of turtles skimming over a soft sea. From within, the house feels both sheltering and airy, its wide overhangs like cap brims shading the eyes.

"Architecture is a process of human ecology," Victor Prus has written. "It is continuous in character, concerned with relationships between man and his environment." With his wife Maria, a landscape architect, Prus has achieved in the Molson house a rare relationship between built and natural forms that draws its inspiration from a rich diversity of cultural memories.

Interior views of atrium and living room.

Bradley House

Architect: Peter Rose
Location: North Hatley, Quebec
Completion date: 1977
Gross floor area: 3300 square feet
Construction cost: $200,000
Client: Tim Bradley
Contractor: Sherma Construction Co.
Design Team: Peter Rose, Erich Marosi

Approach elevation in the snow.

Modern architecture, like the contemporary culture from which it springs, has two historic polarities: the classical and the romantic. Modern classicism was formulated by the Bauhaus. Romanticism was developed by folklorists like Frank Lloyd Wright and expressionists like Erich Mendelsohn.

Good architects feel free to choose whatever elements of style they fancy, whatever the dogmas dictate. Le Corbusier, a Marxist and a Modernist puritan, designed the wildly worshipful chapel at Ronchamp with its crustacean shells assembled by an almost Romanesque nostalgia.

Post-Modernism has released a younger generation of designers into a largesse of eclecticism to rival the late Victorian era. The historic as well as the modern past has become, for them, a supermarket of styles to be consumed at one's pleasure.

One great gain from this fresh freedom is the increase in playfulness. The qualities of irony and wit, neglected, along with several other subtleties, by the modern movement, have returned to enrich the visual vocabulary.

The Bradley house is an excellent instance of this free and playful wit. Sitting on a windy, open hill near Lake Massawipi in the Eastern Townships between Montreal and the international border, it resembles, in its manipulations of scale and detail, nothing so much as a blown-up doll's house.

The house is a comfortable four-bedroom residence with pretensions toward mini-mansionhood. It draws its manner and its idiom from the early twentieth-century clapboard country houses of the American eastern seaboard.

Peter Rose admits the manipulation of scale and style. "Part of the art of architecture," he has said, "is to be able to use the tricks of creating a desired scale...[to make]...a small building in the middle of an open field have an appropriate presence."

The Bradley house, the Marosi house in the same district, and Rose's ski pavilion at St. Saveur, are, in the architect's words, "cousins of the existing local buildings, which are a rich variety of styles." Both these residences are intended for year-round occupation in a region of vacation homes.

The timber-framed Bradley house has a severely symmetrical plan, organized around a central hall that rises three floors above a basement to an octagonal gallery and crowning lookout. However, this symmetry is not expressed in section or elevation. An arcaded entrance gallery beside the garages pulls the roofline low into the prevailing wind, so that snow rolls over the house leaving the decks and entry clear.

The lookout, made playful with chimney turrets and dormers, commands a 270-degree view of lake and woods. The clear-glazed, black-trimmed, aluminum windows contrast with the doll's house detailing of the two-tone pine clapboarding and lookout

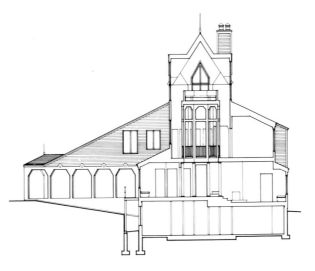

Section and close-up of lookout.

235

The summer landscape.

portholes. Internally there's a free fusion of idioms such as traditional turned balusters and streamlined boarding.

If, at times, the interior detailing lacks invention this is due as much to the scarcity of good craftsmen as to the failure of the designer's verve. Yet this occasional uncertainty lays bare one of the essential vulnerabilities of Post-Modernism: a deeply considered design such as this can slide towards an unwanted cousinhood with developer's mass-produced "Modern Traditional" marketing.

Wit is the crucial ingredient. Eclecticism must be ironic to earn sophistication. Post-Modernism is a playful mode that dances on the knife-edge of cliche with a wry delight.

Central hall.

Floor plans.

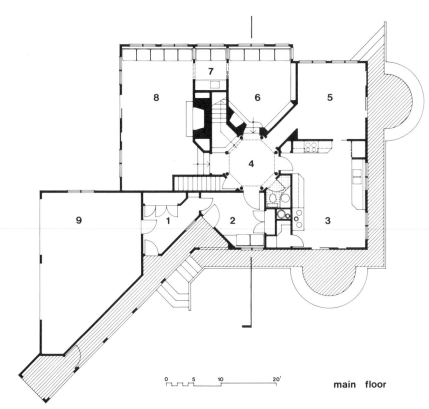

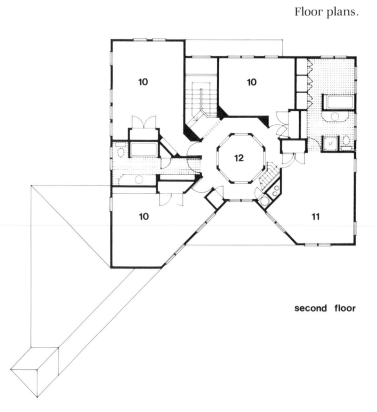

0 5 10   20'

main floor

second floor

237

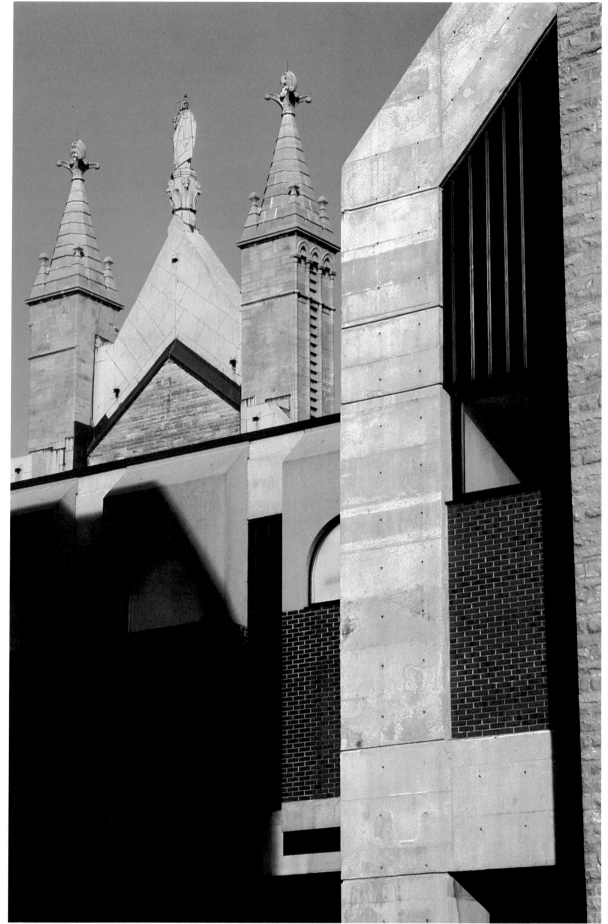

Integration of
old and new.

University of Quebec at Montreal

Architects: Dimitri Dimakopoulos and Partners
Project Architects: Dimitri Dimakopoulos and William Sung
Location: Montreal, Quebec
Completion date: 1978
Gross floor area: 1 million square feet
Construction cost: $65 million
Client: University of Quebec
Structural Consultants: Regis Trudeau & Associates;
    Nicolet, Carrier, Dressell & Associates
Contractor: Donolo Construction Ltd.

A university in the heart of a modern metropolis must strike a complex balance between a cohesive campus and an integration with the city that surrounds it. It has to be at once socially and architecturally distinct, yet take full account of the context of the metropolitan life it serves.

Before the construction of its integrated campus, the University of Quebec at Montreal (UQAM) was scattered across downtown Montreal. The site of the new university, located in the eastern sector of the city's commercial core at the junction of main subway lines, covers two city blocks north and south of St. Catherine Street between Berri and St. Denis streets. A projected second phase of development will occupy a third block along De Maisonneuve Boulevard. The site is historic. Montreal's first cathedral and episcopal palace, burned down in the great fire of 1852, was here. The chapel of Notre-Dame de Lourdes and the steeple and south transept of St. Jacques remain.

This ambience of dreaming spires is contrasted by a subterranean transit network under the site. The northeast corner of the campus sits over a subway station and its underground mezzanines. This connection with the urban transit system links directly with the campus's main circulation pathways. Commercial spaces are distributed along St. Catherine and St. Denis streets, and on a level with the subway mezzanines.

Elevation on rue St-Denis.

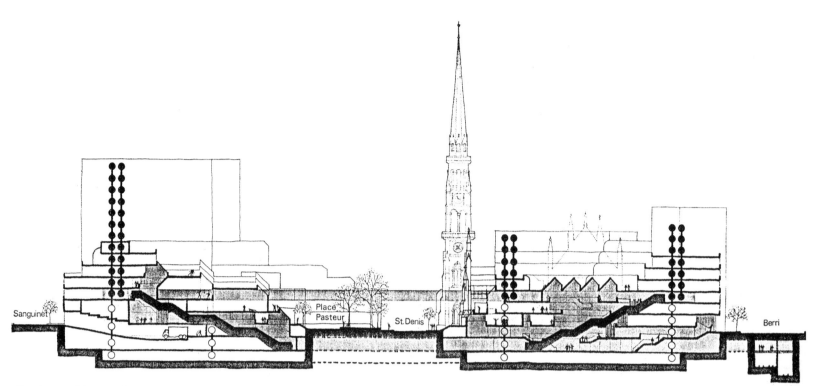

Section and internal court.

Circulation was a major design concern. The planners, faced with the conflict of encouraging easy public access to the campus while preserving academic security, divided movement on two layers. The lower three levels (including grade) have open access from the streets into the inner courts and terraces of the campus. Above this, connected by stairs and escalators, are the specialized university spaces.

The surrounding urban context is respected. Building heights are kept down along St. Denis Street but step up along Berri Street. The steeple and south transept of St. Jacques Church are preserved. The silvered Byzantine dome of Notre-Dame Chapel, not part of the campus, is integrated into the complex with terraced parks.

This sensitivity to context and conservation is a relatively recent phe-

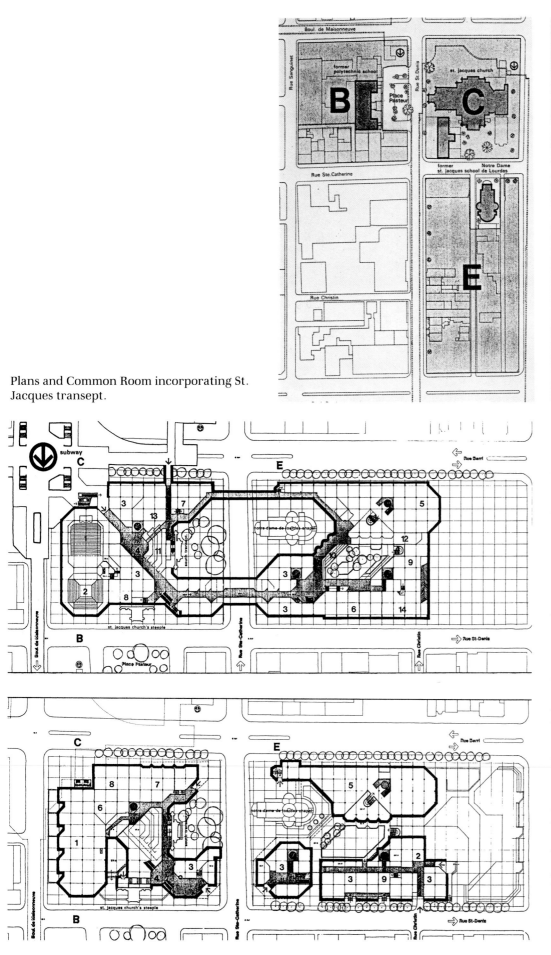

Plans and Common Room incorporating St. Jacques transept.

nomenon in Montreal. The city was, in earlier post-war decades, wide open to developers, who demolished almost a third of the old downtown. However, controls have been tightened under pressure from preservation activists caring for the character of one of the continent's oldest urban centres. UQAM's sensitivity to the historic fabric is one of the major results of this late concern.

UQAM's campus falls into two sections, linked by overhead glass-roofed walkways over St. Catherine Street's commerce. To the north is the cultural centre, an atrium under St. Jacques's south transept surrounded by an auditorium, theatre, arts library and workshops, and student affairs services. To the south is an exterior court enclosed by economics, law, and social science classrooms, a general library, administration offices, and a student lounge.

Construction is of reinforced concrete clad in beige brick. The university's façades are articulated to integrate with the domestic character of its neighbours, broken into bays and balconies to echo the *quartier* idiom. Along Berri Street the scale is more urban, to match the commercial street context. The stone spire of St. Jacques, the rough bulging ashlar of Notre-Dame, provide nostalgic contrast.

Lasalle Metro Station

Architects: Gillon-Larouche
Location: Montreal, Quebec
Completion date: 1978
Construction cost: $4,200,000
Client: Bureau de transport métropolitain de Montréal (BTM)
Structural Engineers: Labrecque-Vézina & Associates
Contractors: Fitzpatrick Ltd.
Design Team: Didier Gillon, Pierre Larouche, Peter Gnass,
    Michèle Tremblay-Gillon

Control mezzanine.

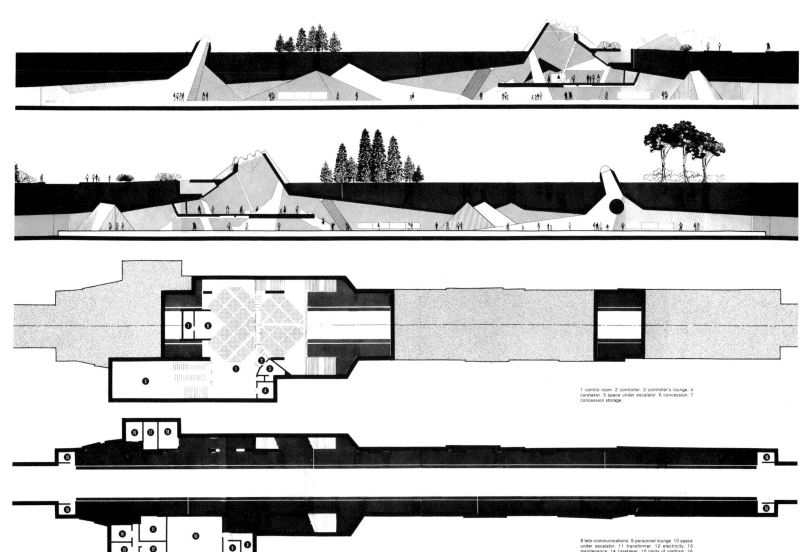

Plans and sections.

There is a natural human resistance to the notion of burrowing underground, except in times of extreme threat from the skies. City dwellers become conditioned to riding subways, but few ever feel quite comfortable. Rapid transit subway riders endure this unease for the sake of speed, but they seldom much enjoy descending beneath the pavement.

The designers of Montreal's Metro seem to have understood this deep reluctance from the inception of the city's system in 1966. From the earliest stations, such as Bonaventure and Peel, to the most recent extensions of the Metro, architects, artists, and engineers have collaborated to produce remarkably enticing underground spaces.

Lasalle Station is one of eight new stops on the fourteen-mile extension of Line Number One, serving sixty-five thousand daily riders from the southeastern suburbs of Saint-Henri, Pointe-Saint-Charles, and Verdun. From the interchange at Lionel-Groulx to the terminus at Angrignon, all the stations are designed to lure the commuter from his comfortable car into the cheaper, more efficient and energy-conserving mass transit.

Lasalle Station is conceived as a subterranean sculpture. At street level, where the station links with bus lines in the old industrial suburb of Verdun, the subway announces its presence with boldly angled thrusts of reinforced concrete. These structures are huge lanterns whose acrylic domes bring natural light and year-round solar rays to the platforms thirty-three feet below.

The passenger descends by escalator to a mid-level, suspended, control mezzanine on which the ticket turnstiles are located. From this vantage point staff can oversee the platforms, and riders can take a breath before descending to the depths. To aid light penetration and airiness, the architects suggested a glass floor to the mezza-

Street level entry,

nine; but this idea was rejected by the client as too bold. Nonetheless this intermediate space is filled with sky light that bounces off the mirrored, stainless-steel mural by sculptor Peter Gnass. This broken silvered surface, contrasted with striated smooth and rough shuttered concrete textures, distracts the subway user from the revulsion of descent, turning entry into the underground into a brilliant act of cinema.

Strong oranges and deep purples set off granite paving at the platform level. The station is oriented north-south, and a south-tilted concrete lantern further down the line brings illumination to the far end of the subway. The tilt of all the lanterns is calculated to bounce sun or moon light into the depth in all seasons, and at all hours of the day and night.

The incised concrete walls and angled ceilings, designed by Michèle Tremblay-Gillon, echo the oblique volumes in a vigorous orchestration of shadows, patterns, and colours so that the waiting passenger's eye is never bored.

Art, architecture, and structural skill have fused in Lasalle to create a drama of travel, transforming the daily act of burrowing underground to go to work, shop, or play downtown into a cinematic experience. This is, as one commentator said, "*un métro sans graffiti.*" More than that, it is both a kinetic walk-through sculpture and an imaginative *coup-de-théâtre*, designed to lighten the hearts of metropolitan moles.

Escalators.

Incised concrete and angled planes.

Nuns' Island Town Houses

Architect: Dan S. Hanganu
Location: Montreal, Quebec
Completion dates: 1980 and 1982
Construction costs: $1.5 million for 18 units per project
Client/Developer/Contractors: Danurb Inc.; Delrive Inc.
Structural Engineers: Alex Stoian; James Teasell
Project Team: Dan Hanganu, Anca Hanganu, Frances Bronet

Corner close-up.

A truly urban domestic architecure is a rarity in Canada. A sense of the city street, a delight in density that is neighbourly without being oppressive, is uncommon. Urbanity implies an acceptance of the collective idiom over individual expression, yet allows each person his own eccentricity.

The *quartiers populaires* of nineteenth-century Montreal provide Canada's most urban housing tradition. Uniform brick façades were elaborated with multilevel balconies and porches with busy balustrades; elevated entrances and outside stairways opened directly onto the sidewalk. Articulated eaves and gables and a screen of trees enriched the idiom. Each floor was an individual apartment; the occupancy was dense. In summer families lived on the balconies, parents watching children play on the street. It was, and is, a style at once very European and particularly Québecois.

In the newly developed Nuns' Island community, close to downtown Montreal and up the St. Lawrence River from the Expo '67 site, Dan Hanganu has designed two sets of townhouses that derive from this urban Montreal tradition.

Each project of eighteen units, on *rue de Gaspé* and *rue Corot*, develops the traditional idiom of neat brick, elevated entrances, sash windows, articulated roofs, and tree screens. Although the setting is suburban, almost semi-rural, the architecture is urbane without being imitative, translating urban history into a Post-Modern manner.

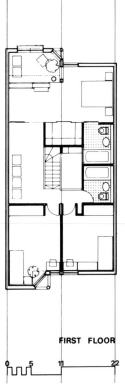

BASEMENT **GROUND FLOOR** **FIRST FLOOR**

0 5 11 22

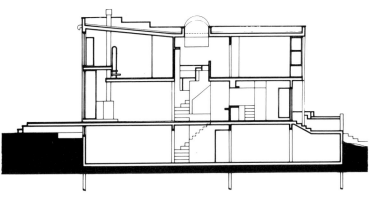

Rue de Gaspé: street elevation, plans, and sections.

The houses in both projects are built with standard twenty-two-foot frontages, grouped in clusters of two, four and six units. Each unit, on two storeys with a basement, contains three bedrooms, two baths, a ground-floor open-plan living-dining space, and a sub-grade garage, furnace, storage, and laundry. Floor area totals 1700 square feet per house.

The plans are neat and economical. A central featured staircase all but eliminates the need for corridors. The constuction is traditional: brick-veneered timber framing for exterior walls, eight-inch concrete-block party walls, and a reinforced concrete basement on piles. An electric furnace fitted with a humidifier recirculates hot air. The sky-lit interiors are sunny and spacious, opening up the narrow widths.

The *rue Corot* lots run down to the river. The *rue de Gaspé* houses open on a forest. These natural milieus set off the urban sophistication of the street façades with a delicious hint of mockery.

Sky lit interiors are sunny and spacious.

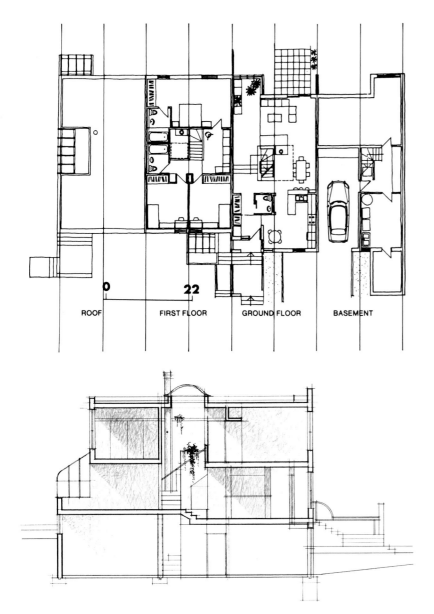

ROOF   FIRST FLOOR   GROUND FLOOR   BASEMENT

Rue Corot: elevation, plans, and section.

The architect has articulated a simple vocabulary of elements into a subtle language at once austere and lively. The capped flat gables are jigged to vary the roof line. Vertical glazing, sash windows, and projecting greenhouses, trimmed in black metal, are carefully judged openings in the beige and rust brickwork. Modern details that recall the classic International Style with a touch of Art Deco add surprise in cutaway corners propped on steel stanchions.

The brickwork is sensitively patterned in panels of stackbond played off against curves. Carved wooden ornaments, saved from demolished buildings, are cleverly inserted. Abstract metal balustrades echo the *quartier* idiom.

Nuns' Island housing is an old vernacular translated by the mind of a Mondrian. The façades are an almost abstract rendering that somehow conjures up a domestic tradition. It is a rare feat of *déjà vu* underlying a look into the future.

249

Poste Viger
Switching Station

Architects: Longpré-Marchand
Partner-in-charge: Claude Longpré
Location: Montreal, Quebec
Completion date: 1982
Gross floor area: 54,000 square feet
Client: Hydro-Québec
Structural Engineer: Fernand Imbeault
Contractor: Duquette Construction Inc.

"Meaning made forcibly plain . . ."

Modern architecture's classic slogan, "form follows function," finds its purest expression in technological structures, where function is so direct it dictates form. Gropius wrote, as early as 1913: "the silos of Canada...the coal carriers on the great railways...offer an architectural composition of such precision their meaning is made forcibly and unambiguously plain." These early grain silos were not "designed" in the architectural sense. Their "natural perfection," as Gropius described it, is difficult to duplicate consciously. Architects seldom achieve the muscular force and simplicity of the potent structures that inspired the fathers of the modern movement.

The Poste Viger switching station for Hydro-Québec comes close. Standing on a tight triangular embankment beside an expressway, this complex gathers the overhead 120- and 315-kilovolt high-tension lines supplying downtown Montreal from the south. The urban site, placed near the centre of the city in an area of mixed industrial and residential renewal, is crowned by a strong symbol of advanced energy.

The site was previously a garbage dump, so special precautions had to be taken to eliminate methane gas seepage. The enclosed and compact switching station is insulated with sulphur hexafluoride, which reduces the surface area required to neutralize heat emission by a factor or six, compared to an open station.

The complex comprises five main elements: switching station, control room, lubrication centre, maintenance workshop, and pylons. These elements are articulated in an L on a grassed embankment built up to allow air currents to circulate under the building.

Concrete, the material of the old grain silos, was chosen to enclose and express the contained force of so much electrical energy. The 39-foot-high, 197-foot-long switching station, the complex's largest unit, is constructed of pale beige ribbed concrete prefabricated wall panels on a poured reinforced substructure and frame. The two- and three-storey ancilliary buildings are constructed in the same method.

The rounded corner, smooth-capped flow of the buildings, empha-sized with horizontal joints incised in the wall panels, is offset by the vertical thrust of the 105-foot-tall pylons that gather in the overhead cables supplying the station. The 200-ton pylons are manufactured of prestressed concrete kept in compression during fabrication to achieve a slim and muscular elegance. They terminate in massive "shoes," as if to trumpet the march of modern energy across the urban landscape.

The massiveness of all this concrete is gentled by landscaping, by wrought-iron fencing, and by brilliantly coloured metal lamp standards. At night, arc lights dramatize the station's sculptural strength, making it a beacon at the gate of the city. The interiors are strictly functional; technology provides its own splendid drama of high power, the humming tension of 315,000 volts with a capacity of 3000 megavolt amps.

In the Poste Viger station form follows function with a "natural perfection" Gropius would have admired for the manner in which "meaning is made forcibly and unambiguously plain." Yet, unlike the grain silos of a less organized age, this structure was designed — which, ironically, makes its formal precision all the more remarkable.

Switching station.

251

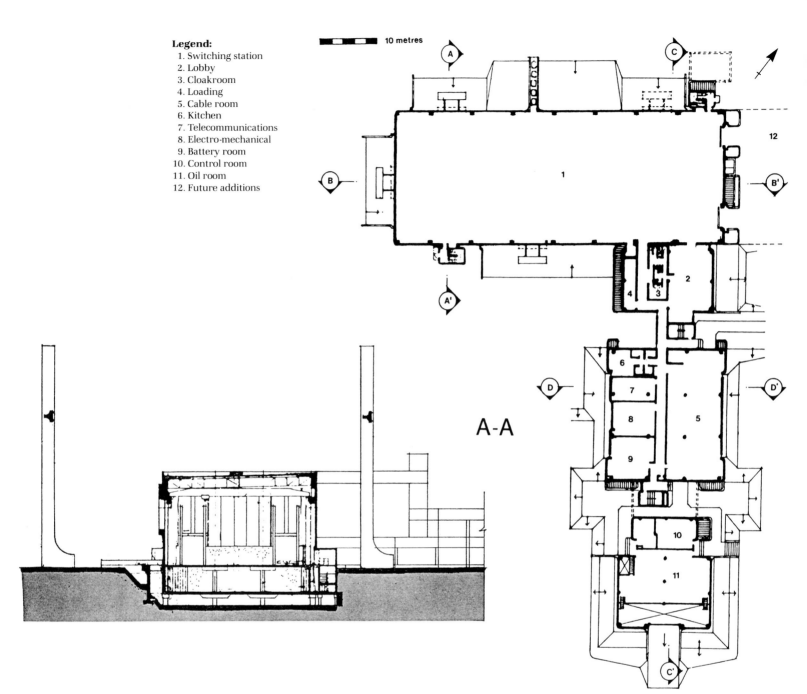

Legend:
1. Switching station
2. Lobby
3. Cloakroom
4. Loading
5. Cable room
6. Kitchen
7. Telecommunications
8. Electro-mechanical
9. Battery room
10. Control room
11. Oil room
12. Future additions

10 metres

A-A

B-B

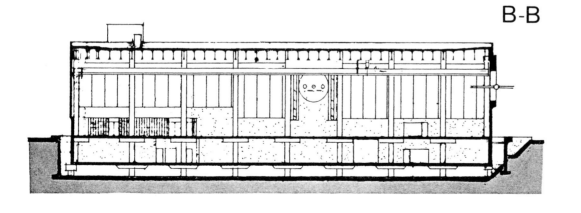

Plans and sections.

10 metres

Pylons gather in
overhead cables.

View from access road.

Fathers of Confederation Memorial Buildings

Plaza and Memorial Hall roof.

Architects: Affleck, Desbarats, Dimakopoulos, Lebensold, Sise,
    with Norbert Schoenauer, Town Planner
Partner-in-charge: Dimitri Dimakopoulos
Location: Charlottetown, Prince Edward Island
Completion date: 1964
Site area: 6.3 acres
Construction cost: $5,600,000
Client: Fathers of Confederation Memorial Citizens' Foundation
Structural Consultants: Adjeleian and Associates
Theatre Design Consultant: George C. Izenour
Contractors: Pigott Construction Co. Ltd.

254

The Centre at night; plan.

The generating impulse for this "national shrine to...the birthplace of their nation" came, ironically, from a group of private citizens who organized a national design competition for this "living monument" to the first Confederation conference held in Charlottetown in 1864.

The "Cradle of Confederation" was the 1847 Provincial Building, a dressed sandstone, three-storey neo-Palladian structure with Ionic porticoes. This solemn civic temple forms the axial focus on Queen Square in the centre of the small city. The new Memorial Buildings complex is asymetrically composed to complement without overwhelming the old capital house.

The design team formulated three planning principles for the complex: first, the historic integration of old and new architectures, which led to the choice of a uniform height matching the pediment of the Provincial Building; second, an acceptance of change and growth in the surrounding city core of which the complex would remain the focus; third, open pedestrian penetration from all points.

The interaction of these three factors encouraged a design that was monumental yet not dead; a cradle that gave a sense of containment while it became the lively heart of a city with a long and significant heritage. The cradle motif is developed by a manipulation of strong horizontal planes stepped up and down from the surrounding streets. In the scooped-out centre, approached down an amphitheatre of steps, sits the low Memorial Hall, the core of the complex. A thousand-seat theatre, a library building, and an archive, museum, and art gallery element occupy three sides of a raised podium confronting the Provincial Building.

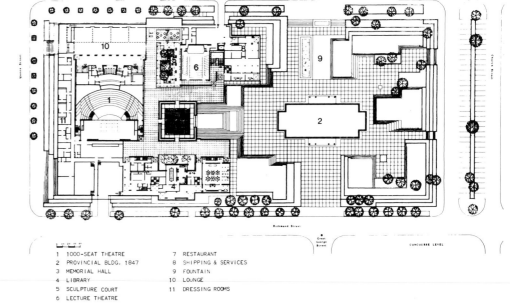

1	1000-SEAT THEATRE	7	RESTAURANT
2	PROVINCIAL BLDG. 1847	8	SHIPPING & SERVICES
3	MEMORIAL HALL	9	FOUNTAIN
4	LIBRARY	10	LOUNGE
5	SCULPTURE COURT	11	DRESSING ROOMS
6	LECTURE THEATRE		

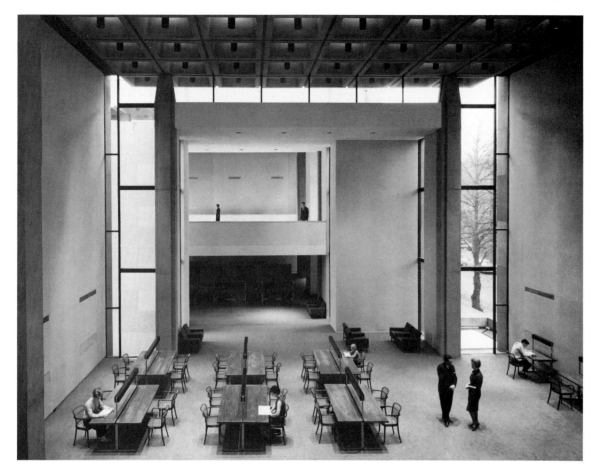

Library.

Sections through theatre
and Memorial Hall.

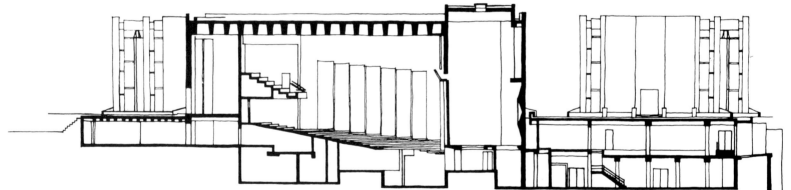

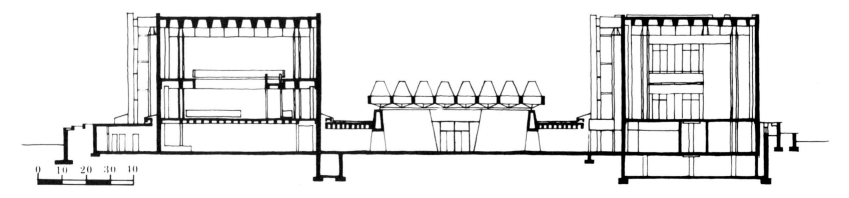

0 10 20 30 40

The enclosing structures are articulated as blank screens of the same reddish-brown Nova Scotia sandstone as the old capital house. Recessed corners with vertical glassed slits lighten the monumentality of these big, dressed stone cubes, which are all the same height. By contrast, the sunken hall is roofed with a crystalline collection of truncated glazed pyramids carried on an open concrete diagrid.

The effect is that of a high-walled cradle protecting a precious jewel, or of a lighted ship in safe harbour. The Memorial Hall is the hub of the complex, surrounded by open-air sculpture courts, connected by underground passages to the other three elements. Its coffered ceiling, flooded by natural sky-light or artificial illumination, casts subtle shadows on the sandblasted exposed aggregate of reddish local igneous beach gravels.

Reinforced concrete rib columns on spread footings support a flat-slab or slab-and-beam structure. The main roofs are eighteen-inch reinforced concrete diagrids at six-foot centres varying in depths of up to sixty-four inches for spans of up to forty-eight feet. Connections with the outer stone skin of the "rain screen" walls are hinged to prevent distortion due to differential expansion. The parabolic theatre roof is post-tensioned with Freyssinet cables.

The stage of the elegant theatre is designed to adapt, with moveable screens and seating, from a conventional proscenium to an apron thrust. Its acoustics, modulated by suspended ceiling baffles, are excellent. The theatre manages to be a performing space at once formal and welcoming.

Detailing throughout is crisp and articulate in a manner of vigorous simplicity set off by an intimate intricacy. No fussiness intrudes to induce premature dating of this "modern miniature acropolis," as one of its designers has dubbed it. The centre functions both as a permanent "homage to the birthplace of a nation," and as the heart of a lively provincial capital.

Theatre.

Brudenell Park Lodge

Architects: Victor Prus and Associates
Location: Brudenell River, Prince Edward Island
Completion date: 1973
Gross floor area: 60,000 square feet
Construction cost: $1 million
Client: Government of Prince Edward Island
Consulting Engineer: L. A. Coles
Landscape Architect: Maria Prus
Contractors: Square-K Construction Co.

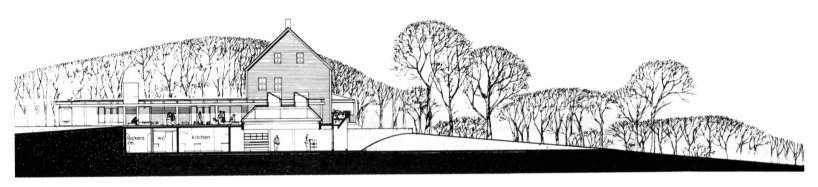

SECTION a-a

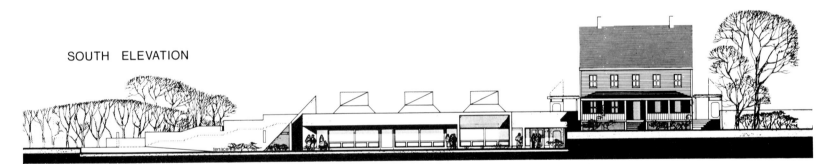

SOUTH ELEVATION

Section and elevation.

Brudenell River Recreational Park occupies the north shore of the Brudenell River twenty miles from Charlottetown, Prince Edward Island's capital. The shore's western marshes give way to tidal beaches in the east. The land rises steeply from the river, then slopes into a central meadowland cut by creeks and inlets, intersected by stands of spruce, maple, and birch planted along former farm boundaries. Coniferous windbreaks cross gentle hills and dales.

In 1970 the architects prepared a study for the region's development as a tourist attraction. The study's overriding concern was to preserve and enhance the park's natural wildness while providing facilities for visiting campers and boaters. Prus aimed for "an inte-gration of natural and human ecology," an enjoyment of this Acadian Eden by motorized tourists.

A complex of "experience circuits" was planned through the park's three main zones — western marshes with nature trails and canoeing; the forested eastern zone reserved for children's summer camps; and a central zone given over to swimming, boating, and golfing. The circuits, projecting beyond the boundaries of the park, allow easy travel with a rich variety of natural and man-made pleasures.

The Park Lodge is the focus of the central zone. An existing three-storey clapboard Georgian farmhouse with a columned and balustraded porch sits atop a rise overlooking a river

Hollowed colonnade surrounding the Lodge.

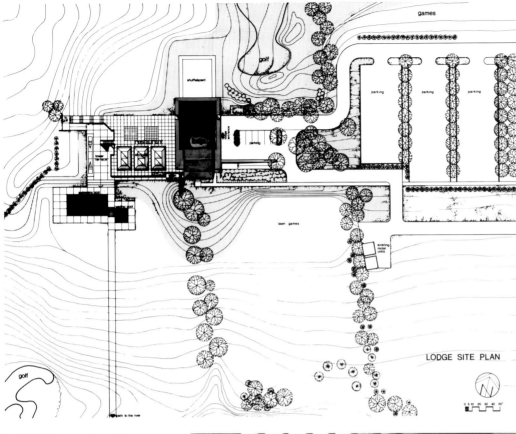

LODGE SITE PLAN

Lodge balustrade and
restaurant skylights.

bay enclosed by a marina. Around this renovated building the architects have designed a modern recreational complex.

The new architecture, though uncompromisingly modern in its use of raw shuttered concrete, complements the old farmhouse and integrates the complex into the landscape's horizontals of ridge, rocky beach, and clouded sky. The house's ground floor is renovated into reception, bar, and lounge areas linked to a new shuffleboard court at the rear and a western terrace that forms a skylit roof over a lower-level dance hall and restaurant beside pools for swimming and wading.

Seen from the shore, the concrete deck horizontals are capped by the three white "sails" of the terrace skylights. The crisp clapboard farmhouse is the "bridge" that crowns this landlocked modern schooner. Up close, the concrete is boldly folded to follow ramped stairs and balustrades, and forms hollowed colonnades supporting pergolas surrounding the lodge. Raw pine softens the cement idiom without distracting from its muscularity.

Prus's design philosophy has been described as an "Architecture of Condition...an interplay between intuition and reason that finds its meaning in experience rather than expedience." Trained in Warsaw, Paris, and London before coming to Canada in 1952, Prus acknowledges the major influences of Le Corbusier and Buckminster Fuller, with whom he studied.

On a deeper level, in Brudenell Park, as in all his designs, Prus reveals an innate European reserve, a respect for the givens of nature and the manmade vernacular, that allows him to be thoroughly modern without trampling the complex natural and human inheritance.

"White sails;" —
terrace and skylights.

Sculptural concrete.

Newfoundland Telephone Company Head Office Building

Architects: Shore, Tilbe, Henschel, Irwin, Peters;
    Sheppard, Burt, Pratt and Short
Co-ordinating Architects: Steve Irwin, John Dobbs
Location: St. John's, Newfoundland
Completion date: 1981
Gross floor area: 240,000 square feet
Construction cost: $12 million
Client: Newfoundland Telephone Co.
Construction Management: Project Management Design Ltd.;
    J. S. Watson and Associates Ltd.

Atrium bridge.

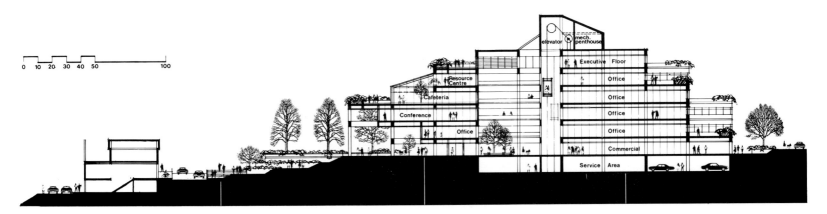

Architectural "good manners" are a relative rarity in contemporary design. Much of the time clients and designers desire distinctiveness rather than discretion. Even in a rapid-growth, highly urban context such assertiveness can be distracting. In the setting of a small, settled city like St. John's the effect of striving to be more striking than one's neighbours could be devastating.

The new headquarters for the Newfoundland Telephone Company is a well-mannered, yet most handsome building. Set on the historic Fort William Hill site, on the boundary between the waterfront city's medium-rise downtown and its residential districts, the building achieves as harmonious a skyline with the existing fabric as such a relatively large structure could manage. Seen from the harbour, the six-storey building's stepped and terraced silhouette, faced with a warm red brick common to the city, is dramatic without imposition.

Glazing, tinted and anti-glare, is kept to a minimum, both to conserve energy and to respect the protective architectural vernacular of St. John's hard climate. The only lavish area of glass is the angled skylight over the double-height cafeteria and lounges of the mezzanine conference centre on the upper floors, giving splendid views over the water. This feature is suspended over the undercut entrance that is approached across a landscaped forecourt and through an open display of the exposed white structural skeleton.

The structure is reinforced concrete with thirty-foot-square column bays. A sixty-foot-square toplit atrium forms the core of the building, rising through six floors. Glass-fronted elevators open

Section and view from waterfront.

on the atrium. The beige plastered parapets are articulated in a series of stepped horizontal bands accented by planting boxes. A fourth-floor bridge links the elevators with the cafeteria.

The major portion of the floor space is given over to offices for the company's seven hundred fifty employees. Conference rooms, a computer centre, equipment spaces, lounges, and ground-floor shops occupy the remainder. Rust-coloured, synthetic fibre carpeting is glued to the screed in all office areas. Parking for thirty-five company cars is provided in the underground garage, with further surface parking at the rear of the building to the north of the four-and-a-half-acre site.

263

Site plan and visual context.

The office lighting is coffered — increasing its relfective efficiency — and controlled by photo-electric dimmers. The illumination areas are zoned and separately switched to allow for the effect of daylight around the perimeter. Heat from the lights is recycled by the ventilation system to the mechanical penthouse, where it is used to pre-heat the fresh-air intake. Waste heat from the computer suite and telephone equipment rooms is channelled to the parking garage. Combined with the building's use of electrical heating, this recycling has held energy consumption

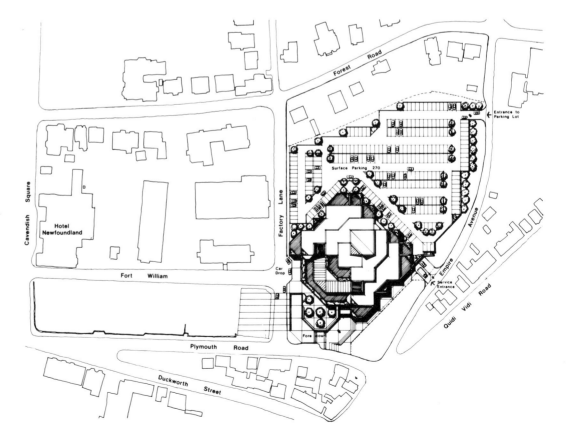

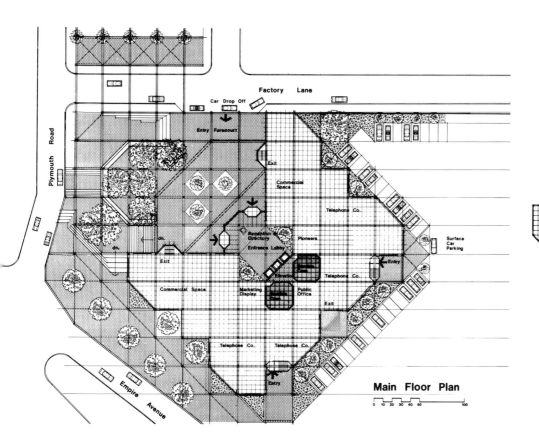

Main Floor Plan

0 10 20 30 40 50   100

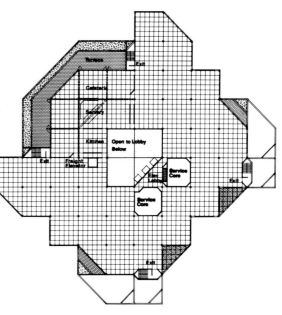

Fourth Floor Plan

0 1½ 3 6   9   20   30

down to a highly economical level of sixteen kilowatt hours per square foot per year. Small-bore ducts and fans aid in reducing energy costs by more than half that of a conventional system.

The massing of the building, whether looked down upon from the vantage of Signal Hill Park, or up at from waterline level, or at grade against the St. John's skyline, is always complex and composed without being overscaled. The structure is handsome and discreet from any angle; it is thoroughly well-mannered.

Plans and cafeteria over entry.

Arctic Research Laboratory

The laboratory in the landscape.

Architects: Papineau, Gérin-Lajoie, Le Blanc, Edwards (PGL Architects)
Location: Igloolik, Northwest Territories
Completion date: 1973
Gross floor area: 5000 square feet
Client: Federal Ministry of Public Works and Housing
Structural and Service Consultants: St-Amant, Vézina, Vinet, Brassard
Fibreglass Contractors: Polyfibre Ltd.
Steel Frame Contractors: Canron Ltd.

Two-fifths of Canada's land mass lies north of the sixtieth parallel. This vast region, one and a half million square miles comprising the Yukon and the Northwest Territories, is inhabited by seventy-thousand people, an ethnic mix of Europeans, native Indians, and Inuit. The region is bisected by the Arctic Circle. Its topography is mostly tundra plains of permafrost formed on the rocks of the Canadian Shield. Its climate is extreme, with low precipitation. Only four months of the year, June to September, have average temperatures above zero Celsius. The settlement of Igloolik is on a small, isolated island at the tip of the Melville Peninsula on Foxe Basin. This is south of Baffin Island and well north of the Arctic Circle.

Such severe conditions require radical architectures. New technologies are needed to replace the Arctic tradition of the Eskimo igloo, the Indian tepee, and the trapper's cabin. In the Igloolik research laboratory, and in other structures at Frobisher Bay further to the south designed by the same architects, steel and fibreglass prefabrication provides a solution.

The laboratory is a circular, mushroom-shaped building on two levels. The lower level houses entrances, storage, service, and equipment facilities. The upper level has a sky-lit, central conference and multipurpose room ringed by cantilevered offices and laboratories.

The steel skeleton was prefabricated in Ottawa, shipped in during the brief open-water summer season, and assembled on site by a field erection crew provided by the fabricator. Eight steel core columns twenty-six feet tall are set in a concrete substructure that allows a two-foot-six-inch space between the slab and the footings to preserve the permafrost.

Eighty-six light-weight steel trusses weighing 500 pounds apiece cantilever twenty feet from the circular perimeter beams to form the upper floor and roof structures. Vertical steel ties join the two levels at the perimeter, forming a rigid frame on which the cladding can be fixed. The upper level is seventy-two feet in diameter. Connections are site-welded or fastened by high-tensile steel bolts.

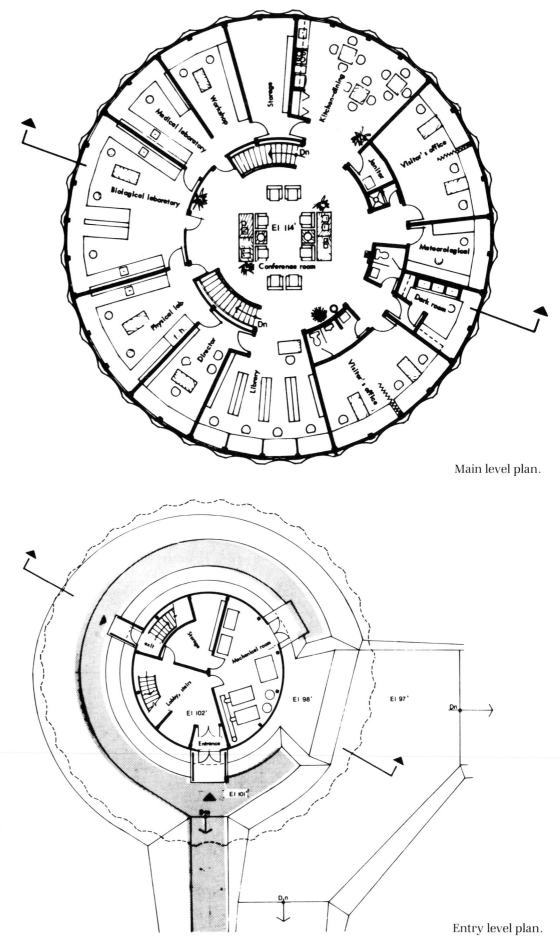

Main level plan.

Entry level plan.

Section.

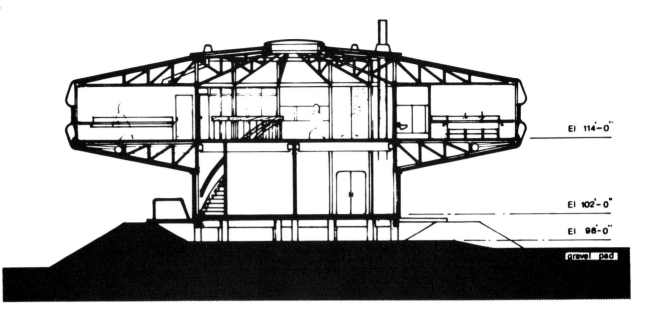

EI 114'-0"

EI 102'-0"

EI 98'-0"

gravel pad

Structural
steel skeleton.

The ground floor is constructed of insulated concrete sandwich slabs. The first floor is twenty-two-gauge, zinc-coated, sheet-steel decking topped with concrete slabs that are either carpeted or exposed and polished. In the labs a full gypsum ceiling is installed for fire and sound insulation.

Fibreglass reinforced plastic (FRP) was chosen by the architects as a skin for its excellent strength-to-weight ratio, its integral rigidity in withstanding windloads of up to hurricane force, its ease of erection with no necessity for heavy equipment by unskilled local labour, and its esthetic and maintenance properties.

The prefabricated fibreglass panels are stressed-skin sandwich units packed with two inches of polyurethane foam. Combined U value is 0.067. Bolted connections are designed in detail to ensure an absolute thermal seal. Interior and exterior surfaces are integrally coloured and polished. The panels are self-supporting between the steel-truss perimeter rings to which they are fixed. Windows are triple-glazed and vacuum-sealed, inserted in the panels in much the same way as windows are inserted in aircraft.

While the base cost of FRP was higher than more conventional materials — $12 per square foot of wall installed — savings were made in speed and simplicity of erection. FRP is durable, light, and uncomplicated. On several sites in Frobisher Bay, including schools and a large arena, Inuit labour was trained to fabricate the fibreglass locally, reducing costs by up to one-third.

Canada's North has a harsh beauty all its own. For much of the year it's an ice desert splendid in its hostility to man. Its silences are resonant, its landscapes magnificently primal. Human architecture, in this Olympian context, faces challenges uniquely physical and spiritual.

The Igloolik laboratory is both technically sophisticated and formally simple. It updates the clear geometry of traditional arctic building forms. Its simplicity of shape and detail, which might seem crude in a gentler region, fits the hard North.

Fibreglass skin.

269

Architects' Biographies

RAYMOND AFFLECK: born Penticton, B.C., 1922; graduated McGill University, 1947; post-graduate studies in Zurich. In 1953 Affleck formed group partnership in Montreal with Desbarats, Dimakopoulos, Lebensold, and Sise to design and administer major projects in Quebec, elsewhere in Canada, and abroad; the core of this partnership was later incorporated as ARCOP Associates. Affleck has also taught architecture at several universities and technical colleges.

JOHN ANDREWS: born Australia, 1934; graduated Sydney University, 1956; post-graduate degree, Harvard, 1958. A finalist in Toronto City Hall competition, he joined John B. Parkin Associates, 1958. Chairman of the University of Toronto School of Architecture. Established own firm in 1962, in Toronto. In 1970 Andrews returned to Sydney where his practice has been responsible for major projects such as the King George Tower and Cameron Offices.

ERNEST ANNAU: born Hungary, 1931; emigrated to Canada, 1951; graduated University of Toronto and Technical University of Munich, West Germany, 1963. A principal of Annau Associates since 1972, Annau has designed a wide variety of projects across Canada and has received many awards. He has also won a number of competitions for social housing and low-energy building design.

ADAMSON ASSOCIATES: founded in 1934 by Gordon Adamson, the firm was expanded in 1962, and includes a section dealing with structures. Gar MacInnes of Adamson is the principal designer of the North York Municipal Building and a graduate of the University of Toronto, 1959.

JOOST BAKKER: born Willemstad, Curacao, 1945; emigrated to Canada, 1952; graduated University of Toronto, 1974. Bakker, whose chief interest is urban housing, became a consultant with Norman Hotson Architects, Vancouver, in 1977.

DOUGLAS CARDINAL: born Red Deer, Alberta, 1934; graduated University of Texas, 1964. Cardinal set up practice in Red Deer then moved to Edmonton. His practice specializes in governmental, educational, and religious facilities, and hospitals; St. Mary's Church, Red Deer, was Cardinal's first major commission.

GUSTAVO DA ROZA: born Macao, 1932; graduated University of Hong Kong, 1955. Da Roza practised and lectured in Hong Kong and California before emigrating to Canada in 1961, where he established the firm of Da Roza Architects in Winnipeg. He has been visiting lecturer and design critic at numerous schools of architecture in Canada, the United States, and the Far East.

DIMITRI DIMAKOPOULOS: born Athens, Greece, 1929; graduate of Athens University and McGill University, Montreal. He emigrated to Canada, 1952. In partnership with Affleck, Lebensold, Desbarats, Michaud and Sise, who have won several major competitions, including Vancouver's Queen Elizabeth Auditorium and Fathers of Confederation Centre in Charlottetown, P.E.I. Collaborated with I. M. Pei in design of Place Ville Marie, 1955 to 1960. Now a principal of Dimitri Dimakopoulos and Partners, Montreal.

MACY DU BOIS: born Baltimore, Maryland, 1929; graduate of Tufts University and Harvard, 1958. Emigrated to Canada, 1958. Established practice of Fairfield and Du Bois, later DuBois and Plumb and Associates, with Helga Plumb. Du Bois has been responsible for many major projects, including the Ontario Government Pavilion at Expo '67, Casa Loma Campus of George Brown College, and the Joseph Shepard Building. He is visiting professor at several universities.

ARTHUR ERICKSON: born Vancouver, 1924; graduated McGill University, 1950. Erickson was a professor at the universities of Oregon and British Columbia. In 1963, in partnership with Geoffrey Massey, Erickson won the competition for Simon Fraser University. In 1972 Erickson formed the firm of Arthur Erickson Architects with offices in Vancouver, Toronto, and Los Angeles. His major projects include Lethbridge University, Alberta, and Roy Thomson Hall, Toronto.

ETIENNE GABOURY: born Swan Lake, Manitoba, 1930; graduated University of Manitoba, 1958. Gaboury joined the firm of Libling, Michener and Associates, started his own practice in 1961, and was associated for a period with Lussier and Sigurdson. Gaboury has designed a number of religious buildings, including St. Boniface Cathedral, Winnipeg, as well as the Canadian Embassy in Mexico City.

GUY GÉRIN-LAJOIE: born Montreal, 1928; graduated McGill University, 1956. Gérin-Lajoie is a principal and founder of PGL Architects, Montreal, and PGL International Ltd.; the practice has completed many major projects in North America and the Middle East, including schools, universities, and airports, and structures designed for arctic conditions.

DIDIER GILLON: born Brussels, Belgium, 1938; graduated, Saint-Luc Institute of Architecture, 1962. Head of department of architecture at Lovanium University, Kinshasa, Zaire. Emigrated to Canada, 1965. Architect and urbanist with several firms in Montreal until the establishment of Gillon-Larouche and Associates Ltd. in 1972.

BARRY GRIBLIN: born Regina, Saskatchewan, raised and educated in Calgary, Griblin graduated from the University of British Columbia in 1965. He joined the Toronto office of Ron Thom, was involved in planning and design of Trent University. In 1969 he formed partnership with Robert Hassell which concentrated on residential projects. Griblin now maintains own practice in North Vancouver.

IRVING GROSSMAN: born Toronto, 1927; graduated University of Toronto, 1950. Grossman set up a practice in Toronto in 1954 concerned mainly with community-oriented projects such as multiple-housing developments like Flemingdon Park and Edgely Village. Has also designed a number of synagogues and senior citizens' facilities.

DAN HANGANU: born Bucharest, Romania, 1939; graduated University of Bucharest, 1961. Emigrated to Canada, 1970. Hanganu worked in several offices in Toronto and Montreal before setting up his own practice in 1976 in Montreal. He has won a number of awards for projects in Romania, the Soviet Union, Morocco, Switzerland, and Canada.

ROBERT HASSELL: born Vancouver, 1940; graduated University of British Columbia, 1967, then set up in practice with Barry Griblin and others, refusing to register as an architect.

PETER HEMINGWAY: born and educated in England, Hemingway emigrated to Canada in 1955 and established his own practice in Edmonton. He has written extensively on architecture for a number of periodicals.

RICHARD HENRIQUEZ: born Jamaica, 1941; graduated University of Manitoba and Massachusetts Institute of Technology, 1967. Henriquez, in partnership with Donald W. Taylor, has designed several prominent projects, including Gaslight Square and English Bay Village, Vancouver.

NORMAN HOTSON: born Toronto, 1946; graduated University of Toronto, 1969; Hotson worked in Toronto with Ron Thom and Crang and Boake Architects before moving to Vancouver in 1971. In 1973 he set up his own practice specialising in urban renewal projects.

RANDLE IREDALE: born Calgary, Alberta, 1929; graduated University of British Columbia, 1955. In practice since 1958, first as Rhone and Iredale, he has carried out projects such as Simon Fraser University's Science Complex and the University of British Columbia's Sedgewick Library. Iredale founded Tecton Structures to develop prefabricated, modular building systems. Merged now with other companies, Tecton became a major contractor for such structures in the province.

STEPHEN IRWIN: born Toronto, Ontario, 1939; graduated University of Toronto and Harvard, 1963. Irwin worked in Sweden and Britain before joining Shore and Moffat and Partners in 1964. In 1971 Irwin was appointed a partner in the firm of Shore, Tilbe, Henschel, Irwin, Peters.

RONALD KEENBERG: born Winnipeg, Manitoba, 1941; graduated Pratt Institute, New York, 1965. A founding partner of IKOY Architects in 1968 with Yamashita, Stratton, Scherle, Ellard and Blakey. IKOY Architects has been responsible for a number of projects on the Prairies and in Florida, particularly in the field of housing.

ROGER KEMBLE: born Hull, England, 1929. Emigrated to Canada, 1951. Registered as an architect in British Columbia, 1959. Kemble commenced private practice in 1960, completing over a hundred custom-designed residences in the lower mainland area for which he has received many awards.

VINCENT KWAN: born Hong Kong; emigrated to Canada in 1966 after graduation from the University of Hong Kong. Established partnership with Roger Romses as Romses Kwan and Associates in 1973 in Vancouver. The firm has designed a number of residential and commercial projects in British Columbia, as well as the Chinese Cultural Centre in Vancouver.

PIERRE LAROUCHE: born Victoriaville, Quebec, 1929; graduated McGill University, 1957, Yale University, 1964. Larouche has been an engineer with various regional planning boards in Quebec and a consultant to a number of official bodies in connection with urban design and revitalization in and around Montreal. Associated since 1972 with Didier Gillon.

JACK LONG: emigrated to Canada from the United States in 1960. Worked with Vincent Kling in Philadelphia, and in New York and Washington, D.C. with I. M. Pei after graduating from Pennsylvania State College. With his associates in The New Street Group, Long has designed the Calgary Planetarium and a prototype neighbourhood improvement program for the Inglewood Community, as well as an urban-space handbook for Calgary's Urban Renewal Area, the site of the Court and Remand Centre.

CLAUDE LONGPRÉ: born Montreal, 1924; graduated L'École des beaux-arts de Montréal, 1951. Partner in a number of firms since 1953, now with Les Architectes Longpré-Marchand, Montreal. Longpré has been design collaborator on numerous projects in the fields of research, power generation, education, residential, commercial, and industrial design in Canada and abroad.

ROCCO MARAGNA: born 1947, Abruzzo, Italy; emigrated to Canada, 1958; graduated University of Toronto, 1971, Harvard University, 1977. Commenced practice in 1974, winning several major design awards. Maragna has also taught at universities in Italy and Canada.

GILLES MARCHAND: born Victoriaville, Quebec, 1924; graduated, L'École des beaux-arts de Montréal, 1950. Senior partner in a number of firms, now with Claude Longpré in Les Architectes Longpré-Marchand.

JEROME MARKSON: born Toronto, Ontario 1929; graduated University of Toronto, 1953. Commenced private practice in 1955. Projects include many private houses and public housing such as the David Archer Co-operative and Market Square, Toronto; the Jewish Community Centre, Willowdale; and group medical centres in St. Catharines and Sault Ste. Marie, Ontario.

MMP ARCHITECTS: successors to Moody, Moore and Partners; Duncan Rattray Peters Searle; Architects Consortium; and McFeetors and Sedun of Winnipeg, Manitoba.

RAYMOND MORIYAMA: born Vancouver, 1929; interned by federal government with other Japanese Canadians during the war; graduated University of Toronto, 1954, McGill University, 1957. Commenced private practice in 1958. Projects include Ontario Science Centre, Japanese Canadian Cultural Centre, Toronto; Sudbury Science Centre; and a master plan for the Meewasin Valley Project, Saskatchewan.

BARTON MYERS: born Norfolk, Virginia; graduated University of Pennsylvania. Worked with Louis Kahn before emigrating to Canada, 1968. Established practice with Jack Diamond in Toronto as Diamond and Myers until 1975. Has taught architecture in Toronto and Waterloo, and lectures widely in North America and Europe.

COSTAS NICOLAIDIS: born Kastoria, Greece, 1937; emigrated to Canada, 1947; graduated McGill University, 1963. Partner in Marshall and Merrett; Stahl, Elliott and Mill; and Stahl and Nicolaidis.

JOHN C. PARKIN: co-founder, John B. Parkin Associates, 1947; partner in charge of design, 1947-1968; senior partner, Parkin Architects, Engineers, Planners, 1968-1971; senior partner, Parkin Architects Planners, 1971-1976; principal, Parkin Partnership from 1976. Parkin's practice has been responsible for a number of highly visible and influential projects, including Terminal One and Control Tower, Toronto International Airport; and Ortho Pharmaceutical (Canada) Ltd.; and, with Viljo Revell, the Toronto City Hall.

HELGA PLUMB: born Bruk, Austria, 1939; emigrated to Canada, 1959; graduated University of Toronto, 1963. Partner with Macy Du Bois in Du Bois, Plumb and Associates since 1979. Plumb has taught in several universities in Canada and the United States.

VICTOR PRUS: born Warsaw, Poland; studied architecture, engineering, and urban design in Poland, France, and Britain before emigrating to Canada in 1952. In 1954 commenced practice with wife Maria in Montreal. Major projects include Bonaventure Metro Station and Montreal's new Convention Centre.

ROGER ROMSES: born Tompkins, Saskatchewan; graduated University of British Columbia, 1962. Worked for various firms in the Vancouver area until setting up practice with Vincent Kwan in 1973, as Romses Kwan and Associates.

PETER ROSE: born Montreal, 1943; graduated Yale University, 1966. Rose was a partner in the firm of Rose Righter Associates until 1976, when he established Peter Rose Architects in Montreal. He is a founder and co-ordinator of the Alcan Lectures in architecture and has been visiting critic at a number of Canadian and American schools.

MOSHE SAFDIE: born Haifa, Israel, 1938; emigrated to Canada, 1954; graduated McGill University, 1961. Worked with Louis Kahn in Philadelphia before setting up practice in Montreal in 1964. Active since then as a practicing professional, a teacher and a writer. In 1970 Safdie was commissioned to design Coldspring New Town, Baltimore, Maryland; he is also engaged in the restoration of Jerusalem's Old City and the planning of a new city in Senegal, and for the North Station Area in Boston, Massachusetts, where his practice is now located.

NICHOLAS STAHL: born Somerset, England, 1923; emigrated to Canada, 1952; registered as an architect, 1964. Joined the firm of Marshall and Merrett (founded by E. I. Barott in 1912) and has held partnerships in consecutive practices until, in 1980, he established the practice of Stahl and Nicolaidis. The firm's major projects include the head office for Gillette of Canada and various technical and educational buildings in Quebec and Ontario.

LESLIE STECHESEN: born Fort William, Ontario, 1934; graduated University of Manitoba, 1957. Stechesen was head of design for Libling Michener and Associates in Winnipeg before establishing his own practice in 1971, later joined by Frederickson and Katz. The partnership is currently Stechesen Katz Architects.

JAMES STRASMAN: born Penticton, British Columbia, 1937; graduated University of British Columbia, 1962. Strasman worked in Montreal for Victor Prus; in Lugano, Switzerland, for Guido Borella; and for Erickson Massey in Vancouver before setting up his own practice in Toronto in 1976.

TED TESHIMA: born Vancouver, 1938; graduated University of Toronto, 1962. Joined Raymond Moriyama's practice in 1962 and became a full partner in Moriyama and Teshima, Architects, in 1970.

RON THOM: born Penticton, British Columbia, 1923. Partner in practice of Thompson, Berwick, Pratt and Partners in 1958. In 1961 Thom won competition for University of Toronto's Massey College and set up practice in Toronto. Major projects include the Shaw Festival Theatre at Niagara-on-the-Lake and many private residences on the West Coast and in Ontario. In 1974 the firm's name was changed to The Thom Partnership.

WEBB ZERAFA MENKES HOUSDEN PARTNERSHIP: established in Toronto and Montreal in 1961, with subsequent offices in Calgary, Vancouver, Boston, Dallas, Houston, and Irvine, California. Major projects have also been undertaken in Europe and the Middle East. The Partnership consists of sixteen principals and ten associates with a total staff, in 1983, of 400.

CLIFFORD WIENS: born Saskatchewan, 1926; graduated Rhode Island School of Design, 1954. Commenced private practice in Regina in 1957. Major projects include the Silton Chapel and a variety of buildings in the province.

EBERHARD ZEIDLER: born Silesia, Germany, 1926; studied at Weimar Bauhaus, graduated *Technische Hoschschule*, Karlsruhe, 1948. Emigrated to Canada, 1951. Worked for Blackwell and Craig, Peterborough, Ontario. Firm became Blackwell, Craig and Zeidler, 1954. In 1962 Zeidler moved his office to Toronto. Practice now called Zeidler Roberts Partnership, is responsible for many major projects in Canada and abroad, and has received over a hundred design awards.